FLYING IN THE FACE OF COMPETITION

I dedicate this book to the memory of my father-in-law

John Zinn

He was a much loved and respected man - not least of all

by me

Flying in the Face of Competition

The Policies and Diplomacy of Airline Regulatory Reform
in Britain, the USA and the European Community 1968–94

ALAN P. DOBSON

Department of Political Theory and Government
University of Wales, Swansea

AVEBURY
aviation

© Alan P. Dobson 1995

Published by
Avebury Aviation
Ashgate Publishing Limited
Gower House
Croft Road
Aldershot
Hants GU11 3HR
England

Ashgate Publishing Company
Old Post Road
Brookfield
Vermont 05036
USA

British Library Cataloguing in Publication Data

Dobson, Alan P.
    Flying in the Face of Competition: Policies and
    Diplomacy of Airline Regulatory Reform in
    Britain, the USA and the European Community
    1968–94
    I.Title
    387.71
 ISBN 0-291-39821-9

Library of Congress Cataloging-in-Publication Data

Dobson, Alan P.
    Flying in the face of competition: the policies and diplomacy
    of airline regulatory reform in Britain, the USA and the
    European Community 1968–94 / Alan P. Dobson
       p. cm.
    Includes bibliographical references and index.
    ISBN 0-291-39821-9: $59.95 (est.)
    1. Aeronautics, Commercial – Deregulation – Great Britain.
    2. Aeronautics, Commericial – Deregulation – United States.
    3. Aeronautics, Commercial – Deregulation – European Economic
    Community countries. 4. Competition, International. I. Title.
    HE9843.A4D63 1995   94-35059
    387.7'1–dc20   CIP

Typeset by John A. Ford, 77A Uplands Crescent, Uplands, Swansea SA2 0EX

Printed and bound in Great Britain by
Hartnolls Limited, Bodmin, Cornwall

Contents

Acknowledgements

I am greatly indebted to the ESRC for funding the research for this book: grant reference ROOO233058, and to all those politicians, government and EC officials and airline executives who allowed me to interview them.

Alan Dobson, June 1994

Abbreviations

AA	*American Airlines*
APEX	*Advance Purchase Excursion*
ATC	*Air Traffic Control*
ATLB	*Air Traffic Licensing Board*
BA	*British Airways*
B.Cal.	*British Caledonian*
BEA	*British European Airways*
BIS	*Bank for International Settlements*
BM	*British Midland*
BOAC	*British Overseas Airways Corporation*
BUA	*British United Airways*
CAA	*Civil Aviation Authority*
CAB	*Civil Aeronautics Board*
CEA	*Council of Economic Advisers*
CIEP	*Committee for International Economic Policy*
CRS	*Computer Reservation System*
DG	*Directorate General*
DOT	*Department of Transport*
DTI	*Department of Trade and Industry*
EC	*European Community*
ECAC	*European Civil Aviation Conference*
EPB	*Economic Policy Board*
FO	*Foreign Office*
GAO	*General Accounting Office*
GATT	*General Agreement on Tariffs and Trade*
GATS	*General Agreement on Trade in Services*
HR	*Heathrow*
IAPS	*International Aviation Policy Statement*

IAPR   *International Aviation Policy Review*
IATA   *International Air Transport Association*
ICAO   *International Civil Aviation Organisation*
IMF   *International Monetary Fund*
NSC   *National Security Council*
NWA   *Northwest Airlines*
OMB   *Office of Management and Budget*
OPEC   *Organisation of Oil Exporting Countries*
Pan Am   *Pan American World Airways*
QANTAS   *Queensland and Northern Territories Aerial Service*
R&D   *Research and Development*
SCO   *Show Cause Order*
TDRs   *Traffic Distribution Rules*
TWA   *Trans World Airlines*
UA   *United Airlines*

Glossary

Behind feed: services from within a country which bring passengers to an international departure point.

Beyond rights: the right to carry passengers or cargo from the bilateral partner to a destination(s) other than the airline's country of origin [see also below - Operating Rights or Freedoms].

Bilateral: an international agreement between two countries.

Cabotage: the reservation of commercial operations between points within a country for its national airlines.

Chosen instrument: an airline licensed by goverment to have the exclusive right to operate either all foreign services, or, foreign services in a defined geographical region.

Code sharing agreement: an arrangement between two airlines to have connecting flights, but with the same code numbers.

Computer Reservation Systems: used by subscribers to book and sell airline tickets and other services.

Double, or multiple designation: the licencing of two or more airlines from one country to operate in competition on the same route.

Frequent Flyer Programmes: discounts and other kinds of benefits offered to those who fly with a particular airline, or group of airlines, frequently and who participate in the scheme.

Gateway: an airport that has international routes.

Grandfathered rights: rights to beneficial positions in market operations, such as the holding of prime time take-off slots at Heathrow, justified on the grounds that the airline has 'always had them'.

Hub and spoke: name derived from the configuration of routes fanning from a major operating airport for airlines.

Mega carrier: a large airline that operates in all sections of the market and consciously strives to enlarge its size to gain further economies of scale.

Multilateral agreement: an international agreement in which more than two countries participate.

Operating Rights or Freedoms:

1. Innocent passage: the right to fly over another state.

2. Technical stop: the right to stop for repairs or refuelling.

3. The right to take passengers and cargo from the airline's country of origin to another state.

4. The right to pick up passengers and cargo in another state and bring them to the airline's country of origin.

5. The right to pick up passengers and cargo in another country and carry them to a destination(s) other than the airline's country of origin.

6. The right to pick up passengers and cargo in one state bring them to the airline's country of origin and transfer them to flight(s) for a foreign destination(s): often referred to as gateway traffic.

7. The right to carry passengers and cargo between two states, neither of which is the airline's country of origin.

8. The right to carry passengers and cargo between two points within a state, other than the airline's country of origin.

Chapter 1
Deregulation and Self-Interest

We must make a reality of a European market in air transport before giving open access to that market to the much larger U.S. carriers with huge domestic feed and strong home bases. (Lord King, 16 May 1991) [1]

'Flying in the face of competition', is as ambiguous as the policies of contemporary governments and airlines. It can mean flying in competition with other airlines, or flying in a manner designed to flout the norms of competition. Some airlines compete, some of the time, in accordance with an approximation to a free market, while others only fly by means of subsidies and protection. Some governments profess a commitment to commercial, free market operations, but they are never entirely consistent in practice, while others openly avow protectionism.

In the 1970s this complex scene of civil aviation was buffetted by radical change. Trying to establish a regime of fair competition for airlines has never been easy, but, under the new dispensation, it became even more difficult to establish a criterion of fairness. It now became necessary to take into account new ideas about airline operations as well as varied practices of different airlines, government policy at both the domestic and international level and inputs from organisations such as the International Air Transport Association (IATA), the International Civil Aviation Organisation (ICAO) and the Commission of the European Community (EC). In this rich milieu of policy sources, the establishment of a level playing field might be a priority for one competitor while, for another, it may not be of such importance as the enlargement of the area over

1

which it can play in order to reap the benefits of economies of scale. Playing fields that seem flat to some appear to slope preferentially to others, or to be too small for the game to be played profitably. Policies which are prudent, sensible, innocuous and in the national interest of one state and which help to nurture a 'fair' opportunity for its airlines, may be regarded as competitive abuses and protectionist by others. In many cases commercial considerations are overruled by political priorities.

Things might be simpler if all states protected and nurtured their airlines in the same way, but they do not. Governments vary in their views of what is an appropriate mixture of the free market and regulation, not only for the airline business alone, but for their economic policies in general, and different national circumstances - economic, political and geographical - dictate different policies of protection. Civil aviation, therefore, is clearly not an island unto itself. Policies which affect its character have their origin in the broader context of the development of a state's economic policies. Since the start of the 1970s, there has been rapid economic change in general and, in particular, in the airline industry. Policy, technical, and economic changes from within and without the industry have transformed the systemic landscape and posed difficult problems for governments. Increased equipment and operating costs have made it difficult to make profits and have also commensurately increased the burden of government subsidies to the extent that for some it has become unbearable. At the same time as this happened, leading aviation nations, such as the USA and Britain, became disillusioned with regulation and moved down the road to a freer market. The impact on the airline industry, especially in the USA, was enormous and the consequences posed major problems for other states' airlines. And finally, as the airline industry in the EC moved towards a single market and as globalisation of the world market gathered pace in the late 1980s and early 1990s, questions arose concerning the efficacy of both the existing state-centred infrastructure and the bilateral system of granting commercial rights which had developed since the Second World War. In addition to trying to cope with these challenges, governments and airlines of the world had inherited a legacy of close government interaction with the industry, which showed just how much politics had always been at the heart of the matter and would complicate any attempts at change.

International civil aviation abounds with a diversity of regulations and restrictions. Airlines are often subsidised to avoid their exit from the market, and, conversely, entry of new would-be competitors is restricted, or, at least, there are difficult obstacles to overcome such as lack of airport landing and take-off slots. Fares, frequencies, capacity and the right to pick up passengers are normally regulated. As well as over wholly desirable matters, such as air traffic control, safety and technical standards, there are successive tiers of government regulation: over domestic operators; over foreign operators in the domestic market; over international operations between two states; over intermediate stops in third countries; over computer reservation systems (CRSs); and over foreign ownership of domestic airlines. The airline business is not just business. It is exceedingly complex in its make-up and highly politicised. Bearing that judgement in mind might help one to understand why there has been so little achieved in terms of liberalisation in the international sphere of aviation despite the fact that countries like the USA, Britain and Holland, the EC and many airlines profess a commitment to that goal.

Explaining why this intensely regulated system came about is not the main purpose of this book, though a brief setting of the international context is given in chapter two and consideration of regulation as a general policy is discussed in several places. The main focus of the work, however, is the 1970s and beyond when the wisdom of regulated aviation markets first began to be seriously questioned and challenged. From then onwards civil aviation policy-makers in the USA, Britain and the EC, especially when they interacted at the diplomatic level over air service agreements, could not avoid the issue of deregulation, whether it involved opposing or promoting it. The story of liberalising or deregulating civil aviation is not one that is told in its entirety here, but some of the most important themes in airline deregulation emerge in the story of Anglo-American, and, in the later period, EC aviation relations. Thus the study of US and British policies and bilateral Anglo-American relations predominates for much of the story, though the triangular relationship and the interaction of policies emerging from the apices of Washington, London and Brussels come ever more into play in the final chapters.

The future of civil aviation is going to be much affected by what happens in the EC. In how it relates to the USA, and with regard to how successful it will be with the liberalisation necessary for creating a single aviation market, the EC will have a major impact on the international system. It may develop precedents with the Single Market which could be applied more widely outside the EC in order to reform civil aviation world-wide. However, the model it has in mind at the moment is somewhat different to what would curry favour in Washington. Europe prefers a more managed development of deregulation and envisages a higher degree of regulation remaining in place at the end of the day than is the case in the USA. Liberalisation, rather than deregulation, is a more appropriate term for the European scene. Recent disagreements, not only over aviation policy, but also in the wider context of the negotiations about a General Agreement on

Trade in Services [GATS] under the auspices of the General Agreement on Tariffs and Trade [GATT], have emphasised the differences between the USA and the EC.[2]

While the impact of the EC has only recently been felt in the world aviation system, Anglo-American relations have been extremely important for many years in determining its character and they will undoubtedly continue to be influential in the future. Britain is the single largest market for the USA in terms of emplanements. It has a large, successful and aggressive airline in British Airways (BA), some promising smaller airlines, and it is an important actor in aviation in the EC. These things will ensure that Britain continues to have a major say about aviation in the future, but perhaps equally important have been its contributions to the system over the years.[3]

Britain, while professing to want liberalisation, and sincerely so, has also been the most successful state in resisting American demands for the deregulation of bilateral air service agreements in order to bring them into a freer market. That has had a major impact upon the civil aviation system. Much of what now exists owes its past to the interaction of the UK with the USA. In particular, in their web of relationships, one of the main issues that needs to be addressed is how it came about that in 1977 the USA entered into the most restrictive agreement it has ever made, with an important bilateral partner, when it agreed to the Bermuda 2 Air Services Agreement. Its predecessor, Bermuda 1, had been upheld as a model liberal bilateral since its negotiation in 1946. Yet, the transition from Bermuda 1 to 2 came at a time when the USA was on the verge of both a revolutionary policy development, namely the deregulation of its internal market, and the promulgation of a new general policy of more, not less, liberalisation for its international bilateral agreements. When one considers that the USA was the most powerful nation in the world at that time and the world's leader in civil aviation, such surprising behaviour as conceding to British insistence on controls clearly needs explanation. The affair is also rich in the political complexities that need to be unravelled if an understanding of the problems of deregulation, civil aviation and its diplomacy are to be grasped.

So far as the USA itself is concerned its importance is self-evident. It has more carriers than any other state and any one of Northwest (NWA), Delta, United (UA), American (AA), Continental, US Air, and Southwest Airlines is bigger than most nation's biggest airline. It has both the largest internal market and aerospace industry. It has an aggressive and clear policy on international civil aviation, which all states have to take some account of, even if they do not agree with it.

These three major forces in world aviation: the USA; Britain; and the Transport Directorate General (DG7) of the EC, all professed their intent to liberalise international civil aviation in the 1990s. In the summer of 1991 the EC Commission forwarded to the Council of Ministers its third package of measures aimed at achieving the liberalisation necessary for the creation of a single internal EC airline market and in a speech in Brussels on 8 April, Frederik Sorensen, head of aviation affairs in DG7, looked forward to future reforms of the EC's aviation relations with the rest of the world.[4] Within eighteen months, much of the reform package had been accepted, though not without some compromises and dilution of its liberalising potency. While DG7 struggles to liberalise on the level of government decision-making and legislation, the Directorate General for Competition, DG4, tries to apply articles 85 and 86 of the Rome Treaty in an effort to make the airline companies compete fairly in a freer market. It is within these two directorates general and in the governments of Member States that the ultimate fate of liberalisation within the EC will be decided. About the same time that Sorensen spoke in Brussels, US Secretary of Transport Samuel Skinner, notwithstanding the difficulties being experienced by airlines because of the economic recession and the Gulf War, emphasised that his department's job was to ensure that the airlines which survived 'compete against each other'[5]. Skinner's Department of Transport repeatedly called for liberalisation and open skies agreements in the early 1990s. That policy was succinctly described by Paul Wisgerhof, Director of the Office of Aviation Negotiations in the State Department, as one that seeks rights in bilateral air service agreements which give US airlines routes completely untrammelled by restraints on commercial operations.[6] For Britain, Secretary of Transport Malcolm Rifkind, in a speech to the Aviation Club in London on 21 May 1991, made it clear that Britain also favoured liberalisation. '"Open skies" in Europe should be an example to the rest of the world and not just an end in itself.'[7]

But expressed intent does not always square with performance and performance may often appear bewilderingly contradictory. For example, few would quibble with the claim that the UK has been in the forefront of those calling for liberalisation within the EC, but it finds itself severely criticised by the USA because of the restrictions that it managed to incorporate into the Bermuda 2 Agreement. Jeffrey Shane, US Assistant Secretary of Transport for Policy and International Affairs during the Reagan and Bush administrations, commented on the character of the Bermuda 2 Agreement as follows: 'We have a more liberal relationship with Japan! I mean the fact is there is nothing liberal about the relationship between the US and the UK except the number of gateways in the US.'[8] Frustratingly for the Americans, when Britain looks to the continent it demands deregulation; when it looks to the Atlantic it insists on maintaining a tightly controlled market.

For their part, the British recall that the USA had a restrictive civil aviation regime too, until the late 1970s. It only changed when the government decided that it was in the general interest of the USA to do so. None of the major US airlines, except UA and Pan American Airways (Pan Am), favoured deregulation and the subsequent attrition rate in the industry indicated that many were not ready for it. In the long run, given the large number of airlines that exist in the USA, the failure of some simply made way for the expansion or startup of others. In contrast, in a country like the UK, where there is a tiny domestic base and only one major carrier, the gamble with deregulation has to be undertaken more cautiously. If BA were to expire there would be no guarantee of a phoenix rising from its ashes nor could it be certain that one of Britain's independents, such as British Midland (BM), could step into the breach. So far as the British are concerned, and BA in particular, their interests do not yet indicate that deregulation, as asked for by the Americans in the international sphere, is desirable. However, that conclusion should not be interpreted to mean that British governments have acted hypocritically or that they are against radical change.

The British also point to the fact that the USA has a protectionist policy on inward investment in US airlines and that it fiercely protects its cabotage rights (operations on domestic routes). In other words, the USA only deregulates in areas which give its industry advantages, and, even when deregulation begins to bite, the pain is often dulled by bankruptcy legislation which provides Chapter 11 protection to US airlines in financial difficulties. One unintended consequence of that has been that Chapter 11 companies can offer discounted airfares to try to claw their way back into a substantial market share. They have only been able to do this because of Chapter 11 protection from their creditors. The net result is that the market does not immediately decide who is to succeed and who is to fail. Quite the contrary, because Chapter 11 allows companies in difficulty to continue their operations and to do so by offering unrealistically low fares. This in turn undermines the position of airlines which are not under Chapter 11 protection as they feel obliged to match uncommercial pricing. This has international repercussions, most notably on the Atlantic where air fares in 1991 dipped to very low levels indeed and angered European and US airlines which were not under Chapter 11 protection. This is not to say that other factors were not at work as well in bringing transatlantic airfares down, but, undoubtedly, low fares by Chapter 11 airlines were a contributing factor. And anything that encouraged deep discounting of fares cannot be ignored during a year when estimates in September 1991 suggested a $2.5 billion loss for the world airline business in the previous year.[9]

Even in more prosperous times, when Chapter 11 protected airlines are not an everyday occurrence, the USA is still seen as having forms of protection which contradict its calls for liberalisation. The maintenance of cabotage is one such matter. The Americans observe that all other countries maintain their cabotage rights and ask why should the USA be any different? An answer to that is that the size of the US domestic market makes it a different case. It constitutes about 40 per cent of what used to be described as the non-communist world's civil aviation business. That was, of course, before the breakup of the Soviet Bloc. Because of its size, the protected US domestic airline market has a qualitatively different impact on the civil aviation business than, for example, the protected British domestic airline market. Speaking about the latter Lord King opined that he did not care what the government did with it: 'I really don't mind ... it's overloaded and it doesn't pay.'[10] One cannot imagine any American airline chief expressing a similar view about the US domestic market: and therein lies the difference. In fact, the USA has recognised that there is some force to the suggestion that cabotage is a form of protection which impedes the development of a market system and yet they are reluctant, to say the least, to countenance change. Skinner ruminated on the matter in the spring of 1991 as follows:

> Some people would argue that cabotage is the long-term solution for increased competition in the airline industry. Right now there are no programs within this department to change the law to allow foreign airlines to participate in the domestic route structure. We've got to take some steps to make sure that we're looking at all the issues. You've really got to walk before you can run. And that would be a very dramatic step ... I don't think it's on the short-term agenda.[11]

Having such a significant share of the market reserved for US carriers not only provides them with an almost invaluable and privileged position, but it also gives US airlines enormous advantages in terms of feed into hubs for their routes which fan out like the spokes of a wheel into the international marketplace. To many minds outside the USA, this gives US airlines an unfair competitive advantage: an advantage that the British counter by maintaining controls on the Atlantic.[12]

While Europeans and others bemoan the protection of the US domestic airline market, the USA regards with apprehension, at least in some very influential quarters, the development of EC policies. Michael Colvin, Chairman of the British Conservative Party Aviation Committee, felt a sense of American paranoia at the IATA meeting in Marrakesh in 1989 regarding EC protectionist aviation policies.[13] More recently in speeches at San Diego, California and at Duke University, in North Carolina, 24 and 28 March 1991 respectively, Robert Crandall, the head of AA, reiterated those fears. Mixing contempt and anger he said:

> Although we hear a good deal about what the Europeans like to call "airline liberalisation", we think the real result is likely to be more along the lines of "fortress Europe", as the European carriers consolidate their already dominant positions - and band together to limit participation by US carriers.[14]

Others in the USA were less worried and felt that the efforts of both Karel van Miert, the EC Transport Commissioner, and Frederik Sorensen, were directed towards genuine liberalisation. Nevertheless, there are doubts about the Commission's ability to push liberalisation forward in the face of a number of recalcitrant Member States. In addition, the scramble to protectionist cover by a number of European airlines during the Gulf War of 1991 dismayed American officials and airline executives. The EC's approval in the summer of 1991 of a Belgian Government subsidy to Sabena in order to rescue it from collapse seemed an ill omen for the future prospects of fair airline competition in Europe to those on the other side of the Atlantic, and worse followed over the next three years.[15]

In the spring and summer of 1991 there clearly existed much resentment, tension and frustration among EC, US and UK officials and airline executives. The European Commission was irritated by the outcome of Anglo-American discussions about succession rights for US airlines to enable them to operate into Heathrow (HR). It feared that the agreement might impact adversely on the aviation policy that it was then trying to develop for the Community as a whole.[16] The British were unhappy with American demands for the liberalisation of the Bermuda 2 Agreement while the US maintained cabotage and restrictions on inward investment. The Americans were stinging from the price that they had had to pay for the rights of AA and UA to take over the routes of Trans World

8

Airlines (TWA) and Pan Am respectively into HR. BA thought that the HR deal had given away an important British bargaining chip in return for little of immediate benefit, so far as its own interests were concerned, but there was also a sense of grievance among US airlines which believed that the USA had been out-negotiated. In particular, UA was unhappy that the Bermuda Agreement prevented it from flying into either HR or Stansted Airport from Chicago. It desperately wanted to do that, partly because AA, its main competitor, could fly Chicago-HR as a result of buying the route from TWA, but the main reason was that Chicago is UA's main hub and it was therefore not able to take advantage, as it felt it should be able to, of its ability to assemble large numbers of passengers in Chicago for London.[17]

These matters, which caused resentment and concern in all quarters in 1991, were only the symptoms of a far more complex number of commercial and political factors that have bedevilled civil aviation as a commercial enterprise since its beginning, and in particular the relations between the USA and Britain since the mid 1970s. They now also pose serious problems for the development of a civil aviation policy for the EC.

Given the ubiquitous sense of unease with the way things were developing, one might be tempted to ask: Is the demand for liberalisation from BA, US airlines, the EC Commission and the US and UK governments anything more than empty rhetoric? How is it that all these parties can profess a commitment to liberalisation and yet find themselves so much at odds with each other? Answers are by no means straightforward.

The viability of major airlines could depend on the method and timing of deregulation. Deregulation of the international civil aviation market can thus have enormous commercial implications and its piecemeal deregulation might provide what one side sees as a liberalisation of the market, while another sees it as providing a competitor with an unfair advantage. The somewhat unpalatable fact is that deregulation does not affect all airlines in the same way and therefore there is much scope for debate about tactics and timing. There are also immense problems to do with infrastructure, which has developed over the years on a state basis, but is now increasingly inadequate for dealing with what has rapidly become a globalised industry. Apart from the commercial and systemic impact of deregulation there is also the political dimension.

There has been some movement to disengage politics from the airline business in recent years, and, in effect, the liberalisers want to nurture and promote that. At the same time some of them want pro-competition legislation to counter predatory behaviour and domination of markets by carriers in a laisser faire system, but their end goal is the same as the other liberalisers: a competitive

9

market as free from government regulation, protection and subsidies as possible. So on the one hand there are those who are doctrinally committed to the view that a freer market system will benefit the public and industry all round, and on the other there are some governments who have stepped back from involvement in the industry for practical economic reasons, even though their economic philosophy might be interventionist and *dirigiste*. Costs of the industry are so enormous that governments have begun to tire of continuously pumping money into them to subsidise operations. This began to tell first among the less prosperous states. As Cyril Murphy of UA pithily put it:

> We used to joke in this industry: first thing a developing country does is buy a steel mill and the second thing it does is to fly an airline. To a large extent, that was true for a number of years. It's rapidly becoming less true. You don't hear about steel mills anymore and we're beginning to see in this industry a move away from the idea that every country has to have its own airline. The airline business is becoming more and more of a commodity that can be bought and sold.[18]

Of course the move towards the airline industry becoming solely concerned with the selling of a commodity was given impetus not just by third world countries pulling out or reducing their involvement in the business, but by the active promotion of the free market philosophy of deregulation in the USA and in the UK. However, although Murphy was correct in identifying the apolitical direction the industry was moving in in 1991, politics still retains a major presence in airline operations, especially in the international sphere, and its exorcism from there will be a complicated diplomatic ritual. Needless to say, it is the political dimension which gives rise to the main difficulties in the drive for reform.

Politics has always been endemic in civil aviation and diminishing its presence will not be easy. The level of difficulty involved is a measure of the hardship the regulatory reformers face. Airlines, since their beginnings, have attracted political attention and intervention. The very nature of flying makes them of concern to governments. They have military and political as well as commercial value and they also need regulation of one kind or another so that safety and operational standards are upheld. Even the commercial side of civil aviation has required government interference in the past (and in the present) because it is not easy to run a major airline and make a profit. Internationally, profit margins and the return on capital investment throughout the industry's history have both been notoriously low. Richard Pryke, in his work on airline competition, shows, with the help of ICAO statistics and his own computations, that between 1975 and 1982 revenue among member state airlines was two per cent above their costs.[19] As a result, governments, unwilling to be in charge of a nation without a major airline at their beck and call, have subsidised and cosseted them and controlled the environment in which they operate to ensure that they survive. Competition at the international level has never been vigorous until recent years and then only sporadically and in certain markets. Competition within domestic markets has varied more from state to state, but within the most important market, that of the USA, until the reforms of the late 1970s, it was one of the most rigorously controlled airline markets anywhere.

Although it remains a difficult job to make airlines profitable, their importance to a nation's economy has grown in recent years. Civil aviation is a major industry in its own right, but it also links with the health and welfare of the tourist industry, with the aerospace industry and through that has impact on the economics of research and development in the defence sphere. Aerospace and tourism are important industries: the latter is already the world's largest and it continues to be one of the fastest growing; an illustration of the significance of the former is that Boeing received orders for $47.7 billion worth of aeroplanes in 1990. For a country to be without a major airline, which is a vital support component of these two industries, is seen as politically undesirable by many governments.

In addition to the commercial reasons for government intrusion into the airline industry, there are important political and strategic reasons as well.

In the early days of flying it was soon realised that planes had military potential. First they were used for reconnaissance and then later for bombing, strafing enemy trench lines and for aerial combat. Although military planes were purpose built machines, it was also possible to convert civilian into military aeroplanes and *vice versa*. The designs of heavy long range bombers, military transports and civilian passenger planes were all closely interrelated: so much so, that one of the stumbling blocks for aerial disarmament at the Geneva General Disarmament Conference, 1932-34, was that no means of controlling civilian planes could be devised to prevent them from being used for aggressive military purposes. The persistence of that problem caused delegates to despair of effectively disarming in the air. It also demonstrated how civilian aeroplanes, and hence civil airlines, could not be divorced from matters of national security.

Over the years as the roles of combat and bomber aircraft have become

11

more and more specialised so have their designs. Consequently, the possibilities for the conversion of civilian to military aircraft have diminished, but they have not disappeared altogether. The most direct way in which civilian airlines now strengthen the military power equation of a state is by their ability to help transport large quantities of combat and support troops and equipment to trouble spots around the world. Jeffrey Shane, touched on this in late 1990 when speaking about foreign ownership of US airlines. He was reported as saying that Secretary Skinner 'is ready to take a "hard look" at foreign ownership rules. Any changes would have to pass two tests, however: first, that national security was not compromised and second that further liberalisation of international services be not restricted.'[20] It is the first condition that reveals the continuing importance attached to the potential military use of civilian airlines. That potential was soon to be called upon. In the Gulf War of 1991 US carriers, with NWA in the lead, transported a large proportion of the US military manpower that was used in the Middle East.

As well as the direct, there are less obvious ways in which civil aviation benefits a nation's military and defence interests. In the 1930s the Roosevelt Administration persuaded Pan Am to help in its shadow war against German and Italian interests in the Western Hemisphere. That kind of covert activity has continued, or at least governments have suspected each other of continuing it, right down to the present. Perhaps the most tragic manifestation of this syndrome was the shooting down of a South Korean civil airliner in August 1983 by the Soviets who suspected it of conducting espionage work.

Another less obvious connection between the civilian and military spheres is research and development (R&D). There is a prolific cross-fertilisation of ideas between military and civilian aviation. R&D in military aircraft can lead to the creation of new generations of civilian aeroplanes which thus gain commercial advantages through the potential for sales. In addition, the end result is that the costs of R&D are shared by the civilian and military parts of the industry to their mutual benefit and the country's civil airlines get easy, if not privileged, access to the latest types of aeroplanes. Economic interconnections between the three industries - military aerospace, civilian aerospace and the airline industry - create interests of state, which, in turn, reinforce the tendency for politics to become involved in the civil aviation business.

States have also been concerned to use civil air routes as a means of encouraging national or imperial unity and for promoting national economic interests. For a great trading country like the UK, the importance of having a national carrier in a prominent position in the international route system is somewhat analogous to the importance of having an efficient infrastructure for the domestic economy. The same rationale applies, in that, it is seen as preferable to subsidise and have a good infrastructure that will enable other parts of the economy to thrive and compete, than to have an inadequate infrastructure that will damage industry's competitiveness. Of course, the free market comment on this is that other nations' airlines could provide the services better and without subsidies if political considerations did not get in the way. The trouble is that they do. States have broader interests than just narrow economic calculations. Sometimes balance of payments considerations may override principles of free competition as they relate to flag flying airlines and sometimes diplomatic considerations, completely lacking in economic substance, may affect the kind of air services bilateral a nation is prepared to accept. States are also still generally unwilling to rely on others to provide air services for them and with good reason. It is not unknown for a state to suspend air services to another country as a way of trying to reprimand it: for example, the suspension of Pan Am services to the USSR after the Soviet invasion of Afghanistan in 1979. In this kind of world to put oneself at the mercy of other states in international civil air services could be said to be politically imprudent.

Finally, despite the tendency previously mentioned for developing states to be now less keen to run commercially unviable airlines, they still remain a major status symbol and one that industrial countries are reluctant to abandon. Sabena has not made much commercial sense for a long time, but it has not been allowed to expire. After the 1991 injection of Belgian Government funds, it eventually struck a deal with Air France which now owns 37.5 per cent of its shares. Co-operation between the two may make Sabena commercially successful, though the evidence of operations in 1992/93 still raises a question mark over its viability. However, this limited erosion of national flag identity is not really an appropriate litmus test for the demise of nationalism, politics and status symbols in the airline business. One would really have to see the disappearance, as a national entity, of a large airline like BA, Alitalia or Air France before one could hazard a pronouncement that political consideration, as an overriding factor in the fortunes of airlines, was dead. There are some signs that the system is moving to free the market and devalue the role of nationalism and politics in the airline business: for example the Scandinavian airline SAS is a truly international company and has been for several years. There, national politics do not determine things. It is the airline of Denmark, Sweden and Norway. Perhaps that is the way things will develop in the future. If that kind of development were to gain momentum and particularly if two major national airlines were to follow such a precedent, then the road would be opened to the beginning of the end of national politics determining and moulding the character of international civil aviation. But that at the moment is not likely of immediate realisation. The character of the industry is determined by the large and successful and the large and subsidised airlines not by those which are less successful or those which have had to find a niche, protected or not, in order to survive. However, in the opinion of some airline executives, the force of the market, if unleashed through deregulation, or even by the liberalisation espoused by the EC Commission, would provide a dynamic that would force airlines to respond in more purely commercial terms. Competition and the economies of scale that can be enjoyed with the development of a hub and spoke system lead to a greater differentiation between competitive and uncompetitive airlines. If that stage were reached, the cost of subsidies to governments would become prohibitive. Then the market would decide and politics would be forced to retreat.[21] But, of course, the key to this scenario is the achievement of deregulation, or at least liberalisation, in the first place and that logically entails a political willingness to downgrade the role of politics in the airline business. Governments, however, will be unwilling to take that step unless they believe that their national airlines will benefit from deregulation. It would be a brave government that favoured reform knowing that the cost of following that path would be the demise of its airline as an independent entity. For the deregulators and the liberalisers this is a classic catch-22 situation. The solution to part of the problem of the airline industry is to reduce the role of politics in its operations. But, to bring that about, it is necessary either for politicians to take decisions which will be contrary to their own national interests, or for a situation to be created where all key players believe that they have a comparative advantage, at least in a niche of the market, that will enable them to prosper.

In 1994 the situation in the international civil aviation system was not one where deregulation prospered. Regulations motivated by a host of political considerations existed in abundance. Exceptions to the regulated model were few and far between. They were to be found in US bilaterals with Israel, Holland, Germany and several South American states, in the liberalised EC airline market and in the domestic markets of a number of states, most notably of all in the USA. But, on the whole, the pattern world-wide was of regulated markets and of a renewal of interest in protectionism.

Thus to observe that Britain the USA, the EC, and major airlines were all calling for liberalisation has to be placed in context before it becomes meaningful. That context-setting requires consideration of three important matters.

Firstly, the character of the international system as it existed in the early 1970s and the problems it posed for deregulation need to be described. Secondly, the policies of Britain, the USA, the EC, and the major airlines need to be explained as they developed through the 1970s and 1980s. And thirdly, the reaction against the ethos of economic regulation that took place in the 1970s must be discussed in order to appreciate the impact on the industry of wider political and economic developments. Once the context is clearer then it will be possible to explain the growth of the reform movement and how diplomacy has tried to square national and EC self-interest with regulatory reform. For the calls for reform are not composed of empty rhetoric, but the commercial and political issues at stake in deregulation make the matter highly complex and difficult to resolve despite the profession by various parties that they wish to achieve an end goal that is at least similar, if not identical.

Notes and References

1. Remarks by Lord King, Chairman of BA, at the Royal Aeronautics Society 125th Anniversary Banquet, 16 May 1991: text supplied by courtesy of BA.

2. Drake and Nicolaidis (1992), pp. 37-100.

3. For the historical background see Dobson (1991 A).

4. Presentation by Frederik Sorensen, 'European Airline Traffic after 1993', Brussels, 8 April 1991, text supplied by courtesy of Mr. Sorensen.

5. *Washington Flyer Magazine*, March-April 1991, B. Cook interview with US Secretary of Transportation, Samuel Skinner.

6. Interview with Paul Wisgerhof, Director Office of Aviation Negotiations, US Department of State, 4 April 1991, conducted by the author.

7. Malcolm Rifkind, 'Secretary of State's Speech to Aviation Club, 21 May 1991: Aviation: A Framework for the Nineties', text by courtesy of the UK Department of Transport.

8. Interview with Jeffrey Shane, US Assistant Secretary of Transport for Policy and International Affairs, 5 April 1991, conducted by the author.

9. By February 1992, after US airlines alone had recorded operating losses of well over $2.5 billion in 1991, concern about Chapter 11 bankruptcy

protection law became acute in the industry: see report of 'blistering attack' on Chapter 11 by AA Chairman, Robert Crandall in *Flight International* (hereafter, *Flight*), 19 Feb. 1992, p. 14.

10. Interview with Lord King, Chairman BA, 17 May 1991, conducted by the author.

11. *Washington Flyer*, Skinner interview.

12. Cabotage was on the agenda for US-Canadian talks in 1991 in the context of the North American Free Trade Area. That fact made it more difficult to defend US cabotage in principle, despite people like Wisgerhof saying that any exchange of cabotage rights with Canada would not be accepted by the USA as any kind of precedent: to date, 1994, nothing substantial has come of the US-Canadian talks. Interestingly, cabotage was also allowed onto the table by the USA in subsequent liberalisation talks with the British (Wisgerhof Interview), but BA's main concern became inward investment - the right to buy into a US airline, rather than with gaining cabotage rights.

13. Interview with Michael Colvin, MP, Chairman of the Conservative Backbench Aviation Committee, 7 Dec. 1989, conducted by the author.

14. Remarks by Robert Crandall, Chairman and President AA, at Allied Pilots Association Banquet, San Diego, California, 24 March 1991, and at the Fuqua School of Business, Duke University Durham, North Carolina, 28 March 1991: texts by courtesy of AA.

15. Shane Interview; and interview with Charles Angevine, US Deputy Assistant Secretary of State for Transportation Affairs, 29 July 1991, conducted by the author.

16. Interview with Frederik Sorensen of EC Commission DG7, 21 May 1991, conducted by the author; and other official EC Commission sources.

17. Interviews with Robert Ebdon, BA Head of Government Affairs, 5 Aug. 1991, and Cyril Murphy, Vice President of UA for International Affairs, 1 July 1991: both conducted by the author.

18. Ibid.

19. Pryke (1987), p. 17.

20. *Flight*, 28 Nov. 1990, p. 13.
21. Murphy Interview.

Chapter 2
The Bermuda 1 System

There should be a fair and equal opportunity for the carriers of the two nations to operate on any route between their respective territories. (Bermuda 1, Air Services Agreement)

The development of international civil aviation in the inter-war years was based on a kind of bilateralism in which political rather than commercial considerations predominated. The result was unsatisfactory. The operation of airlines was determined by subsidies and the political power of their host state rather than by their efficiency and performance. That situation, while the range and size of aircraft were severely limited by technical constraints, was galling but tolerable. It ceased to be so when major technical advances were made at the end of the 1930s and during World War Two, which enabled manufacturers to design aircraft that were larger and had longer range. Pressure for reform of the international aviation system now became irresistible. With these new aircraft the possibilities for mass travel and cargo operations were increased enormously, but for them to be realised the problem of national restrictions on commercial operations had to be modified.

The most ambitious attempt to deal with the problem was the Chicago Conference of 1944 when the Americans tried to get the world to accept a free market system. Its adoption was prevented by opposition led by the British. They feared that the Americans, with the monopoly that they then held in modern civil aircraft, would establish an unchallengeable dominance for their airlines, if they were allowed a free rein by the international community. The British, therefore, used their political influence and the bargaining power that their control over a world-wide system of bases gave them to oppose the American proposals. Nevertheless, the British did not want a return to the days of highly political bilaterals. There had to be some form of order in the system.

That order came to be expressed over the years by the notion of freedoms, or privileges as they were sometimes called. All in all, they have come to number eight. The Chicago Conference achieved acceptance of the first two: innocent passage of aircraft over foreign countries; and technical stop for refuelling or servicing without entering into any commercial transactions. The conference also set up the ICAO, a specialised agency of the United Nations which acted as a forum for discussion of technical and safety matters.[1]

The third, fourth and fifth freedoms were not accepted by the majority at Chicago. Those rights respectively were: the carriage of passengers from an airline's country of origin to a foreign destination; the carriage of passengers from a foreign country to an airline's country of origin; and beyond rights, which allowed the picking up of passengers after completing a third freedom flight and taking them to a destination other than the airline's country of origin. These third, fourth and fifth freedom rights soon became the subject of bilateral negotiations. The other rights were: sixth freedom rights, enabling an airline to carry passengers from country x to country y by the use of a connecting flight in its country of origin - often referred to as gateway traffic; seventh freedom rights for an airline to operate between two foreign countries without originating or terminating the flight in its country of origin; and eighth freedom rights to operate between two points within a foreign country - usually referred to as cabotage. These rights and various arrangements for determining fares set the framework within which the character of commercial relations in international civil aviation have been and still are worked out by states.

In 1944 all that was in place were the first two freedoms and the Provisional ICAO. The stalemate at Chicago caused by the clash of British and American interests prevented anything more constructive coming into being and so, in effect, the commercial side of international civil aviation remained to be shaped by bilateral agreements. The danger of the prewar system being resurrected was immanent. However, largely because of political and economic factors outside of civil aviation, the two leading air powers, Britain and the USA, reached a compromise at Bermuda in 1946. The detailed reasons for this do not concern us here, but the general landscape of the compromise involved a British need to accommodate the Americans so as not to jeopardise a much needed line of credit from the USA of $3.75 billion, which had been negotiated with the Truman Administration, but still had to be approved by Congress; a shift in American attitudes prior to Bermuda which made them more willing to accept fare controls than they had been at Chicago; and a mutual desire to avoid friction and to co-operate because of the deteriorating world situation. The outcome was the Bermuda Air Services Agreement of 1946 which governed civil aviation between the USA and the United Kingdom until it was denounced in 1976 and expired as a result of that in 1977. It was then superseded by the Bermuda 2 Agreement, and so, for convenience sake and to avoid confusion, the 1946 agreement is referred to as Bermuda 1.[2]

Although Bermuda 1 was a bilateral agreement and therefore, *prima facie*, no different from the interwar experience, in fact it was not just another bilateral. In 1946 and thereafter on several occasions both the USA and Britain reaffirmed their commitment to Bermuda 1 and presented it to the rest of the world as a model agreement. If the world could not make a multilateral arrangement to govern world aviation then at least some order and conformity might be achieved through trying to get nations to follow good practice as established by Britain and the USA.

Although references are often made to the Bermuda Model, it is significant that opinions vary concerning its character and the extent to which it has been followed. Paul Wisgerhof of the US State Department said in 1991 that: 'It's fair to say that Bermuda 1 set the basic international aviation relationship among most nations, which in many parts of the world still obtains today. That is to say that Bermuda 1 still tends to be an ICAO model agreement.'[3] More or less at the same time Jeffrey Shane, of the US Transportation Department, gave his opinion that:

> From 1946 on, or when we really moved into other negotiations after Bermuda 1 was concluded, we moved away immediately from the Bermuda 1 model. I mean Bermuda 1 is a model in terms of a variety of ... provisions, you know, fair and equal opportunity to compete - a lot of the broad principles that are applied to civil aviation services in the market - but the most important part of the bilateral is the route description. That's what it's all about. And to that extent it's never been a model.[4]

Different perspectives give different views on Bermuda 1. Some of the different emphases can be explained by the contrast between those Americans who assess things in the light of the radical commitment to deregulation policies, which developed from the late 1970s onwards, and those who bear in mind the advance that Bermuda 1 made on previous practice when it was first negotiated. Another factor at work here is that, even before the 1970s, there was American dissatisfaction with selective aspects of Bermuda 1 and a US tendency to construe the Bermuda Model in a more liberal way than other countries.

21

Nevertheless, it is a fact that American criticisms of practices in international civil aviation were couched in terms of alleged departures from Bermuda principles until 1977. In the early 1970s, the US continued to reaffirm its commitment to the Bermuda Model. The Nixon Administration's Statement of International Air Transportation Policy approved by the President on 22 June 1970 stated: 'The basic system of exchanging air transport rights through a structure of bilateral agreements embodying the Bermuda provisions should be continued although further studies should be made as to the feasibility of exchanging rights on a multilateral basis.'[5] So, although Shane is undoubtedly reflecting American official views when he says that Bermuda 1 was never a model in certain respects, it was the only working model to which repeated reference was made between 1946-77. It was never wholly ideal for the Americans, nor for that matter for the British, and, as will be seen, it was possible to interpret the broad provisions of the Bermuda Model in ways which the Americans found unsatisfactory. Nevertheless, more than any other agreement, it set the tone and character of the postwar international civil aviation system.

The Bermuda Agreement set out general principles, but it is important to remember that the agreement was a compromise between Britain and the USA, even though the latter gained more of what it wanted than did the former. The net result was an agreement that worked for a long period of time, but it contained some vague provisions which were subject to various interpretations. Also, in the opinion of some, a bilateral system has a natural propensity to conservatism, to political intrusion into commercial affairs and to state protectionism.[6]

Bermuda 1 governed the operation of airlines between Britain and the USA and required them to be under the effective control, or substantial ownership, of British and American nationals. It stipulated that: 'there should be a fair and equal opportunity for the carriers of the two nations to operate on any route between their respective territories'. This was intended to outlaw the kind of political pressures used to extract excessive commercial rights from weak players in the aviation field, which had been so common in the interwar period. There was both a strong element of reciprocity and a commitment to the equitable exchange of commercial rights in the agreement. This was fine for protection against exploitation by political power in order to gain unfair commercial aviation advantages, but problems arose later with the potential for protection against more efficient airlines of the bilateral partner. Gaining commercial advantages because of political pressure was one thing, gaining them because of efficiency, high standards of service and fare competitiveness was another.

The capacity provisions set broad guidelines and were permissive, but they were also somewhat vague and, when read in conjunction with other clauses, it was possible to construe Bermuda 1 in a less liberal manner than might first appear likely. Capacity was to be related to:

> ... traffic requirements between the country of origin and the countries of destination
> b) to the requirements of through airline operations; and
> c) to the traffic requirements of the area through which the airline passes after taking account of the local and regional services.[7]

These provisions created much more scope for competition than the system of rigid capacity control and the division of traffic that was so common in the interwar years. US airlines could now calculate their capacity levels for Britain on the basis of the Bermuda definition of primary traffic, which consisted of passengers destined for both London and onward destinations of the route in Europe or elsewhere. However, British airlines had virtually no commercially viable destinations beyond the USA and thus found themselves disadvantaged in terms of primary traffic levels. They could not justify as much capacity for their operations to the USA as US airlines could justify for flights to Britain and eventually this was to cause problems. In any case, if things began to get out of hand, there was always what was known as the undue effect clause.

> That in the operation by the air services of either Government of the trunk services described in the Annex to the Agreement, the interest of the air carriers of the other Government shall be taken into consideration so as not to affect unduly the services which the latter provides on all or part of the same routes.[8]

Generally, during the life of the Bermuda 1 Agreement, the combination of these two clauses - capacity and undue effect - were taken to mean that there should not be any predetermined capacity level. Capacity could only be adjusted *ex post facto* on the grounds that it was excessive, that it was compromising the principle of fair and equal opportunity, and having an undue effect on the operations of one of the airlines. At least this was the position of the USA and, for most of the life of Bermuda 1, of Britain as well.

Within these general principles, the USA and the UK mutually extended the five freedoms to each other, with some restrictions on the use of the fifth. Most notable was that any change of gauge [i.e. change in the size of aircraft at the point at which a third freedom flight becomes a fifth freedom flight] should be tailored to the number of passengers being brought from the USA for onward carriage and should not provide excess capacity which would allow the US airline to prey upon local traffic. In addition to these operating principles there was also an understanding about the control of fares.

Immediately after the Chicago Conference steps were taken to establish an organisation of scheduled airlines. That culminated at Havana in April 1945 with the establishment of the IATA. This non-governmental organisation was to play a major role in modern aviation. It revolutionised airline ticketing; acted as a forum for discussion and a centre for gathering economic and technical data on the civil aviation industry; and has made a major contribution to the process of setting international fares. It was to this organisation that the British and the Americans looked for help on the sensitive issue of pricing.

The question of fares was a difficult one for the USA. By 1946 it favoured some form of management, but was in danger of running afoul of antitrust laws. In the end the two sides agreed that fares should be dealt with through IATA rate conferences. They would then be subject to approval by the US Government before being applied in the USA: in effect this involved two stages of approval. The first was given of the IATA machinery on an annual basis up to 1955 by the US Civil Aeronautics Board (CAB), which was the relevant US regulatory agency. Thereafter, the CAB gave its approval for an indefinite period until it spearheaded the deregulation movement in the 1970s. CAB approval was necessary in order to extend exemption to the airlines from US antitrust legislation, which would have otherwise challenged the practice of controlling fares in the marketplace. The second stage was CAB ratification of specific recommended rates. In Britain only the second stage was relevant as it had no antitrust legislation from which to exempt its airlines. Both sides committed themselves to IATA as the first line of approach to fare setting. If one side objected to the proposed rates then bilateral negotiations would attempt to resolve the problem. If that failed provisions for non-binding arbitration from ICAO was a further possibility. But, in the end, although they established an orderly procedure for setting rates, the bottom line was that it was a double approval arrangement: one side could not set a rate without the consent of the other.[9] Thus, the competitive aspect of the

Bermuda 1 model was provided by the frequency and capacity provisions rather than by the pricing regime.

An overall impression of the Bermuda 1 model is not easy to give. Generally, it was regarded as a major step forward towards developing a more open, competitive and liberal system for civil aviation. However, the liberal spirit of the Bermuda model was not always adhered to and some people believe that any bilateral system has a natural propensity to conservatism and protectionism.[10] British and American officials who deal with negotiating air service bilaterals have expressed the view that no agreement can work unless both sides believe that they are benefiting more than they would if it did not exist. There has to be an element of mutual benefit and in terms of the Bermuda Model that has meant interpreting Bermuda 1 agreements in different ways according to circumstances. The flexibility of the Bermuda Model gave it a strength which enabled it to survive for a long time, but it also provided scope for countries, which were less liberal in their outlook than the USA, to interpret matters in a way that was often objectionable to the Americans.

What happened with Bermuda-type agreements, according to one well informed airline official, was that 'airlines and governments sat down and said whatever this agreement meant to say we aren't going to let you do more than we want to do.'[11] Setting bilaterals with the USA aside for the moment, the general practice world-wide was for agreements that predetermined capacity at the official level, which was largely the case outside of Europe and the norm for Italy and France. Alternatively, things were left to the airlines to arrange pools where traffic and revenue were divided between them. This prevailed in Europe where, for example, every British European Airways' (BEA) route was in a 50/50 pool with its foreign counterpart, and it was also common within the Commonwealth, most notably between Qantas and the British Overseas Airways Corporation (BOAC). These agreements were disliked by the USA, but there was little that it could do except tolerate them. Its own bilaterals were more liberal, but then it was in the best position to exploit a more competitive market.

Although Britain and the USA were the authors of the Bermuda Model, their relations within its framework were by no means always smooth. There were periodic disputes over fares in which the US CAB generally supported lower fares. The most serious argument was the so-called Chandler fare controversy of 1962-63, named after the IATA rate conference in Chandler, Arizona. There were also problems over routes, particularly involving Hong Kong.[12] However, these disputes did not really strike at the overall character of the Bermuda 1 Agreement in the way that the dispute over National Airlines' route from Miami to London in 1972 did.

The episode involving National's route from Miami to London illustrates the chameleon-like character of Bermuda 1 and anticipated some of the problems that were soon to arise in a more dramatic form between Britain and the USA. For some, Bermuda 1, if not exactly an ideal liberal bilateral, was at least a permissive agreement that rendered liberal practice possible. Its flexibility, however, also allowed it to be used in a restrictive way as well. Towards the end of the 1960s and in the early 1970s pressures built up which led to serious questions about the state of international air service agreements, which eventually threw everything into the melting pot for a re-fashioning, including Bermuda 1. Those questions brought forth several different answers. Some involved liberalisation, others more regulation and protection. Just to add confusion to this, governments and the airlines often juggled with contradictory courses of action simultaneously or, at least, in rapid succession. Even in the USA, which is widely viewed as the champion of deregulation, governments in the 1970s were never unanimously in favour of it, neither was Congress and, certainly, neither were the major airlines with the notable exceptions of UA and Pan Am, though even the latter had reservations.

The pressures that built up and stimulated new thoughts about the operation of international airlines came from various sources, but they all had a similar impact in that they put the profitability of the airlines in jeopardy. The rapid expansion of charter services in the 1960s and the growth of subsidised Third World airlines challenged the market of the established scheduled carriers like TWA, Pan Am, and BOAC. The cost of re-equipping with the new generation of jet aircraft, in particular the Boeing 747, was astronomical and damaging to the profitability of the airlines. The rise in fuel prices which resulted from the Middle East wars of 1967 and 1973 had a dual impact upon the airline industry. They raised the costs of flying and the general economic recession which followed the increased price of energy cut back on the number of people travelling. All these factors added to the economic problems of the airline industry and caused people to rethink strategies for the future. At the same time, the wider economic problems of the 1970s and later on the 1980s began to cause politicians and economists to challenge the prevailing Keynesian consensus about social and economic policies and to resurrect notions of a freer less regulated market. In the USA, in particular, there was growing disillusionment with federal regulatory agencies and that was to prove an enormously important catalyst in the eventual restructuring of the American airline industry. But this is to anticipate the story somewhat. The immediate concern is with National's route from Miami to London and the questions that it raised about the character of the Bermuda 1 Agreement in the light of changes in the industry that were then gathering pace. Those questions did not result in radical changes in 1972, but they foreshadowed problems that were to reappear in a more acute form a few years later.

In June 1970 the Miami-London route was opened by BOAC and National Airlines. National was a newcomer to the international system and that in itself was important for American policy and had significant consequences for Britain. In the late 1960s the USA had come under considerable pressure from a number of countries, most notably Italy, to revert to a chosen instrument policy, which it had formally rejected in 1945 because it was anti-competitive. The question was basically to do with the right of multiple designation, i.e. having more than one airline serve a route, or a country. For a while it looked as if the State Department might acquiesce to Italian demands, but at the end of the day multiple designation was maintained. One consequence of this was that National joined Pan Am, TWA, and Seaboard (an all-cargo carrier) on routes between the USA and Britain.[13] That exacerbated a problem already perceived by the British who felt that their competitive position *vis-a-vis* the USA was being eroded by the introduction of more US scheduled carriers and more US charter operators, both of which added to the over-capacity on the Atlantic route, reduced load factors and increased the competition for BOAC. Capacity/frequency was one of the main ways of competing under the Bermuda model. Eventually these all became serious problems, but the immediate cause of concern was the capacity issue, which raised its head in relation to National's operations within two years of the Miami route being opened.

On 25 May 1972 National changed over from narrow bodied jets, DC-8s, to Boeing 747s for its daily service from Miami to London. BOAC began Boeing 747 flights the following day on the route, but only for three days a week. On other days the route was serviced by narrow bodied aircraft. BOAC was concerned about over-capacity on the route. If it had matched National with seven flights by 747s a week, capacity, as compared to the state of affairs before the introduction of the wide bodied jets, would have been raised from 3,724 seats a week in both directions to 9,786. The British Department of Trade and Industry (DTI) calculated that under those circumstances peak period load factors would decline from the previous year's 60 per cent to a little above 40 per cent.

BOAC was neither willing to mount a daily 747 service nor allow National to do so. The company was backed by the Conservative Government, even though it generally favoured more competition. The Department of Trade and Industry Minister, John Davies, unilaterally restricted National to four 747 flights a week and allowed BOAC the same, with narrow bodied jets operating on the remaining three days. US authorities were outraged. They felt that this was contrary to the Bermuda Agreement, which they interpreted as only having provisions for adjustments of capacity *ex post facto* and then only after consultations between the two governments. So far as they were concerned this was a highly illiberal, restrictive and illegitimate use of the bilateral. They argued that there would not be over-capacity because the attractiveness of the 747s would help to stimulate more demand, which they also claimed was set to expand in any case.

The British position was that interpreting the agreement as only allowing *ex post facto* capacity adjustments, although adhered to for a long time, was mistaken. Given the American insistence at Bermuda in 1946 and in subsequent talks with the British that there should be no predetermined capacity limitations, the British, in terms of the historical record, appear to have been on very weak ground. The USA retaliated through the CAB on 12 July insisting that BOAC file all its flight schedules into and out of the USA within seven days and cautioned the company that any new schedules would have to be submitted for prior approval.

The situation remained fraught throughout July and for most of August. Then on 23 August a compromise was agreed whereby National proposed operating 747s five times a week until the end of September after which it would revert to the use of narrow bodied jets for the winter. On that basis the British withdrew their unilateral controls and the US CAB abandoned its insistence on BOAC filing new schedules for approval. In April 1973 National reintroduced 747s on a daily basis and the increase in traffic both in 1972 and early 1973 allayed the fears of BOAC and the British Government concerning over-capacity and no further action was taken. For a few months, at least, capacity matters were allowed to rest.

Despite the specific problem of the Miami route fading away, there remained a number of matters of principle that had not been resolved. The British had refused to accept the American contention that Bermuda only allowed *ex post facto* adjustment of capacity, although in the case of National and the Miami route they claimed that the reduction they had insisted on was in fact the result of a review of actual practice. The British concern about over-capacity seemed to have been justified as the load factor, when 747 flights were restricted to 4 per airline a week, was only just over 43 per cent. Nevertheless, their actions had been high-handed and had exposed not only an illiberal side to the Bermuda Agreement, but also an unsettling uncertainty about what capacity airlines could actually offer. It also exposed the growing concern with over-capacity on the Atlantic and begged the question as to how that problem should be dealt with in general: should it be done through regulation or should the market have a greater say in allowing the efficient to prosper and the less efficient to contract their operations. Finally, given the strain that had been placed on Anglo-American civil aviation relations by what amounted to a fairly small matter, namely the local problem of capacity on a single route, one might be prompted to ask what hope was there for the continuance of the Bermuda Agreement if more serious, and more general problems arose, particularly if a less free market oriented government came to power in Britain, as in fact happened in 1974?[14]

The Bermuda Agreement alone did not dictate civil aviation policy. For one thing it was too flexible and too subject to varying interpretations to do that. Changing government policy was still the overriding determinant. In Britain, policy outwardly changed little from the Second World War until the 1980s in the sense that the country's main airlines BOAC and BEA were nationalised and cosseted to one degree or another by the government through subsidies and protective regulation. This set-up made it possible for the government to require the companies to perform certain non-commercial activities on political grounds and also insist that they equipped their fleets with British aircraft. Both these requirements had a significant adverse impact on the profitability of BOAC and BEA even though they were compensated with subsidies and enjoyed regional chosen instrument status in their respective geographical spheres of operation. There were differences between Labour and Conservative Governments in terms of the emphases they placed on the value of competition, but such differences were not really telling until the end of the 1960s, when various pressures mounted in the airline industry generally, which prompted governments to reconsider their policies on commercial civil aviation.

The responses made by Conservative and Labour governments during the late 1960s and in the 1970s cannot be summarised as consistent sets of policies. In particular Labour, while generally favouring a more regulated market, was also responsible for the Edwards Report, which was the overture to a more competitive British international policy (even though it was sometimes a case of one step forward two steps back); for effectively abandoning the equipment policy of 'buy British' after insisting upon it; and for the start of Laker's Skytrain, which helped to revolutionise the fare structure on the Atlantic route.

In terms of the history of British deregulation the Edwards Report is as good a place as any to begin. It has already been noted that charters, which by 1970 accounted for about a quarter of the transatlantic traffic, Third World Airlines, rising costs of equipment and fuel were all creating adverse economic pressures for the airline industry in the 1960s. In addition, the USA was becoming less and less happy about the IATA procedures for setting rates. In Britain, as elsewhere, these factors pushed government into reconsidering aviation policy.

The Labour Government of Harold Wilson was not generally regarded as being well disposed to the idea of allowing the free market a larger say in the operations of BOAC and BEA. The tendency of the Government to favour regulation and intervention in the industry was demonstrated by a number of decisions in the late 1960s. Firstly, the government insisted that BEA acquire British aircraft it did not want to buy and then to sweeten the pill it extended a subsidy to the company. Secondly, the Air Traffic Licensing Board (ATLB) in 1968 refused to allow British Eagle and Caledonian Airways to operate on the Atlantic in competition with BOAC. It accepted the argument presented in submissions from BOAC that they could only succeed by taking traffic away from the nationalised corporation.[15]

In the light of those developments one might think that the Wilson Government had set its face against any radical changes in the civil aviation sphere. Effective regional monopolies were being maintained for BEA and BOAC and the uncommercial nature of the airline industry was apparently being perpetuated by the government foisting uncompetitive aircraft onto the airlines. However, the year before the ATLB decision, the Government had set up a committee under the chairmanship of a leading industrial executive Sir Ronald Edwards. It reported in May 1969.

Formally named 'The Committee of Inquiry into Civil Air Transport', the brief of the Edwards' Committee was: 'To inquire into the economic and financial situation and prospects of the British civil air transport industry and the methods of regulating competition and of licensing currently employed.' The Government White Paper which resulted from the work of the Committee made suggestions which began a long process which radically altered both Government policy and the character of the airline industry. The proposals marked a move away from stringent regulation to a more competitive dispensation and held out the hope for further liberalisation. The Edwards Report made some deference to the postwar achievements of British airlines, but, rather worryingly, noted that their productivity was only in the middle range of European carriers. No comparison was made with their American competitors, but quite clearly some changes were needed if British airlines were to thrive either on the Atlantic or in Europe.

The Government declared that the purpose of British civil aviation was to provide services to meet demand at the lowest cost compatible with safety, an adequate return on investment, and the stability of the industry. Its contribution to the welfare of the British economy and in particular the balance of payments would also have to be taken into account.

> In setting these objectives for the industry, the Government consider that the minimum of restriction should be imposed on it or on the users of its services, and that arrangements which restrain competition or innovation should be tolerated only to the extent that they are necessary to achieve the main objectives of policy. Thus, as will appear later in this White Paper, the Government favour the licensing of a second British carrier on a scheduled service route, where it can be shown that such competition would be in the public interest.[16]

This was not a radical form of deregulation, but it was a definite step in that direction. The declared intention to cultivate more competition was qualified with various things that could modify or even prevent the pursuit of that goal, such as, balance of payments considerations, or, failure to demonstrate dual designation was in the public interest. Nevertheless, the general tenor of the White Paper was clear. The Government intended to move, whenever possible, towards more competition and a less regulated market. This was quite a departure for the Labour Government. It recognised that the industry would continue to be highly regulated because of safety, environmental factors and the need to maintain stability and regularity of public service. In addition, international services could only be operated through negotiations with other countries and this was a further reason why regulation would continue to play a major role. However, even here the Government was optimistic about making a constructive, competitive impact on the international system.

> The need ... is to operate within this framework in such a way as to give the [British] industry the biggest possible opportunities in the expanding world market. At the same time, however, this framework of regulation can be modified by international bargaining, by both the airlines and the Government. This applies to fares as well as to traffic rights. Britain's bargaining power is far from negligible.[17]

The White Paper also proposed administrative changes as a result of which a Civil Aviation Authority (CAA) was established to perform a similar role to that of the US CAB, and an Air Holdings Board was set up to oversee the operations of BEA and BOAC. These changes were in fact put into effect by the Government of Edward Heath after the surprise victory of the Conservatives over Labour in the 1970 General Election.

The CAA was subject to policy guidance from the government and had considerable powers over technical matters, economic and financial fitness of airlines and licensing policy, though over the latter there was a right of appeal to the minister. In 1980 the CAA acquired greater and more independent powers. Generally, under Heath, civil aviation was upgraded in importance and by the summer of 1971 Michael Hesseltine had become Minister of Aerospace with responsibility for air transport. These changes, particularly the impact of the CAA in the long-term, were significant. They immediately created a new sense of purpose and a renewed sense of the importance of the industry, especially as they were accompanied by statements by Heath advocating a more commercial approach to the operation of airlines.

Heath's Government followed the recommendations and the overall spirit of the Edwards' Report by attempting to cultivate a more competitive environment for British airlines. In retrospect, what appears as the rather inevitable logic behind the creation of the Air Holdings Board was followed in 1973 when the Board proposed the merger of BEA and BOAC. The Secretary of State for Trade and Industry agreed and, as of 1 April 1974, the two companies were succeeded by BA. Britain now had an airline with the most extensive international route system in the world and the potential to compete with any airline that then existed. And compete the government deemed it must do.

The most radical development from the Edwards Report was the adoption of a policy of dual designation involving the creation of a second force British airline. The airline was created by Caledonian taking over British United Airways and becoming British Caledonian (B.Cal.). The route network of the new airline was expanded by the CAA under the authority of the 1971 Civil Aviation Act and the Policy Guidance White Paper of February 1972. Routes were taken from BOAC, notably those to Nigeria and Ghana, and given to B.Cal., which was also licensed as a second carrier to operate alongside BOAC on the London-New York-Los Angeles route. Furthermore, the CAA licensed Freddie Laker's Skytrain, after lengthy deliberations, to operate as from 1973 between Stansted and New York. Previously Laker had operated charters to the USA, but now he could mount a scheduled operation that was revolutionary both in terms of fares and the walk-on, walk-off approach to bookings. Ultimately, Laker and his operations were one of Britain's main contributions to the liberalisation of the transatlantic aviation market.[18]

During the first three years of the Heath Administration significant changes occurred in British civil aviation policy. These developments will be considered in more detail in chapter four, for the time being suffice it to say that although there was no radical transformation, possibilities for such change seemed to exist. Then the Yom Kippur War threw everything into confusion, highlighting the problems that had been mounting in civil aviation since the mid 1960s. British policy now underwent a temporary reversal and its drive toward liberalisation was blunted. Britain's answers to the problems of the 1970s were not couched in terms of further deregulation except in one or two exceptional cases. It was left to the government of Margaret Thatcher, which came into power at the end of the decade, to bring about a greater degree of doctrinal harmony with the USA and her close friend President Reagan. Britain then began to reconsider things along liberalisation lines, but by that time it found itself some way behind its close ally and ideological bedfellow the USA on the road to a more deregulated system and was confronted with specific difficulties which made it difficult to follow in America's footsteps.

Before turning to examine the course taken by deregulation in the USA, one further development in the European sphere needs to be considered as it had the potential to pose a number of challenges to Anglo-American air service arrangements and to the bilateralism of the Bermuda system.

In 1973, after two abortive attempts by previous prime ministers, Edward Heath successfully took Britain into the EC. Between 1973 and 1993 there was a long and rather tortuous path to the Single European Act [SEA] and the Single European Market [SEM]. The SEA, among other things, revived the admonition to the Member States in the Treaty of Rome to create an integrated Community transport system. The creation of appropriate policy proved to be a difficult task, but eventually it became an important factor in the development of international civil aviation policy both in the Community and between the Community and the rest of the world.

As early as the Messina Conference of 1955, the Europeans realised that transport would be just as important to the future development of integration as any transport system is in the life of a nation state - in fact possibly more so. On political, social and economic grounds, transport was deemed to be of major importance. Politically it would help to bring the Community together and help nurture a sense of collective identity. Economically it would facilitate the growth of Community-wide trade, investment and movement of labour. All of which would be vital if the Community were to benefit from economies of scale, an enlarged consumer market and concerted efforts at R&D. In addition, a Community-wide policy would encourage rationalisation, greater efficiency and competitiveness in an industry which produced six per cent of the Community's GDP by the mid 1980s: a greater percentage than agriculture's. Socially, it would be beneficial by helping to create a more uniform level of economic activity throughout the Community and by ensuring that the less developed south and regions on the periphery ceased to be disadvantaged by poor communications. The potential advantages of a Community transport policy were self-evident, but that did not make it easy to achieve. The long-standing existence of national transport policies and the highly political nature of civil aviation meant that transport was one of the slowest policies to develop within the Community.

In 1962 the Council of Ministers recognised that harmonisation would have to proceed in stages and that until some progress had been made the fundamental law of the Community - the Rome Treaty - could not be applied fully in the transport sector. In fact for a long time sea and air transport were considered to be outside the Community's jurisdiction.

As the Community developed and transport policy gradually evolved two administrative departments or Directorates of the European Commission became involved: DG4 in charge of the Community's competition rules and DG7 in charge of transport. In very simple terms, DG4 looks after the rules of competition that govern relations between companies in the Community, and DG7 looks after broader policy issues and relations between the Member States and the Commission with regard to developments in civil aviation and other areas of transport. So far as liberalisation of civil aviation is concerned, it is the job of DG7 to try to create a harmonised, common policy acceptable to Member States in the European Council. After that, it is then the job of DG4 to ensure that the system operates fairly in accordance with the Community's competition rules.

The competition rules are embodied in articles 85 and 86 of the Rome Treaty. The general principles are expressed in the opening paragraph of each article.

85.   The following shall be prohibited as incompatible with the common market: all agreements between undertakings, decisions by associations of undertakings and concerted practices which may affect trade between Member States and which have as their object or effect the prevention, restriction or distortion of competition within the common market, ...

86.   Any abuse by one or more undertakings of a dominant position within the common market or in a substantial part of it shall be prohibited as incompatible with the common market in so far as it may affect trade between member states.[19]

The Rome Treaty envisaged the eventual emergence of a competitive and largely, though not entirely, deregulated common market. If this were applied to civil aviation much of the regulated side of the industry would have to go, such as pooling arrangements, price fixing, capacity restrictions, controls over entry into the market and so on. This scenario looks very similar to what happened in the USA once momentum for deregulation built up in the 1970s. However, the Council of Ministers decided in 1962 that the competition rules could not be applied to transport until substantial progress on harmonisation had been achieved.

As a result of that decision policy developed in stages involving the different categories of transport. Road and rail transport developed first and the competition rules came into operation there in 1968. In 1973 the European Court ruled that sea and air transport were also subject to the Treaty of Rome.[20] However, it was one thing to declare that airlines should be subject to competition, it was another matter to implement this. In fact the means were lacking and attempts by the Commission to develop airline policy were largely unsuccessful and a decade slipped by without significant progress being made.

It was not until the 1980s that the potential for a competitive single airline market in the European Community began to be realised. Much of the impetus for change came because of what had happened in the USA and because of initiatives taken by Britain, Holland and a more assertive Commission. In 1986 competition rules were applied to sea-borne transport and then in 1987 the first step was taken to bring aviation under Community regulation. Developments in the EC were to become of more and more importance in the 1990s though the character of the system that would finally emerge is still not certain at the time of writing (1994).[21]

So far as the origins of civil aviation deregulation were concerned in the 1970s, the EC played no part. Or at least it played no positive part in the move towards deregulation. On the contrary, its contribution was to present the world with a picture of a highly regulated and protected European system that for the time being took no heed of the competition rules of the Rome Treaty because they were deemed inapplicable until policy was harmonised and there were no moves in the 1970s to change European civil aviation policy such that the competition rules could operate.[22] The idea of deregulation lay dormant in Europe and posed little challenge to the Bermuda system. In Britain there had been some changes, mainly prompted by the Edwards Report, but, with problems becoming acute in the industry in the mid 1970s and with the return of a Labour government in 1974, further liberalisation was delayed. There were some developments within the market, namely the challenge to the established system posed by Laker, and there were growing strains within the Bermuda 1 framework as Britain and the USA gave it different emphases and interpretations. Eventually the divergence in British and American policies was such that the Bermuda Agreement had to be renegotiated. As Britain moved towards a more regulatory stance, the USA began to move decisively in the opposite direction. Initially this was confined to the US domestic context, but the momentum for change gathered pace as the 1970s developed and soon there was also major impact on the international scene as well.

Notes and References

1. For more detail on the background to and developments of the wartime period see Dobson (1991 A), chs. 1-5.

2. Recent accounts of the Bermuda Conference may be found in ibid., ch. 6; Mackenzie (1991); Dierikx (1992).

3. Wisgerhof Interview.

4. Shane Interview. In fact, 'fair and equal opportunity to compete' was the language of the generally more restrictive Bermuda 2. In Bermuda 1 the equivalent phrase was 'fair and equal opportunity to operate'.

5. National Archives of the USA, Alexandria Virginia, The Nixon Project (hereafter, Nixon Project), Papers of Hendrix S. Houthakker, box 51, folder: Transportation, International Aviation Policy (Interagency Committee), 'Statement of International Air Transportation Policy of the United States, 22 June 1970'.

6. Cmd. 6747, 1946, 'US, UK, Civil Air Services Agreement, Bermuda'; Haanappel (1984), pp. 34-58; Hans A. Raben, Director General Netherlands Civil Aviation Authority, 'Deregulation a Critical Interrogation', in Wassenberg and van Fenema (1981), p. 18.

7. Ibid.

8. Ibid.

9. Chuang (1972), ch. 2.

10. Raben, in Wassenberg and van Fenema (1981), p. 18.

11. Ebdon Interview.

12. Dobson (1991 A), ch. 7.

13. Nixon Project, WHCF CA, box 12, folder: CA 7/UK beginning 7/16/69, memo. attached to W.S. Street to John Ehrlichman, 28 April 1969.

14. Ebdon Interview; *Flight*, 29 June, 20 July and 7 Sept. 1972.

15. For much of the background concerning BOAC, BEA, and BA, I have drawn liberally from Penrose (1980) and Sampson (1984). For problems involved in the postwar buy-British policy see Lyth (1990).

16. Cmd. 4018, 1969, 'Report of the Committee of Inquiry into Civil Air Transport [Edwards Report]'; Cmd. 4213, 1969, 'Civil Air Policy'.

17. Ibid.

18. Ebdon Interview; Interview with Raymond Colegate, former member of the UK CAA, conducted by the author 25 March 1991.

19. Treaty of Rome 1957, text taken from Swann (1983), appendix.

20. European Court of Justice Law Case 167/73, 1974.

21. European Commission Official Source; Nicholl and Salmon (1990), pp. 185-89.

22. European Commission Official Source; The European Community's Transport Policy, Periodical 3/84, European Documentation, Official Publication of the EC.

Chapter 3
Early Moves in the USA Towards Regulatory Reform

The euphemisms of government press releases notwithstanding, the basis of regulation is armed force. At the bottom of the endless pile of paper work which characterises all regulation lies a gun.[1]

US regulatory reform began in a wider context than the civil aviation industry and the diplomacy that it spawns in the international realm. Politicians and economists started to question what for many years had remained unquestioned, namely the various justifications of regulated markets.[2]

Why do governments regulate markets? The reasons are legion and the kinds of regulation that they demand vary by industry and by country. To eradicate corruption; to prevent exploitation of consumers; safety reasons; competency; to halt the decline of public services; to exercise public control over industries on the basis of political doctrine; and defence, strategic or other national interest considerations: these are the usual justifications cited for introducing regulation.

The most fundamental disagreement with regulation comes from free marketeers who believe that the interplay of impersonal forces of supply and demand is the best and most efficient economic system and, moreover, a necessary complement to a free political system. According to them, political freedom and a free market cannot be divorced from each other. A more moderate free market view sees some virtue in government regulation, especially in the form of antitrust laws to ensure against monopolies, predatory behaviour and exploitation of the consumer. Those who are sceptical about the benefits of the free market support regulation in order to achieve, not only economic but also social, political and national interest benefits. The spectrum range of these views can be demonstrated by reference to arguments by Alan Greenspan who was to have a long career at the heart of economic policy in Washington, and by Stuart G. Tipton, who was Chairman of the US Air Transport Association in the early 1970s.

As early as the 1960s, Greenspan attacked the theoretical and historical justification for the USA's antitrust legislation. He alleged that the abuses that antitrust laws were supposed to deal with were caused not by the free market but by public policy. For example, the need to tie California to the east coast resulted in subsidies, land grants and a *de facto* form of protection to encourage the construction of the transcontinental railroad. Greenspan argued that problems in the market which arose from monopolistic railroad companies came about because of such government action and not because of operations of the market. Problems were then compounded by people in government concluding 'that a free market by its nature, leads to its own destruction [competition creates a tendency to concentration and eventually to take-overs and a monopoly emerging] - and they came to the grotesque contradiction of attempting to preserve the freedom of the market by government controls'.[3] Greenspan's panacea was to exclude public policy decisions from the realm of economic activity and to safeguard free entry into the marketplace in order to avoid the establishment of monopolies.

In contrast with that view, Tipton defended airline regulation to Transport Secretary Volpe in February 1971 when the Nixon Administration began to call for regulatory reform. He argued that the basic purpose of regulation was to ensure:

> Provision of regular air service under a system designed to meet a variety of needs in an undertaking by each of the carriers forming a part of the scheduled system to fulfil public service obligations in both high and low volume markets. In other words, regulation makes certain that the scheduled carriers provide adequate, reliable service day in, day out, over both profitable and unprofitable routes, in periods of both peak and off-season traffic demand. Although regulation entails control of market entry, such control is vital to achieving the necessary cross-support of profitable and non-profitable routes.[4]

These views of Tipton and Greenspan by no means exhaust the arguments of either side, but they highlight the irreconcilable doctrinal positions of those for and against regulation.

In the USA, government moves to control transport originated in the late nineteenth century in response to abuses in the marketplace. For example, as one economic historian has written, the railways:

> ... charged such high rates on the monopolistic Southern Pacific that one group of merchants calculated it would be cheaper to send a cargo of nails from New York across the Atlantic to Antwerp, thence by boat around the Cape of Good Hope to San Francisco, rather than ship directly across the nation.[5]

Whether or not this is an exaggeration, it certainly captures the flavour of the problems that afflicted US railways. When those problems were aggravated by corruption and political bribery, the need for legislation became compelling. Regulation of the railways, and indeed transportation in general, began with the 1887 Act to Regulate Commerce and the coming into being of the Interstate Commerce Commission. These developments and the Sherman Antitrust Act of 1890 became the model for regulation in general. Unlike Europe, where nationalised industries provided direct government control, US strategy was to control private sector companies via antitrust legislation and independent federal agencies or commissions.

In 1938 civil aviation was added to those industries already under government control. Although the original impulse for reform came from concern about how the Hoover Administration had awarded airmail contracts, the need for regulation was primarily justified by the need to foster a viable and efficient national airline system. It was the classic argument about the need to foster infant industries, though, as always with airlines, there was also a host of political matters involved which inclined government to support and nurture the industry.[6]

Regulation was achieved by the Civil Aeronautics Act of 1938 and developed in the Federal Reorganization Act the following year. The CAB was created, given independent status and charged with managing the economic side of civil aviation, which included licensing airlines for all domestic and all foreign routes to and from the USA: a role it retained until December 1984. The Civil Aviation Authority had control over aircraft licensing, navigational and some safety matters, and the Commerce Department had a watching brief over the structure of regulation. That arrangement remained in place until the Federal Aviation Act of 1958 established the Federal Aviation Administration. However, it was not until 1966 that really radical organisational change came with the creation of a separate Department of Transport that took over transport duties from the Commerce Department: with the demise of the CAB in 1984 it gained further authority over the airlines.

Under this system, which, at the policy as opposed to the bureaucratic level, remained largely unchanged from 1938 to 1977, a highly restrictive regulatory regime developed. Alfred E. Kahn, a leading proponent of deregulation and chairman of the CAB under President Carter, described what the CAB did as follows:

> The Civil Aeronautics Board controlled the number of major air passenger carriers and the specific routes each airline could fly. The CAB controlled entry into any and every market between two cities, whether by existing carriers or new ones. And for the most part it exercised that authority restrictively ... for five or six years in the early 1970s, the Board refused as a matter of policy to entertain any applications for new route authority. In addition, the CAB fully regulated air fares and exercised some control over the quality of service.[7]

Kahn attributed whatever economies and benefits were made during the period of the CAB regime to improvements in aircraft performance and comfort and not to any dynamic existing in the controlled operations of the market. However, in the early 1970s the force of such an analysis escaped many people who viewed the airline industry favourably. That posed a problem for the deregulators who had to create a situation in which deregulation became politically possible and for a long time that condition eluded them.

Opponents and proponents of deregulation were often at ideological loggerheads with each other and issues seemed impossible to resolve one way or the other to an impartial observer. Attorney at law, William G. Mahoney, speaking on behalf of the transport unions before the House Subcommittee on Aviation during the Hearings on the 1978 Airline Deregulation Bill, used the example of the modest reform of the railways by the 1958 Transportation Act as evidence of the damaging effects of abandoning regulation. Mahoney alleged that, because freight was more profitable than passengers, management downgraded the latter in favour of the former. After deregulation management was only responsive and accountable to the demands of the stockholders and, as a result, profit became the overriding motive and dramatic changes occurred.

> In 1958, there were many first quality passenger trains in this country. A number of these trains were operated on a break-even basis or at a slight profit. By 1968, as a direct result of the enactment of Section 5 of the Transportation Act of 1958, passenger train service was virtually extinct, and two years later, this Congress had to enact the Rail Passenger Service Act of 1970 to preserve, at taxpayers' expense, what little passenger service was left.[8]

There was quite clearly a problem. The market might fail to provide goods and services that were viewed by many as valuable on social and political grounds, and, moreover, which could be provided at a small profit, or on a break-even basis, provided there was some regulation by government. The workings of the free market were viewed with a degree of suspicion after the failures of the 1930s. The market's tendency to boom and bust and its failure to provide infrastructure services and facilities, which only had small margins of profit and then often only realised on a long-term cycle of investment and return, were seen as serious flaws. These deficiencies were threats to the overall system of capitalism and were socially and politically unacceptable in the eyes of many. It was this kind of view, notwithstanding the mild deregulation of the 1958 Act, that prevailed from 1933 to the end of the 1960s. It is important to understand the force of that position if the challenge that confronted the deregulators is to be fully appreciated.

In the 1930s the system of liberal democracy and economic capitalism was challenged in its economic form by the experience of the Depression and in politics by totalitarian regimes in Europe, the Soviet Union and Japan, which seized the political initiative in world affairs. Western liberals were forced to rethink and respond with new economic ideas and a reinvigorated political agenda. In the two decades that followed the simultaneous coming to power of Hitler in Germany and Franklin Roosevelt in the USA a world drama unfolded and in the crucibles of economic depression and hot and cold wars a new vision emerged to inspire the liberal democracies: it dominated the free world throughout the middle of the twentieth century.

The political perspective was provided by the impact of British liberal and socialist thinkers such as T.H. Green, William Beveridge, the Webbs and R.H. Tawney, by Europeans such as Jean Monnet and Henri Spaak and by men in the

USA such as the Philosophical Pragmatist John Dewey and the liberal intellectuals including Raymond Moley, Rex Tugwell, Samuel Rosenman and Adolf Berle, who helped to make up Roosevelt's 'brains trust'. Their effect was to enlarge the liberal socio-economic paradigm so that government's role embraced more social and economic responsibilities. The new economic ideas which underpinned this were provided by both John Maynard Keynes and by what emerged from the pragmatic experimentalism of Roosevelt's New Deal. At more or less the same time, the enormous success of the USA's war production revived confidence in industry and management and helped to rekindle the flame of capitalist fortunes. On the domestic front in the 1930s, Roosevelt and his lieutenants introduced a series of regulatory commissions and agencies to ensure that the less attractive aspects of the free market would be controlled by government. Capitalism was to be responsibly managed, made more responsive to the needs of the people and more accountable to government. The general character of this macro-economic management was the fine tuning of the economy by the use of interest rates and changes in government spending policies. In times of rapid economic growth the government would rein in expenditure, removing demand from the economy thus damping down inflation and accruing a surplus of revenue over expenditure. In times of recession the government would spend more through infra-structure projects, public works, and by increasing salaries of public employees in order to increase demand and pump-prime a recovery. This swinging pendulum of government economic policy would result in the cancelling out of periods of deficit spending by periods of surplus revenue and result in financial equilibrium in the long term.

Counterparts to regulatory agencies and positive government management of the domestic economies were to be found in the international realm in the forms of the International Monetary Fund (IMF) and the GATT and in organisations such as the IATA and the ICAO, which attempted to bring order to specific industries or areas of economic activity. This more regulated form of capitalism was at work in some domestic economies from the 1930s onwards. Confidence in its merits grew during the war and, although it did not develop entirely as planned and envisaged by the American and British policy makers and theorists who did most to create it, it was expanded into the international realm after the war and was never under serious threat until the late 1960s.

Welfare liberalism at home in various degrees; regulation and Keynesian economic policy both at home and abroad; trade liberalisation through the GATT; international monetary stability nurtured by the IMF and by the link between the US dollar and gold; and leadership, provided by the USA: these were the ingredients of the political and economic consensus that reigned in the West from World War Two to the end of the 1960s.[9]

In the 1960s things started to change as the US economy began to falter. It now had to face competition from Japan and Europe and had to come to terms with the fact that they were gaining comparative advantages over the USA in many spheres of industrial production. These developments were reflected in America's growing balance of payments difficulties, but there were even more serious problems looming. Rapid growth and high government spending for both domestic reform and overseas defence, especially in Vietnam, along with its balance of payments deficit, led to strains developing in the USA and the international economy. Among other reasons for the problems was the fact that the Kennedy and Johnson Administrations appeared to ignore Keynesian strictures about reining in expenditure at times of high levels of economic activity. There gradually built up inflationary tendencies that were later exacerbated by the rise in energy prices because of the 1967 and 1973 Middle East conflicts and the emergence of the OPEC cartel. The dollar now came under increasing pressure and the Western world slipped into recession. The postwar framework began to crumble and with it the postwar consensus.

The crumbling took quite a while, but from it there emerged an alternative put forward by neo-conservatives, who were anything but conservative in economic policy. They called for radical changes involving supply side economics, monetarism and deregulation. It amounted to more than an economic doctrine. It was also a backlash against the promiscuous sixties in Britain, the counter culture in the USA, Johnson's Great Society programme and Wilson's and later Callaghan's versions of democratic socialism. High taxation, high levels of regulation and of government intervention in the economy, and expensive welfare policies - all these Keynesian shibboleths had been seen by many as the measure of a civilised society in the postwar period - were gradually cast aside or cut back. This development was accompanied by the decline of the atmosphere of tolerance, at least in its most pervasive form. The ideologues of the right asserted the inextricable link between a free economy and a free people, but they were not noticeably libertarian in their attitudes towards cultural, educational, moral, and social matters as they were on economic questions. However, even though the more strident of the neo-conservative voices were raised in the USA and even though the USA had stuck closer to the pre-Keynsian free market and anti-welfare doctrines than most western countries, it still experienced difficulties in ushering in the new free market policies championed by Milton Friedman and others of what came to be known as the Chicago School.[10]

45

When Richard Nixon took office as President of the USA in 1969 doubts were already being expressed about the Western economic and political system. At first the attack had come from the left, but now the forces of the right were mustering their strength. Social, civil rights, economic and political problems all seemed to be getting out of hand. The response of the Nixon Administration to those problems was conservative pragmatism rather than doctrinaire neo-conservatism. The administration favoured regulatory reform in general, but it achieved little except with the system of international exchange rates.

The people concerned with economic matters in Nixon's team held fairly diverse views. They ranged from the iconoclastic and sometime liberal White House Counsellor Patrick Moynihan, to the avid deregulator Richard McClaren, Assistant Attorney General in charge of the Justice Department's Antitrust Division. The Council of Economic Advisers (CEA) was also largely composed of people who favoured deregulation, though Chairman Paul McCracken tended to moderate between the Keynesian fine-tuners and the free traders of the Chicago School. Arthur Burns, a close friend of Nixon's and another influential figure in economic policy-making, was regarded as conservative in the Nixon Administration, but with his belief that government should be an employer of last resort and his concerns over social policy he was by no means on the far right. In Gerald Ford's team, which was closer to the neo-conservatives, he was regarded as a middle of the road man. Peter Flanigan, Assistant to the President, was in charge of aviation matters in the White House. He was a close friend of Nixon's and had helped in his election campaigns going back to 1960 when he organised 'citizens for Nixon' in New York. Flanigan was a powerful man who pushed policies with vigour, though, at the same time, he was a pragmatist. He never allowed commitments to policies to override his sense of what was politically feasible. He was regarded as Nixon's 'Mr. Fixit'. Ultimately, regarding airline regulatory reform, he failed to live up to his title, but he was a strong influence in favour of that policy. In short, the economic policy makers under Nixon were not a homogeneous group either in policy or personality and not surprisingly, differences emerged about deregulation. Those differences contributed to the failure of regulatory reform proposals in the early 1970s.[11]

There were other reasons for lack of success. The erosion of the liberal, welfare, Keynesian consensus in the early 1970s was nowhere near as self-evident in the minds of moderates and conservatives as it became for them by the latter part of the decade. In any case, in 1973, the Nixon Administration began to lose its ability to take any radical initiatives because of the growing and debilitating effect of the Watergate affair.

Congress and industry - management as well as labour - also posed obstacles to the adoption of radical deregulation. The Congress was a difficult problem both because it was in the hands of the generally more pro-welfare, and more liberal Democrats (though one of the most influential forces for deregulation in the Congress in the late 1970s was Senator Edward Kennedy a leading liberal Democrat: Nixon was Republican), and because the executive branch had offended and alienated many of its members who, if they had been cultivated in the right way, might have been supportive. The unions feared for jobs and wages, but perhaps more surprisingly companies often feared for their market share and their profits. Ironically, the heart of the world's free-enterprise system was awash with companies that actually feared the free market. They opposed deregulation with only one or two exceptions in the airline industry. In addition to these factors, some of which changed over the years of the midseventies, there was also consistent opposition to airline deregulation from: the representatives of small communities who feared that they would lose their commuter services; economists who pointed to the dangers of takeovers and a few airlines coming to control the market in their own interests at the expense of the travelling public; and an influential safety lobby who alleged that deregulation would lead to declining safety standards in a rush to achieve greater profits. All of these things interacted in ways which prevented major deregulation being achieved in the transportation field during the Nixon period.

Nixon's own position both on politics and economics could be described as moderately conservative and there are good grounds for defending that characterisation of him. He had little time for the doctrinaire right and showed it both through his hesitation in supporting the right wing Republican presidential candidate Barry Goldwater in 1964 and by his self-proclaimed adherence to moderate conservatism. Nixon did not challenge the basic postwar assumptions in any concerted way. Quite the contrary: Nixon believed that he should simply redress the imbalance caused by the over-radical liberalism which could be severally found in the counterculture of the 1960s, President Johnson's civil rights, law and order and economic policies. The most radical response that Nixon orchestrated was the disengagement of the dollar from gold and its devaluation and eventual floating on the foreign exchange markets. But in doing that he was partly following the lead taken by Britain and other countries and partly he was succumbing to necessity: the Bretton Woods fixed exchange rate system was no longer sustainable.[12]

Elsewhere, in areas where Nixon had greater control, his policies were more moderate. At least they were moderate in terms of policy substance. Nixon's radicalism lay in his desire to shift the emphasis of the existing politico-economic consensus by handing over management to conservatives who would direct things more efficiently, approach things in a more hard-nosed way and cut costs. The attitude that government was a provider of all was to be changed by the use of less flamboyant rhetoric and by setting a good example of careful housekeeping. Nixon had little desire to cut back radically on liberal economic and social welfarism in the system, but he wanted it to work more cost effectively and in greater harmony with the free market. In bringing these attitudes to bear on economic problems in the transport sector the result was a series of rather half hearted attempts at reform. The impetus was not sufficient to oust vested interests. For that to happen circumstances needed to be different on a broad economic front and the radical reformers had to be allowed the initiative.

Following Nixon's victory in the November 1968 presidential election, he followed established practice by setting up various transitional taskforces to consider policy problems. They did their work between November and Nixon's inauguration on 20 January 1969. One, chaired by C.L. Miller, Head of Civil Engineering at the Massachusetts Institute of Technology, was to do with transportation.

The last time that any major proposals for change in transport policy had been made was in the early 1960s. Following John Kennedy's 1962 statement on transportation there followed two years of activity. In 1963 the Administration issued a declaration on US international civil aviation policy, which advocated a larger role for market forces and competition. On the broader transportation front things culminated in a 1964 bill in Congress, which actually went further than either the Kennedy or Johnson Administrations really favoured. However, opposition to the proposals gathered strength and in the end the whole thing petered out in the House Rules Committee. Now the Nixon taskforce took up the issue of transport reform once again.

Its report raised two themes that became part of the standard language of regulatory reform: consumer interests and the benefits of private enterprise. The report's summary stated that: 'Our national transportation policy should place principal emphasis on the individual, his need for mobility, and on the quality of his life.' It concluded:

> Finally, we urge the new Administration to take a fresh and objective look at the role of private enterprise in transportation. The Task Force is convinced that it is in the public interest to have private enterprise play

a much larger and more efficient role .... Reduction of existing barriers and the keys to progress involve government policies and actions.[13]

In August 1969 the Nixon Administration decided that US international aviation policy should indeed be reviewed because things had clearly changed since the 1963 policy statement. The 1969-70 review was prompted by the Task Force Report, by the problem of terrorist hijackings and by various pressures that had built up over recent years in the industry. Those pressures arose from: IATA fare setting; the impact of charter operations on scheduled carriers; and restrictive tendencies developing in the existing bilateral air services system. The industry was also still suffering from the effects of the fuel price rise and the economic downturn caused by the 1967 Arab-Israeli War which affected the industry in a particularly damaging way because of the costs of re-equipping airlines with jumbo's and inaccurate projections of passenger growth which had already resulted in excess capacity problems.

In mid November 1969 Herbert Stein of the CEA received a memorandum on the problems of the air transportation industry.

In the last eighteen months, the Air Transportation Industry has experienced decreasing load factors and an adverse profit performance. The problem that this memo addresses itself to is the continued high investment plans of the industry in the face of the significant decrease in capacity utilization.[14]

This situation was complex and not easy to deal with politically. Although regulation came under critical scrutiny in the 1970s, even the radical reformers acknowledged that difficulties within the international sphere were intractable. Care had to be taken not to disadvantage US airlines by forcing them into more free market practices when other foreign airlines continued to operate in a restricted and protected environment. The USA could neither unilaterally stop foreign governments subsidising their airlines nor guarantee to craft a competitive regime that all players would abide by. It was no good espousing competition if the actions of other states undermined its rationale and, furthermore, by doing so damaged US airlines. How to cope with this situation, at a time when US airlines were economically vulnerable and when balance of payments problems troubled the USA, was a question of some magnitude and one that caused hesitation about implementing free market solutions.

Some problems were largely of America's own making. In the 1960s, as the European economies began to thrive, the USA experienced a gradual decline of its proportion of the world passenger market. Admittedly this was from the artificially inflated level of the early postwar period, but nevertheless, it troubled successive US governments. One response to this was a policy, developed by the CAB, to nurture charter operators. This was popular because it provided cheap mass transport and also introduced an element of price competition previously lacking.

Charter were kept distinct from scheduled operations. They were not allowed to sell tickets to individual members of the public. They did not operate a regular timetable. Blocks of seats or a whole aircraft had to be booked by groups with a common purpose or 'affinity'; ticket purchases had to be so many days in advance; and there were also length of stay requirements. Despite the differences imposed upon two supposedly different types of travelling public, the charters were so successful that they began to affect the fortunes of the scheduled operators. The fact was that it was not possible to draw a clear distinction between charter and scheduled operators and their respective travelling publics. Charters were so successful that they contributed to the destabilisation of the fare regime that IATA had developed since 1946 and they also added to the general over-capacity problem that had developed in the late 1960s. That problem then became worse as a result of international economic problems and the appearance of even more charter capacity released from military service with the winding down of the Vietnam War. In the eyes of many non-Americans the USA had contributed substantially to the problems of over-capacity and low scheduled prices. Countries were thus unresponsive to US allegations that the problem was caused primarily by subsidised foreign flag carriers and they resented American attempts to get them to reduce the capacity that their airlines mounted.

Reform of the domestic US regulatory system was easier to justify politically in Washington because the government had the scope to determine the overall character of what went on there. On the other hand, there were many vested interests that defended the existing system and there were also difficulties that arose from the autonomous nature of the CAB. Compounding the problems were divisions of opinion within the Nixon Administration about the principles of deregulation, about the political prudence of reform and about the speed with which things should be changed.

US policy generally tried to do a number of rather incompatible things from 1970-76. It continued to encourage charters, but wanted to keep them distinct from scheduled operators as, in fact, was required by US law. This brought it into conflict with the Europeans, who had more liberal charter rules than the USA, but operated with price minima, a policy frowned on by the Americans. They wanted charters to function in a free price regime so long as it could be restricted to the bulk passenger market: the scheduled operators would cater for regular travellers at cost related fares which would enable them to remain economically viable. The two types of operators had very different costs and the USA believed that that needed to be reflected in the types of fare structures under which they operated. The problem was that charter and scheduled operators gradually became virtually indistinguishable in what they did as the 1970s progressed. Thus low fares desired by the USA for charter operators inevitably had a downward price effect on the scheduled operators. As deregulation developed, the distinction that had been artificially maintained between charter and scheduled operators became ever more difficult to sustain and that posed many problems for US policy makers.

Secondly, the USA attempted to propagate the value of a more competitive international airline system. But, while the USA tried to proselytise the world to competition, it also felt constrained to respond to what it perceived as unfair competition from subsidised state airlines and foreign discriminatory practices. The USA began to negotiate on the basis of an 'equal exchange of economic benefits'. To foreigners this seemed an ill disguised form of protectionism. The USA was keen to restrict others in their operations, for example the garnering of sixth freedom traffic by the Dutch carrier KLM for its routes across the Atlantic, but was loath to see its own fifth freedom rights out of London cut back. The Americans argued in their own defence that access to the huge US market was of much greater value to European countries than US access to their smaller markets and, thus, it should be partly compensated by being given extensive beyond rights. On charters, the USA pushed for uplift ratios which would favour its airlines so long as US travellers to a country exceeded travellers from there going to the USA. Such actions suggested that passengers originating from the USA were a national asset for its airlines, to be traded only for reciprocal and equal economic benefits received from foreign countries. That was to some extent true, but interpreting US action further becomes rather more problematic. Instead of it being seen as essentially protectionist, it could be viewed as wanting to open up equal opportunities for airlines to compete on a more level playing field and to recapture American passengers wooed away

51

by subsidised foreign carriers, often with discriminatory advantages *vis-a-vis* US carriers. The fact was that in the harsh economic climate of the 1970s and with America's economic and domestic problems, no matter how keen administrations might have been on moving to a freer market, problems with the intractability of the international system often made it take protective measures instead. They were justified in American minds as retaliation for unfair foreign practices. At other times actions were genuinely aimed at forcing future liberalisation, but they were sometimes misinterpreted outside the USA. There was no simple line of policy that the USA could adopt to push forward liberalisation. Although its general disposition was to move toward a more free market dispensation, there were limits both to the sacrifices that US airlines could be expected to make and to the potential damage to US national interests that could be absorbed for the sake of encouraging a free market airline system.[15]

Transportation Secretary John Volpe was placed in charge of the Nixon Administration's international aviation review. It was hoped that it would yield some strategy by which US airlines could increase their share of the world market. Robert Henri Binder, the Director of the Office of International Transportation, took departmental responsibility for overseeing the review and Paul Cherington was at the work face as Chairman of the Steering Committee. Cherington, DOT Assistant Secretary for Policy and International Affairs, had participated in the work of the Transitional Task Force and favoured some measure of regulatory reform. The Steering Committee was established by Flanigan, who played an important role as he liaised between the White House on the one hand and Cherington and his colleagues on the other.[16]

On 24 July Flanigan began to circulate information and guidelines to the interested departments and agencies about the coming review. It was to be comprehensive in its scope with special emphasis on those things which inhibited or threatened to undermine the potential for competition and the expansion of US airlines. The Bermuda Model was to be examined, in particular, deviations from its principles and the way it dealt with sixth freedom rights, multiple designation, capacity and routes. The relationship between charter and scheduled airlines, rate setting and the role of IATA, competition between US carriers and with foreign carriers, pooling arrangements and other forms of protectionism, balance of payments implications, technical problems and bureaucratic fiefdoms were all included in the brief of the Steering Committee.[17]

On 4 August Flanigan, in his search for a picture of civil aviation that would help him with his input into the formulation of new policy, wrote to Dr.

Ernst van der Beugel in Holland. Van der Beugel was a Professor of International Relations who had much practical and business experience. He had been involved in the Marshall Plan as an adviser to the Dutch Government and was President of KLM, the Dutch flag carrier, in the early 1960s. His views, while not accepted in their entirety by Flanigan, provided another warning about dangers to US airlines.

After referring to the bilateral jungle, which he believed had existed since the end of the war despite rules derived from the Bermuda Model, Van der Beugel went on to suggest that things were about to get even worse, particularly for the USA.

> I have no data available but I am practically convinced that the international position of American Civil Aviation has been adversely affected and surely will be so even more in the coming years by the pure bilateral approach based on the equitable exchange of economic benefits. Because of the greater strength of US civil aviation which cannot be matched other countries are forced to take defensive measures. .... I think it would be a constructive initiative of the Nixon Administration to call a government conference (probably in the framework of ICAO) ... to study the possibility of a substantial liberalisation of international air policy and the creation of a much stronger multilateral instrument of reference.[18]

The idea of a multilateral agreement was never regarded as a practical possibility by the higher echelons of the Nixon Administration, but the sense that US aviation interests were not being served by the existing system did have purchase on many minds. This was not so much an ideological as a pragmatic view. Nixon's advisers believed that a liberalisation of international civil aviation would benefit US airlines. They believed, despite temporary setbacks for Pan Am, that US airlines had a competitive edge that would allow them to increase their market share. More competition was to replace political agreements that divided markets on the basis of criteria that did not yield fair economic benefits for the USA. This reasoning was adopted by Flanigan and others, but implementing change proved to be difficult.[19]

The Steering Committee, into which no less than nine working groups fed their views, came into being in August. Cherington, as he was to confess the following June in an article in *The National Journal*, was a moderate in terms of regulatory reform. 'I favored a go-slow process - creeping deregulation if you will.' That attitude prevailed in the DOT where the first draft of a policy declaration was drawn up in October. By that time differences of emphasis were beginning to emerge between the two most influential groups involved in the review. The moderates stood on one side led by the DOT and supported by the CAB. Those advocating extensive reform were led by the CEA, and Flanigan with strong doctrinal support from the Justice Department's Antitrust Division. Thus, as soon as the draft appeared, Binder began to receive politely phrased, but clearly critical comments concerning its lack of emphasis on the interests of the consumer and the benefits of greater competition.[20]

On 3 October Hendrik Houthakker, the CEA representative on the Steering Committee, wrote to Binder saying that he thought that the draft was OK, but that 'a few major factors should be included.' His comments proceeded to spell out the need for low cost air travel and competition. Three days later Flanigan wrote to Binder in a similar vein. He clearly felt the need to point out that the present draft did not even go as far as the 1963 statement with regard to the need for competition.

> The October 1st draft of your statement on aviation policy seems excellent to me. My only suggestion is that we emphasize a little further our interests in the competitive aspects of this industry. .... I would ... state that we are on the side of expansion rather than restriction, of innovation rather than status quo, of reducing prices rather than otherwise. These are generally ... included in the third paragraph of the '63 statement.[21]

Concern continued to be felt in the CEA over the next two months despite revision of the policy document. There were fears about proposals to give the CAB more control over fares. Ostensibly this was to enable it to deal more effectively with foreign countries that were undermining competition by the use of subsidised or other unjustifiable low fares, but members of the CEA feared that the CAB might misuse such power in an anti-competitive way itself. On 28 November Chairman McCracken, Houthakker and Stein sent a memorandum to Cherington expressing their concerns over this and called for a statement that would be generally more competition oriented and less prone to include clauses that would open the door to regulation on grounds not directly related to the commercial operations of the airline market. On the question of the future role of charter operations, the CEA favoured allowing the market to decide the relative size of operations between scheduled and non-scheduled services. However, while the CEA clearly wanted liberalisation, it was prepared to concede that protectionism might be necessary in 'extraordinary circumstances' involving the balance of payments.[22]

The effect of the representations from the CEA and Flanigan, and the known preferences of the President for regulatory reform had considerable effect on the draft policy proposal. In some ways they had too much effect because when the draft was made public in January 1970 there was strong adverse reaction in many quarters, and especially from US scheduled airlines and from Europe where there was deep concern that aggressive competition from US charter and scheduled operators would reduce the market share of their own operators on the Atlantic. The outcome of this was redrafting and the CEA again found itself fighting to prevent the watering down of its ideas about a more open and competitive international civil aviation policy for the USA.[23]

The final statement approved by President Nixon on 22 June 1970 was moderate and rather lacking in force. In its general principles it reaffirmed much of what had been declared in previous statements. The themes of consumer interests and benefits from competition were well in evidence:

> It [i.e. US policy] should promote an expanding, innovative, economically and technologically efficient international air transport system which (1) provides that passengers and shippers share in the benefits through improved services and reduced fares and (2) assures U.S. air carriers a fair and equal opportunity to compete in world aviation markets so as to maintain and further develop an economically viable service network wherever a substantial need for air transportation appears.[24]

The statement then elaborated on the general principles that were to govern US policy.

> Our international air transportation policy must recognize a number of other U.S. objectives or principles; these may at times be served by the policy or at times be constraints upon it. Thus, the policy must be appropriately mindful of U.S. strategic and political interests, the international military air transportation interests of the U.S., and the prospective effect of the policy on the U.S. balance of payments. It must also take into account legitimate air transport interests of other countries and recognize that in the final analysis the policy cannot be viable without international acceptance. It

55

should recognize that the United States historically has believed that the economic and technological benefits we seek can best be achieved by encouraging competition (the extent of competition to be determined on a case-by-case basis) and by a relative freedom from governmental restrictions. [25]

The policy included many compromises because of the differences between agencies and departments and because of the criticisms of the January draft. It threatened action both against those who would depart from the kind of liberalism sought by Bermuda-style agreements, at least as interpreted by the USA, and those who sought to restrict US rights granted by bilateral agreements. Nevertheless, the USA endorsed the system that had developed under the auspices of the Bermuda Model and offered nothing more radical than a vague commitment to investigate the possibilities of multilateral agreements. Competition between charter and scheduled airlines was praised and was to be encouraged, but not to the extent of developing a totally free market: 'where a substantial impairment of scheduled services appears likely, it would be appropriate where necessary to avoid prejudice to the public interest, to take steps to prevent such impairment.' Similar action was advocated in the case of scheduled threatening to impair charter operations. Nevertheless, it seemed clear, despite some backtracking from the January draft, that US policy was committed to nurturing the non-scheduled airline market as a means of promoting both competition and the expansion of the US share of the international market. One further point on this was that the USA declared its desire to include general conditions for charter services in future air services agreements: this became of great importance in the future for trying to keep some balance between the scheduled and charter parts of the industry. On fares there was criticism of IATA, especially in the Pacific, but the USA pledged continued co-operation with IATA fare setting 'subject to continuing safeguards, but supplemented by increased direct informal exchanges between governments.' The unease with which the Administration regarded IATA fare setting was thus expressed, but no real alternative was put forward.

'As a rule', the US condemned pooling arrangements, but kept the door open for emergencies. It did not condemn all types of co-operation. Some were seen as being in the public interest: others were not. There was a clear and forthright statement on the right of multiple designation - a policy which some departments feared the State Department had placed in jeopardy in the course of difficult negotiations at the end of the 1960s. 'The concept of a single carrier or chosen instrument for the United States remains as undesirable today and in the future as in the past.' The general principle was clear. Perhaps it might not be economically viable to have dual designation competition on a point to point basis in every case, but the broader conception of dual designation should be possible. In other words two US airlines serving one foreign destination from different regions of the USA.[26]

Compared to what was to happen eight years on, this policy statement represented only very modest progress in terms of turning the tide against regulation. The Administration declared its intent to pursue a more competitive aviation policy specifically through multiple designation, nurturing charter operations, and resisting protectionist and restrictive pressures from abroad, but much of this was hedged with qualifications and as things transpired the impact on actual policy was not all that great. However, there were other developments which require some attention. One involved the gradual change of personnel in the main regulatory agency, the CAB; the other was the debate that took place within the administration on a number of fronts that involved the question of deregulation. Those debates were to keep the idea of deregulation very much alive even though further formal progress was negligible with regard to civil aviation during the lifetime of the Nixon Administration.

Appointing those with a conservative free market disposition to positions of management was one of the hallmark's of Nixon's economic policies. In 1969 Nixon appointed Secor Browne to the chairmanship of the CAB in the hope that he would bring a more pro-competition flavour to the Board and also gradually change its composition. Browne turned out to be somewhat more moderate than the Administration might have wished, though he continued to liberalise the operations of charters. On 14 August Flanigan wrote about Browne: 'he talks well, but there is no obvious change in the Board. The staff needs changing and the President wants them changed.' Gradually, there was a shift of emphasis, but the economic problems that afflicted the airlines in the 1970s were such that it needed a more doctrinally convinced man than Browne to move things unequivocally towards more competition. Instead, the CAB's policy was somewhat inconsistent. Sometimes it favoured more competition, at others it resorted to capacity agreements, and other restrictive measures. Flanigan thought that:

Browne should *continue* to clean out the staff to provide the most competent people who agree with the free enterprise philosophy,

57

according to the President. Then the Board's policy is to provide the greatest freedom possible to make its business decisions. The lines, not the Board, should run their business.[27]

In 1973 Browne resigned from the CAB and was replaced by Robert Timm who was less inclined to reform. However, even if he had been differently disposed, his room for manoeuvre was very limited as the situation of the airlines deteriorated badly during 1973 and hopes for deregulation were largely replaced by a series of emergency measures to try to salvage the fortunes of the US industry. In any case, the initial drive within the Administration for regulatory reform was already stalling by this time. The debates that had occurred in Nixon's first term as president were petering out by 1973 with not a lot to show from them in terms of concrete results.

Another stage for those early debates was Nixon's general policy of administrative reform. In April 1969 Roy Ash was appointed chairman of Nixon's Advisory Council on Executive Reorganization. One of its many tasks was to look into the operation of regulatory agencies. In January 1971 the Ash Council issued its 'Report on Selected Independent Regulatory Agencies'. The reaction among members of both the CEA and the Justice Department's Antitrust Division was not favourable.

On 18 March McCracken wrote a memorandum that was highly critical of the Ash Council's proposals. The report had taken the line that the defects of the regulatory agencies were primarily due to poor management and organisational defects and thus, with regard to the whole field of transport regulation, it recommended the creation of a single regulatory agency to replace the Maritime Commission, the Interstate Commerce Commission and the CAB. McCracken's view of the defects of the regulatory agencies was that: 'The more basic cause is the very existence of decision-making by government in areas like rates, entry and exit, and services when such decision-making could be done in today's circumstances, in the market place.'[28] In contrast Secor Browne, while harbouring some reservations, chose to emphasise his agreement with the main recommendation of the report that a single regulatory agency should be created.[29]

The strongest opposition came from the Antitrust Division of the Justice Department. Its head, Richard W. McClaren, wrote: 'In our view the Council has failed to recommend a meaningful program in the regulatory area.' In a blistering attack McClaren drew on CEA's Economic Reports for the President for 1970 and 1971, which pointed to the need for policy as opposed to organisational and management changes in the regulatory agencies.

McClaren thought that this was a better focus than that of the Ash Council for the real problem lay in substantive policy which needed to be more competition oriented. Dissatisfaction with the report rumbled on into the summer. In August, Houthakker told McCracken that: 'This report needs a very thorough critique. I hope it is not too late to stop it in its tracks.'[30] In fact apart from arousing hostility in the CEA and McClaren's Antitrust Division the report had little effect. Meanwhile, by early in 1971 the pace of the debate on regulation was speeding up, but its main format was determined elsewhere and not in the context of the Ash Council Report.

There were two other possible vehicles for the development of regulatory reform within the Administration in the early 1970s. Soon after taking office Nixon asked Volpe to prepare a comprehensive statement on transportation policy. That task was undertaken first by Paul Cherington 1969-70, and then, after he left the DOT, Assistant Secretary Charles D. Baker took over. Later, in May 1970, the Cabinet Committee on Economic Policy formed a subcommittee on transportation under the working chairmanship of Hendrik Houthakker. These two somewhat overlapping groups - Houthakker's subcommittee and Baker's people in the DOT - worked on policy and took up the issue of regulatory reform. Or rather it might be better to say that Houthakker's subcommittee tried to force the pace, though in its final report it bowed to what were seen to be the constraining realities of political and economic circumstances, whereas the DOT policy report never really took on any kind of definite form at all.

In September Houthakker's subcommittee completed its report entitled 'Improving the Performance of the Transportation Industries'. It reaffirmed the Administration's commitment to move 'toward a more deregulated transportation system', but because of the growing financial difficulties airlines were experiencing and because of likely opposition in Congress 'we feel that a program for deregulation in the transportation industry requires further detailed developments, especially with respect to phasing.' Faint hearts never win out against strong opposition and already those most committed to deregulation were losing conviction, with the exception of the Antitrust Division.[31]

At a meeting of the Cabinet Committee on Economic Policy on 4 December 1970, Houthakker's subcommittee's proposals advocating deregulation of surface transportation were considered. 'Considerable interest' was shown, but the Cabinet Committee went along with the caution of the subcommittee and requested further analysis of the positions of the interested parties before moving to the legislative stage. While that investigation was underway it became public knowledge that the CEA and the Antitrust Division were advocating regulatory reform. The reaction in the industry and from government departments was mixed, and on balance adverse. By 11 March the assessment called for by the Cabinet Committee had been more or less completed, but by then the chances for reform already looked bleak. As Baker explained to McCracken:

> We have a great idea here (in some measure) of deregulation. Unfortunately the Administration's less-than-co-ordinated efforts are resulting in a disappearing constituency; e.g. shippers - marginal, truckers opposed, barge lines opposed, railroads - fading fast! (Who is for us?). This thing has got to be brought back into focused orchestration if we expect to get any hearings, let alone legislation.[32]

Ironically, one of the culprits in the failure to focus things was the DOT itself.[33] The following month there were discussions about legislative proposals and some optimism was expressed by those congressmen in favour of reform, but problems and disagreements soon plagued progress. The DOT, which was cool toward reform made it clear that it was prepared to sacrifice reform of entry provisions into the marketplace if route rationalisation could be achieved. Flanigan also was willing to make that sacrifice. Samuel Peltzman of the CEA summed up his dissatisfaction about this by saying: 'In sum, DOT's proposal [on entry provisions for truckers] is substantially as restrictive as current act.' The talking continued for some time, but it was to little effect.[34]

Perhaps the most disappointing thing for the reformers was the lukewarm attitude of the DOT. One thing that might have reinvigorated the faltering moves for deregulation was the National Transportation Policy Statement that had been under preparation in the DOT since 1969. The origins of the idea behind the proposal of the statement had become obscured by the passage of time by the spring of 1971, but it was thought that the initial request had come from Nixon to Volpe via Arthur Burns. Whatever the case might have been, the progress of the Statement was a catalogue of delays, incompetence, differences between agencies, partisan pettiness and a lack of drive on the part of the DOT.

Originally the report was scheduled for 31 December, but when it did not appear Congress amended the Airport and Airways Development Act of 21 May 1970 so as to require that the report be completed within twelve months. Cherington produced a first draft, but it was not acceptable to others within the DOT, nor to either the domestic affairs staff of John Ehrlichman or the Office of Management and Budget (OMB). The main objections from Ehrlichman's people and OMB were to do with the absence of any mention of revenue sharing in the statement. One of Nixon's major proposals for innovation involved a greater devolution of power to the states by handing over a certain percentage of federal revenue directly to them. This New Federalism was supposed to inform all aspects of domestic policy, but the DOT had clearly failed to take the message on board.[35]

The DOT re-write under the guidance of Charles Baker was a painful and uninspiring long drawn out process. After much time had passed all the DOT managed to come up with was two general policy chapters: no progress had been made on detailed policy proposals. Peter Flanigan, the Domestic Council, the CEA and the OMB all thought:

> The draft was not a statement of policy, all but ignored revenue sharing and reorganisation, lacked perspective, organization and focus, and was too long and poorly written, containing excessive extraneous material.[36]

The excessive extraneous material was a reference to quotes from a report drawn up by ex-Transportation Secretary, Alan Boyd, for the Johnson Administration, which, in terms of quality, made for an embarrassing contrast with the present effort. The partisans in the Nixon Administration did not want such comparisons to be possible and so, while acknowledging the superiority of the work in the Boyd report, they wanted it exorcised from the draft and references to the Nixon Administration's successes in transport policy written in.

The National Transport Policy Statement was a fiasco. It was sent to Congress on 8 September after further redrafting, but it remained anodyne and vacuous. In the end, as one official put it, a major consideration seemed to be that 'there is something to be said for a general statement which avoids the kind of heated controversy the enumeration of specific policy would arouse.' The statement was in fact 'a harmless, vague product'.[37] By the end of 1971 there was value in being harmless because the 1972 Presidential election campaign was about to get under way.

A year later in January 1973 a report from the Aviation Advisory Commission presided over by Crocker Snow, summed up how aviation policy was developing. The report was over two hundred pages long and was directed primarily at domestic policy. Snow's comment that: 'None of the recommendations are radical ....' was bad enough for the regulatory reformers, but what was even worse for the industry itself was the judgement that: 'We also learned that there had been no overall planning for U.S. national and international

air service which is the keystone of a civil aviation system.'[38] In fact the
continuing deterioration of the finances of the airline industry inhibited
policy makers from coming forward with strong recommendations for regulatory reform. The Nixon Administration found it difficult to keep a clear
purpose in focus. Differences within the administration, opposition from
the transport industry, prospective problems with Congress and the difficult financial situation of the airlines, especially that of the international
carriers, complicated the situation and put radical change out of the grasp
of the would-be reformers. That is not to say that some changes were not
achieved within the existing framework, or that ideas for change were not
developed. For example, in early 1972 Peter Flanigan explained to Henry
Kissinger that it had been the Administration's policy to pursue bilateral
air service agreements on the basis of economic and not political criteria
as had been the case in the past. He pointed out that the USA had offended
the Australians by this policy even though they were of great political importance because of their military contribution to the war in Vietnam. There
were other areas of progress as well: the 1970 International Aviation Policy
Statement; the Airport and Airways Development Act of 1970 which
pumped substantial amounts of money into the infrastructure of civil aviation; some progress on drawing up criteria for airline mergers; and in
early 1974 the State Department brought in a private consultancy firm,
Harbridge House, to look at possible alternatives to the Bermuda Model in
preparation for further changes in international aviation policy.[39]

Nevertheless, despite these things there was a lack of consistency in US policy
and even the general commitment to a more competitive approach in civil aviation was compromised. Future direction of policy was unclear and the early
1970s were plagued by contradictory developments. On the one hand the Americans pushed for more capacity in the controversy between BOAC and National
in 1972. In part they argued that the introduction of Boeing 747s would attract
more traffic. On the other hand the previous year they had been encouraging
arrangements to reduce capacity. In 1973 the CAB in an unprecedented move
vetoed the introduction of low APEX fares proposed by BOAC and Lufthansa
and would not accept the argument that these low fares would attract more
passengers and help to solve the under utilisation of capacity. One might sym-
pathise with the British in wondering why it could be suggested that Boeing
747s had the ability to attract more passengers while low fares did not. This
was not the only anomaly that the CAB produced within the context of the
stated policy of the USA to strive for more competition in international aviation.[40]

In September 1972 the US was engaged in reviewing its bilateral with the Soviet Union. There were serious problems with the Soviets who cheated and gained more economic advantage from the bilateral than Pan Am did. In the review, the Americans cast around for some way to rectify this and pooling was suggested. Secor Browne, however, wrote a long letter to Flanigan arguing the disadvantages of adopting pooling. Among other things pooling would be a departure from US principles and would set a dangerous precedent. In early 1973 Browne left the CAB and was replaced by Robert Timm. Under Timm the attitude towards pooling changed. Both in the continuing talks with the Soviets in 1973 and for talks with Czechoslovakia in 1974 the CAB proposed that pooling on a limited basis should be allowed in order to enable the USA to gain equitable benefits from bilaterals with those two countries. The State Department, Justice and DOT all opposed this and in the end pooling was rejected, but the episode disclosed a distinctly uncompetitive attitude in the CAB.[41]

Timm's philosophy toward US airlines was 'Thou shalt not erode thy yield'. In the economic circumstances of 1973-4 economic survival took immediate precedence over moves for regulatory reform. Timm's policy was to protect and improve the profitability of US airlines. In early 1974 that even extended to putting pooling on the agenda for co-operation between Pan Am and TWA on the Atlantic routes. In the end it was disallowed, but only after the DOT came out unambiguously against it and after a decisive intervention by the Justice Department.

> Despite signs of approval from the CAB, the Justice Department declared that the proposed "pooling of revenues" was unjustified. The interests of all persons affected by the international air transportation industry are better served by the present system of competition ... than by pooling.[42]

Although Timm and the CAB were rebuffed here, Timm pursued other policies of aid to the airlines. The CAB reversed its traditional low fare policy and worked consistently for higher fare structures for scheduled airlines. Rationalisation of routes and capacity reductions were both pursued and the possibility of direct subsidies were at least agreed to in principle by Timm as a last resort for helping the beleaguered airlines, though they were never allowed in practice. In the first two months of 1974 US airlines clearly needed help: the CAB estimated that in that short time the five biggest lost $75 million. Help was given with fuel costs and a 20 per cent capacity reduction was agreed between BA, Pan Am, TWA and National on the Atlantic route and this was condoned by the CAB. While the CAB tried to alleviate the problems of US airlines by supportive action and a move towards more protection, at the same time it vigorously criticised foreign carriers for dumping subsidised seats onto the market and for discriminating against US carriers. In May 1974 the CAB proposed new powers for itself to take retaliatory action against foreign carriers whose governments discriminated against US airlines. That caused much resentment abroad, but President Ford was later to approve the proposal.

In the summer of 1974 the CAB refused to allow Laker to start his transatlantic low fare Skytrain operation on the suspect grounds of unfitness. The judgement was particularly galling to Laker as the US authorities had approved of him as a charter operator. The problem of low fare foreign competition that Laker posed so starkly also troubled the DOT and led Secretary Brinegar into thinking about policies which were contrary to the international aviation policy statement of 1970. Brinegar in early 1974, for example, was considering a reversion to the old policy of chosen instruments to enable the USA to compete more profitably with foreign airlines which had that same privilege and/or which were subsidised. The CEA, the Justice Department and White House officials were all against this. And so the twists and turns of policy and the rivalries continued. On negotiating charter rights there were also differences in Washington, this time between the State Department and the CAB, which is a further illustration of the contending factions within the Nixon Administration concerning regulatory reform.[43]

The bilateral jungle that van der Beugel had spoken of to Flanigan in the early days of the Nixon Administration when there was hope for change in the regulatory system now seemed to be re-asserting itself and was strangling the movement for reform. In the economic difficulties of 1973-74 the USA, like other countries, ran for regulatory protection in the civil aviation market.

On 9 August 1974 Richard Milhouse Nixon thirty seventh President of the USA resigned because of the threat of impeachment arising from the Watergate affair. His five years in office had not achieved a lot in terms of shifting US aviation policy towards regulatory reform and more competition. The 1970 International Aviation Policy Statement was the most concrete achievement, but its principles had been compromised by political difficulties from within and without the administration and by the economic problems that afflicted the industry at that time. Debate on the issues of regulatory reform had been joined,

but not won decisively or otherwise. Opposition from the transport industry, Congress and from the regulatory agencies and the DOT still had to be
contended with in various forms of strength.

Factions for and against regulatory reform still existed uneasily side by side
in the Nixon Administration in 1974. The CAB was still an obstacle to deregulation and the DOT was nothing more than lukewarm regarding the more
radical kinds of reform. In fact, the CAB, under Timm, retreated into
policies of tighter control and more intervention than had been the practice under Secor Browne. This was despite the fact that onlookers perceived
Timm as being more conservative than Browne and in this context one
would have thought that this would mean that he would be more favourable to competition. The apparent anomaly here can be puzzling unless
attention is paid to the meaning of some of the terms used.

To be conservative during the Nixon era meant having a disposition inclined
to the free market. At the same time it was not a highly doctrinal commitment. It was tinged with the remnants of Keynesian economic welfare values
and spiced with a heavy dose of political pragmatism. In this kind of conservative political milieu commitment to the market could be tempered by
concern for the survival of companies under economic threat, particularly
if they were also deemed to be important on national interest grounds. The
myriad connections the Nixon Administration had with the business world
encouraged this tendency to be sympathetic to the plight of industry, even
when it meant compromising commitment to the free market.

Ironically, for regulatory reform and more competition to be pushed forward
ruthlessly, two different and somewhat incompatible political types were more
appropriate than those generally found in the Nixon Administration. The first of
these were the neo-conservative ideologues who shunned pragmatism and
brought a moral fervour to the call for a return to the free market. 'Capitalism is
based on self-interest and self-esteem; it holds integrity and trustworthiness as
cardinal virtues and makes them pay off in the market-place, thus demanding
that men survive by means of virtues, not of vices.'[44] The second disposition
was more socially liberal or collectivist (though in the US context this is very
mild collectivism), which did not feel a close identity with the business community in the way that such feelings existed among Nixon's conservatives. At the
same time it admired the benefits competition yielded for consumers. This kind
of politician can be seen in the characters of President Carter and Edward
Kennedy: members of the doctrinaire right could be found in the administration
of Gerald Ford. These two political types successively carried the regulatory

reform movement along after Nixon's departure. Despite all the political infighting, it became a bipartisan affair.

Notes and References

1. Greenspan (1963), 'The Assault on Integrity', in Rand, (1967).

2. Much of my thinking about regulatory reform developed during the course of the interview programme upon which much of the second half of this book is based. For the wider context of regulatory reform I am indebted to: Swann (1988) and (1983); Majone (1990); Noll and Owen (1983); Pryke (1987); Ashworth and Forsyth (1985); Baldwin (1985).

3. Greenspan, in Rand, (1967).

4. Nixon Project, Houthakker Papers, box 51, folder: Transport Regulation 1970-April 1971, S.G. Tipton to John A. Volpe, 10 Feb. 1971.

5. Cramer (1973), p. 492.

6. See ch. 1 and Dobson (1991 A), ch. 4.

7. Alfred E. Kahn, 'Deregulation and Vested Interests: The Case of Airlines', in Noll and Owen (1983), p. 135.

8. *Congressional Digest*, June-July 1978, pp. 187-191, W.G. Mahoney, statement before Subcommittee on Aviation of the House Committee on Public Works and Transportation, Hearings on H.R. 8813, 11 Oct. 1977.

9. For further aspects on this see Dobson (1988) ; Spero (1990); Gardner (1980); and Ikenberry (1992), the notes of which provide a useful bibliography.

10. See Friedman (1981), Friedman's ideas on monetarism were developed whilst he was among sympathetically disposed colleagues at Chicago University, hence the Chicago School. Ideas from there were transmitted across the Atlantic, notably by Professor Brian Johnson, and fell on receptive ears, especially those of Alan Walters and Sir Keith Joseph. There were also more specifically political thinkers behind the economic movement such as Ayn Rand and the Objectivists in the USA, and disciples of Frederich von Hayek in the UK, *The Road to Serfdom* (1945), and *Constitution of Liberty* (1962). For perspectives on how these policies impacted on British and American government

policies see respectively: Keegan (1984), Stockman (1987); and Krieger (1986).

11. Reichley (1981), ch. 18; Shoenebaum (1979).

12. White (1965); Nixon (1978).

13. Nixon Project, Transitional Taskforce Reports 1968-9, box 1, folder: Report of President Elect's Taskforce on Transportation.

14. Houthakker Papers, box 51, folder: Transportation General, Robert deCotret to Stein, 14 Nov. 1969.

15. As well as drawing on primary sources for arguments about US general policy in the early 1970s, I am also much indebted to the impressive work in this field by Wassenbergh (1976). Wassenbergh, however, places more emphasis on the legal than the political and is, to my mind, over optimistic about the possibilities of multilateral solutions for the problems of protectionist regulation. Both these aspects of his work lead him to a more critical attitude toward US policy than mine and to discount American profession of support for a freer airline market and to see in their actions naked protectionism and the pursuit of US interests. While I also see these aspects of US policy, I think that in essence the US did strive for a more free market system but in circumstances which forced it into some policies which were not consistent with that goal.

16. 'Shaping a New Transportation Policy', *National Journal*, 26 June 1971; Houthakker Papers, box 51, folder: Transportation - International Aviation Policy (Interagency Committee), Flanigan to McCracken, 24 July 1969.

17. Ibid., attached 'Outline of a Review of the International Aviation Policy of the United States'.

18. Nixon Project, WHCF, CA, folder: CA 5/20/69-12/31/69, Flanigan to van der Beugel and his reply 4 Aug. and 19 Sept. 1969.

19. Ibid., folder: CA 1/1/72 (2), memo. Erb to Flanigan, 22 Feb. 1972, which was written in the context of highly political air services negotiations with the Soviets.

20. Houthakker Papers, box 51, folder: Transportation - International

Aviation Policy (Interagency Committee), Flanigan to McCracken, 24 July 1969, 'Outline of Review'; *National Journal*, 26 June 1971.

21. Houthakker Papers, box 51, folder: Transportation - International Aviation Policy (Interagency Committee), Houthakker to Binder, 3 Oct. 1969; Nixon Project, WHCF, CA, box 1, folder: CA 5/20/69-12/31/69, Flanigan to Binder, 6 Oct. 1969.

22. Ibid., folder: Aviation General, Binder to Chairmen of the Working Groups, 7 Oct. 1969; ibid., folder: Transportation - International Aviation Policy (Interagency Committee), McCracken et al to Cherington, 28 Nov. 1969; see also Houthakker 'Memorandum for Steering Committee, International Aviation Policy Review Committee', 8 Jan. 1970.

23. *Flight*, 29 Jan. 1970, pp. 140-1 and 2 July 1970, p. 7; Wassenbergh (1970), pp. 156-8.

24. 'Statement of International Air Transportation Policy of the United States', approved by the President 22 June 1970, text taken from official copy in Houthakker Papers, box 51.

25. Ibid.

26. Ibid.; for State Department and multiple designation problem see Nixon Project, WHCF, CA, box 12, folder: CA 7/UK beginning - 7/16/69, memo. attached to W. Street to Ehrlichman, 28 April 1969.

27. Nixon Project, WHSF, WHCF, CF, box 3, folder: Civil Aviation 1969-70, Flanigan to Nixon, 14 Aug. 1970.

28. Nixon Project, Papers of Paul McCracken, box 87, folder: Ash Report on Regulatory Agencies (1), McCracken memo., 18 March 1971; ibid., 'A New Regulatory Framework: A Report on Selected Regulatory Agencies by the President's Advisory Council on Executive Reorganization, January 1971', Chairman, Roy Ash.

29. Ibid., folder: Ash Report on Regulatory Agencies (2), Secor Browne to Flanigan re Ash Report.

30. Ibid., folder: Ash Report on Regulatory Agencies (1), memo. McClaren for Attorney General, 'Comments on the "Ash Council" Report on Selected Independent Regulatory Agencies', 17 May 1971, and Houthakker to McCracken 12 Aug. 1971.

31. Ibid., folder: Ash Report on Regulatory Agencies (2), Houthakker,

Chairman Subcommittee on Transportation, for Cabinet Committee on Economic Policy, 23 Sept. 1970, transmittal of 'Report on Improving the Performance of the Transportation Industries'.

32. Houthakker Papers, box 51, folder: Transportation Regulation (2) 1970-April 1971, Baker to McCracken and Houthakker, 11 March 1971 and 11 March memo. by Baker for members of the Transportation Subcommittee; for public reaction to deregulation proposals see: *Journal of Commerce*, 9 Feb. 1971, *Wall Street Journal*, 3 Feb. 1971, and *National Journal*, 26 June 1971.

33. Nixon Project, Papers of Egil Krogh, box 36, folder: National Transportation Policy 1971, Charles L. Clapp to Ehrlichman, 15 July 1971: this memo. illustrates some of the problems that the DOT had with regulatory reform.

34. Houthakker Papers, box 52, folder: Transportation Regulation, April 1971 - (1), Samuel Peltzman to Don Rice, 29 April 1971, Peltzman to Houthakker, 9 June 1971; ibid., box 51, folder: Transportation Regulation (2) 1970-April 1971, Flanigan to Houthakker and Carlson, 1 Feb. 1971, re feeling in Congress.

35. Ibid., box 52, folder: Transportation Regulation, April 1971 -, various items bearing on development of transportation policy and role of DOT.

36. Krogh Papers, box 36, folder: National Transportation Policy 1971, Clapp to Ehrlichman, 15 July 1971.

37. Ibid., and also at same location Clapp to Cole, 1 Sept. 1971.

38. Krogh Papers, box 33, folder: Aviation Advisory Commission: Report of Aviation Advisory Commission, and Snow to Nixon, 3 Jan. 1973.

39. Nixon Project, WHCF, CA, box 1, folder: CA 1/1/72 (1), Flanigan to Kissinger (undated); ibid., box 2, folder: CA 4/1/74, generally, and for Harbridge House, Niehuss to Flanigan, 15 May 1974; for some detail on Airport and Airways proposals see Nixon Project, WHCF, CA, box 1, Nixon to Congress, 16 June 1969.

40. Lowenfeld (1975); Penrose (1980), p. 277; *Flight*, 8 March, p. 321.

41. Nixon Project, WHCF, CA, folder: [EX] CA 1/1/72 (1), Richard Erb to Flanigan, 22 Feb. 1972; ibid., folder: [EX] CA, 1/1/72 (2), Browne to Flanigan, 18 Sept. 1972; ibid., box (2), folder: [EX] CA 6/1/73 -

3/31/74, Niehuss to Flanigan, 8 March 1974; *Flight*, 8 March 1973, p. 323.

42. Ibid., 11 April 1974, p. 448, 18 April 1974, p. 469, and 23 May 1974, pp. 650-1.

43. Penrose (1980), p. 277; *Flight*, 8 March 1973, p. 321, 18 April 1974, p. 469; Nixon Project, WHCF, CA, box 2, folder: CA 6/1/73-7/31/74, Niehuss to Flanigan, 27 March 1974, 'Recent CAB Policy Developments in International Aviation'; ibid., folder: CA 4/1/74, memo. for Eberle, 17 July 1974, 'CAB Rejected Laker Application'; ibid., WHCF, FG-11, box 5, folder: FG 11 State Department 6/1/72-6/31/72, Erb to Flanigan, 16 June 1972; ibid., WHSF, WHCF, CF, box 20, folder: FG-25 DOT 1971-74, Duval to Cole and Mead, 28 Feb. 1974, 'Storm Clouds on the Horizon', which refers to Brinegar's 'chosen instrument policy'.

44. Greenspan, in Rand (1967).

Chapter 4
Two Steps Forward
One Step Back

1974: Thirteen carriers operating with Boeing 747s flew the equivalent of 25 out of every 51 of them empty across the north Atlantic.

The generic term 'western liberal democracies' tends to disguise the fact that the means of doing things in such states vary substantially. This is important as procedural differences are often a key to understanding matters of substance. Policy-making processes are not the same in the USA, the EC and Britain, but the former two have much in common in that they have a dispersed power system which necessitates compromise and accommodation. Those needs can often inhibit the development of new policies, or, at least, result in lengthy delays and significant modification of initial proposals. Testimony to that in the USA is provided by the experience of the Nixon Administration and its attempts at regulatory reform in transportation and in the EC by the painfully slow way that transport policy in general has been developed.

In the EC, once policy has been determined and accepted by the Council of Ministers, there may arise problems of execution because of second thoughts by Member States, or else the European Court of Justice may take a hand by interpreting things rather differently than some states might have wished. In the USA matters are rather similar. Agency and departmental conflicts can continue to affect matters even after policy appears to have been clearly established. Also, Congress may act contrary to the wishes of the Executive and change policy, as may the Supreme Court with its extensive role in the political realm, which culminates in its power of judicial review.

It is not easy to generalise about any complex system of government regarding the way it develops policy and the way it conducts international discussions. The case of the EC is doubly difficult to talk about in this way as it is so relatively new and, in the international sphere, there is very little substance upon which to draw in order to characterise its actions. For the time being that problem will be left alone, but with regard to the USA and Britain a few more general remarks can be offered.

The US system of government allows much more diversity within its make-up than does the British. The processes of creating and implementing policies often have to contend with a recalcitrant Congress and conflict and dissension between departments and agencies, some of which have independent status. Thus it can take a long time to build up congressional and agency support for radical change in Washington. Once that has been achieved, it does not necessarily mean that everyone has been brought on board and sniping at policy and attempts to modify or change it may continue for a lengthy period. This rather cumbersome process does, however, have some advantages.

When policy finally starts to roll, notwithstanding the dissension that may continue for some time, it generally has a head of steam that carries it forward. There may be sidesteps to the right and sidesteps to the left, but rarely are there abrupt 'u-turns'. At the same time the US system, which is more open than Britain's and only loosely regulated by party politics, has weaknesses that affect its diplomatic negotiating position. At the extreme is the danger of the Executive being unable to control the Senate and force it to ratify treaties, as was the case with both the Versailles Treaty of 1919 and the SALT 2 Agreement. But, a much more common problem, especially in the low politics of commercial negotiations, is that US teams lack unity because they frequently include a wide range of contending interests not only from government agencies, but also from labour, business and other parties from outside government. Of course, companies like BA also have a say in the way Britain negotiates air service agreements, but the impact of BA on British politics and its ability to get its voice heard and adhered to is not always as great as that of American airlines which operate in a system that is more amenable and vulnerable to lobbying in the legislature and which has a larger input from the world of business and commerce. Even when BA has had a decisive voice, it has, at least until the introduction of other

British international carriers, been a single voice and not part of a cacophony from numerous airlines as is often the case in the USA.

Rather ironically, the party political domination of the British system tends to allow the negotiating officers of the bureaucracy more initiative and scope within international diplomatic negotiations than is the case on the US side. Once the political contours of a subject for discussion have been set by the politicians, then officialdom is granted considerable leeway for achieving those goals in whatever way it can. There is a conscious acknowledgement in the British system that compromise and accommodation, in the give and take of the pursuit of national interest, have to be made. Furthermore, much of the give and take in technical and commercial discussions is best done by the department most specialised in the subject. So, on the British side in civil aviation negotiations, the Department of Transport (DOT) takes the chair with the Foreign Office (FO) taking second place, observing and advising.

The American style is quite different. At times it appears almost as if politics is so diffused throughout the system that it continues to intrude at levels where its absence might be more beneficial. The USA does not have the same tradition of vocational professionalism in its bureaucracy as in Britain. Instead, civil service appointments have often been political. Although there has been a move away from that in modern times, politics still tends to be more intrusive in the US than in the British bureaucracy. Relationships between US departments are more political and that, in conjunction with the system's great openess, means that there is not the same clear cut division between politics and administration as in Britain.

The net result of this is that US diplomatic teams are generally less homogeneous in their views and more political than UK delegations. For example, of the US Bermuda 2 negotiating team Alan Boyd, its head, has said: 'We had all these people and this great cacophony of sound, very discordant sounds, and we'd have fifty battles within our delegation about what we were going to be doing.' In that kind of situation there is more need for political control from above and that is often manifested by the lack of negotiating discretion allowed to delegations. Unlike their British counterparts, the US DOT is not in charge of civil aviation discussions: the State Department has the chair and the DOT supplies it with information and policy objectives. That in itself suggests the more political approach of the US at the negotiating table. The sense of dealing with technical problems within a set political context which prevails on the British side is replaced in US delegations by a more fluid political situation, often coloured by a sense of moral rectitude in support of US aims. Thus an interesting contrast emerges. In Britain the domestic system is characterised by lack of accommodation and compromise because of the unitary character of the state and the dominance of party politics. The situation in foreign negotiations is different. The ability of government clearly and decisively to determine policy and the knowledge that it has complete control over acceptance and implementation of whatever emerges from international talks, allows it to grant considerable discretion to negotiating teams for compromise and accommodation. In a sense, after a certain stage of policy development by politicians, matters are handed over to the experts in the DOT who, with the help of the FO, negotiate agreements.[1]

In the USA matters are the other way round. Compromise and accommodation is essential in its domestic system of diffused power, if government is to function successfully, but in the international realm there is less flexibility. This is partly because too much compromise and accommodation can lead to immense trouble with the Congress, which the Executive cannot control in the way that the Prime Minister and the Cabinet can control Parliament. This inability can result in the Executive having to change policies in response to political pressure even after agreement has been reached with foreign governments and that adds a degree of uncertainty, which can be frustrating for the US and foreign governments alike. One should add though that American negotiators are fond of invoking difficulties with Congress as a means of strengthening their bargaining hand in situations where they do not wish to give ground. In addition, where political differences continue to vie for favour, as they often do in US teams, then it is necessary to keep a firm hand on things by the political leaders in Washington. The fear of failing to achieve political objectives in a system where there is no clear division between politics and administration tends to politicise the situation in a way which engenders inflexibility.

In Britain, policy making is more single-minded. The dominance of the system by whichever political party is in power contrasts sharply with the diffused and institutionally separated power structure in Washington. Westminster has no institutional separation of powers between the executive and the legislature, which are both composed of and commanded by the party in power. The judiciary intrudes less into the political realm than in the USA, but is arguably less independent. Also in the UK far less use has been made of independent regulatory agencies. Instead, control has been exercised more politically and more directly through nationalisation. One of the notable exceptions to this has been the CAA with its semi-independent status and quasi-judicial role.[2]

The unitary political power structure in the UK has facilitated more decisive action than in systems with a diffused power structure. Once policy has been decided upon there is less chance that the legislature or outside bodies such as airlines and pressure groups can challenge or change things. There is less opportunity for interdepartmental differences weakening or obstructing implementation of policy. The government's negotiating stance in diplomatic negotiations tends to be united and purposeful. However, just as this unity favours decisive adoption and the vigorous implementation of policy, it also means that if there are changes, either within the ruling party, or, if one party succeeds another, then it is relatively easy to alter policies. Even when leaders commit themselves to no 'u-turns', the temptation to do just that when circumstances beyond political control change is often irresistible. And part of the irresistibility is that the system provides the means for rapid change - the option of trying something different when things go wrong, even when it directly contradicts what has gone before.

These differences in the British and US political systems, although presented here in a highly abbreviated and general form, do give some perspective on their decision-making processes. In doing so, they will help to explain the sharp divergence of international civil aviation policy that occurred between Britain and the USA in the mid-1970s. The latter continued to build up a head of steam for regulatory reform even after the change from the Republican Ford to the Democrat Carter. The UK on the other hand moved away from the competitive programme of the early 1970s, with Labour, under Harold Wilson, taking over from the Conservative government of Edward Heath in 1974. Ultimately the two sides clashed in the Bermuda 2 Talks of 1976-77, and the advantages and disadvantages of their respective policy-making systems were, at least partially, responsible for the somewhat unexpected outcome.

When the Heath government came into power in 1970, the Edwards Report had already suggested an agenda for change in civil aviation policy. That agenda harmonised well with Heath's call for a more efficient market oriented economy with greater emphasis on technological change. The Secretary of State for Trade and Industry, John Davies, pledged that the discipline of the market would be allowed to have its way in the British economy and that there would be 'no propping up of lame ducks'. As with the conservative government of Nixon in the USA, the Heath government adopted a number of policies which departed from past practice, but it also discovered that adverse and intractable circumstances often conspired to modify its goals. Perhaps the single most dramatic pressure to navigate a 'u-turn' came as early as February 1971 with the collapse of Rolls Royce. Heath and his colleagues decided that to allow such a concentration of engineering excellence to disappear was a price that their commitment to the free market was not prepared to pay. Nevertheless, despite this early reversal of declared policy, floating exchange rates, entry into the EEC and more emphasis on market forces and less intervention by government set the early tone of the Heath government. It was not as radical as later Conservative governments, nor was it as doctrinal and inflexible, but the pragmatic flexibility for manoeuvre sought by Heath and his colleagues was consistently for reform and change. Civil aviation was no different than any other policy: a more competitive industry was to be encouraged. The questions were: how far and by what means?

The answer to those questions were provided from three sources. Firstly, there were pronouncements by Heath and John Davies about the benefits of competition, though, as time went by and economic circumstances deteriorated, some modifications were made to the competitive dispensation that was initially promoted. Secondly, the 1971 Civil Aviation Act established the official framework for the industry's operations and in particular created the CAA, which was to play a major role in the development of policy over the coming years. Thirdly, there was a provision in the Act for the Secretary of State for Trade to give 'policy guidance' to the CAA and this also was to be an important feature of the new regime.[3]

During the last months of the Labour Government, development of a more competitive aviation system looked distinctly unlikely despite what the Edwards Report had had to say. On the international front, the Wilson Government made it known that it had growing reservations about the suitability of the Bermuda Agreement for existing circumstances. Any changes were unlikely to be liberal and market oriented. On matters that were more under domestic control, the signs were also somewhat negative regarding the possibilities for liberalisation. If progress were to be made, then issues involving the structure of the airline industry would have to be addressed. There had to be some changes wrought to the protected status of the nationalised corporations, BOAC and BEA, which dominated both domestic and foreign routes. British United Airways (BUA) had mounted some pressure in the light of the Edwards Report for a dispersal of routes from the two preferred airlines and in 1969 it applied for a wholesale transfer of BOAC's southern network, but the Labour Government would not allow that. By 1970 BOAC was counterattacking and BUA found itself under threat of a take-over. If Labour were to have been returned in 1970, it is highly unlikely that the more competitive aspects of the recommendations by the Edwards Report would have been implemented, but, even with a Conservative government in power, there remained a number of thorny technical and tactical problems to solve before advances could be made.[4]

The *Flight* editorial of 2 July 1970, noted that for once aviation had someone who was technically able:

> For the first time since Sir Sefton Brancker in 1922, British civil aviation has a minister who knows about civil aviation. Mr. Fred Corfield will be entrusted with all airline affairs by the new President of the Board of Trade, Mr. Noble.[5]

After a decade of neglect and considerable muddle in British civil aviation policy, the Heath Government was determined to upgrade it, and the knowledge that Corfield had would certainly be valuable for the difficult decisions that had to be made as to how competition was to be encouraged. For example, a viable independent, or second force airline, to compete with BOAC and BEA, would have to be conjured up as well as a new licensing policy and, although the forward looking editor of *Flight* balked at the idea of wholesale transfer of routes to a second force airline, in the end that is what the Heath Government decided that it must do in a modified way. Such changes needed new laws. In the 1971 Civil Aviation Act, Heath's Government laid out its plans. In Section 3(1) four broad objectives were set:

> a)   to secure that British airlines provide air transport services which satisfy all substantial categories of public demand (so far as British airlines may reasonably be expected to provide such services) at the lowest charge consistent with a high standard of safety in operating the services and an economic return to efficient operators on the sums invested in providing the services and with securing the sound development of the civil air transport industry of the United Kingdom;
>
> b)   to secure that at least one major British airline which is not controlled by the British Airways Board has opportunities to participate in providing, on charter and on other terms, the air transport services mentioned in the preceding paragraph;
>
> c)   subject to the preceding paragraphs, to encourage the civil air transport industry of the United Kingdom to increase the contribution which it makes towards a favourable balance of payments for the United Kingdom and towards the prosperity of the economy of the United Kingdom; and
>
> d)   subject to the preceding paragraphs, to further the reasonable interests of users of air transport services.[6]

To help implement these aims the Act created the CAA as an independent regulatory and licensing body to which the minister was to issue guidance from time to time. The CAA was to play a major part in the development of policy over the following years and much of the way it had effect was determined by the policy guidance promulgated by the minister.

By February 1972, when Secretary of State for Trade and Industry, John Davies, issued the first policy guidance, the Heath Government had already contrived to create a viable independent competitor for international routes by the take-over of BUA by Caledonian Airways to create B.Cal. This new airline was allocated some of BOAC's routes to West Africa and under the ATLB, the CAA's predecessor, a limited form of regional favouritism to help the new competitor to gain a market share was adopted. So, the first prerequisites of a more competitive system were in place. It was now the purpose of the guidance to move things along. The general aim was to impose the least restraint possible on the industry and its users compatible with the aims of aviation policy set out in the 1971 Act. 'Arrangements which restrain competition or innovation should be accepted only so far as they contribute to the realisation of the objectives and this guidance.'[7]

The policy guidance had to weave a rather precarious path between the interests of the nationalised companies, the second force independent airline, the other independents and the consumer. For scheduled services, BOAC and BEA were to remain the principal providers and B.Cal. the main independent provider. To ensure that these airlines could compete effectively in the international sphere, licensing of other independents for international services was to be limited for some years. B.Cal.'s position was to be boosted by a degree of preferential licensing for double designation, for new routes, and for charters. Some review of further rationalisation of route structures was also to be undertaken with the possibility of further transfers to B.Cal. Quite clearly, the preferred instrument status of BEA and BOAC was now under challenge.

In the long run the most important and controversial change introduced by the 1971 Act and the first policy guidance was the emphasis given to the second force airline, not only with regard to its being strengthened by receipt of preferred treatment, but also by the role it was to play in the government's desire for double designation and hence competition between British airlines on the same routes. Admittedly, the government did not envisage double designation on many routes, but it was a very important development because of the principle it embodied. There was to be double designation provided:

a)   the traffic is likely to be sufficient to support competing services profitably within a reasonable time, b) the choice and standard of services available to the public are likely to be improved and, in the case of an international route, either c) the aggregate share of total traffic that is secured by the British airlines is likely to be increased to an extent that will more than offset any lasting diseconomies, or

d)   where the British share of capacity is predetermined, the licensing of a second airline within that share is likely to increase the total traffic secured by British airlines more rapidly than would otherwise be likely.[8]

While government remained committed to a more competitive dispensation, the tensions between some of the provisions of this policy guidance could be kept in balance; for example, the relationship of the CAA with those who held political power, and the preferences for B.Cal. and the pronouncement that BOAC and BEA were to remain the main scheduled carriers. What was needed was pragmatism and some room for manoeuvre in trying to nurture more competition within an industry which still had the hallmarks of domestic governmental and international control imprinted upon it. For a while those needs were met.

Raymond Colegate, a long-standing senior member of the CAA, believed that between government and the CAA there was 'a honeymoon period because most of the people in the CAA had come from government.'[9] There existed a good rapport and, furthermore, in the early days, there was a clear consensus on the role of the CAA: it was to liberalise regulation and encourage competition. It pursued those goals by several means.

Firstly, the CAA introduced new types of fares for both charter and scheduled airlines. Advance Booking Charters were approved internationally in November 1972 by the Ottawa Declaration of Agreement, and Advance Purchase Excursion Fares were introduced in 1973 after bilateral talks between Britain and the USA and discussions in IATA. In both these cases the initiative was taken by the CAA, whose aim was to try to enable the schedules to compete effectively with low price charter fares wherever possible and to replace the discredited affinity rule. For many years charters had been controlled, in theory, by a requirement that they had to be booked by people belonging to a distinctive group or organisation. This had led to some very imaginative categories being invented such as the 'left-handed society'. Problems arose from this and the British charter carriers, Laker, British Midland, Dan-Air and Lloyd International were all taken to task by the US CAB for alleged violations of the affinity rule. In 1972 BM responded by going to court and getting an injunction against the application of restrictive measures that the CAB had proposed. This was just one symptom of US sensitivity about keeping charters distinct from scheduled operations. So far as the British CAA was concerned, the episode highlighted the need for reform to enhance the position of British charter companies which were very price competitive. In fact, although the US percentage of world scheduled traffic was declining, its overall percentage improved because of the success of the big US charter operators, the biggest of which, and in fact the world leader, was Pan Am, but British charter operators were garnering a pleasing measure of success as well both in Europe and on the Atlantic. Despite their respective success, however, there was considerable conflict between the US and Britain over how charters should be regulated. The British were apprehensive of US potential capacity, especially with the winding down of the war in Vietnam, which released charter capacity from military to civil use. However, British charters could be highly price competitive and it was not politically feasible in Britain to impose too many restrictions upon a branch of the airline industry which was well regarded because of its role in the mass market of cheap foreign package holidays. The whole business of charters was soon to be raised again in the Bermuda 2 Talks, and afterwards, and the US pushed for and paid a considerable price for a more liberal charter regime, but, unperceived though it was at that time, charters had by then largely had their day because of the introduction of innovatory low fares on the scheduled airlines.[10]

The CAA also moved to enhance fare competition by licensing Laker's Skytrain, thus reversing the more cautious policy of the old ATLB. Laker was licensed in August 1972 to begin operations from Stansted to New York in 1973, but the vigorous opposition that BOAC had mounted to this was by no means over, even though Laker had won this particular round of the battle. While BOAC's successor, BA, licked its wounds, the US CAB took up matters and then proceeded to procrastinate and then finally to refuse Laker traffic rights. However, all other agencies in the Ford Administration opposed the CAB judgement that Laker was unfit to mount the Skytrain operation. By the summer of 1975 Ford was at the point of overriding the CAB's decision, but a new Government and a new Secretary of State for Trade in London pre-empted such action. Peter Shore pulled the rug from under Laker by proposing to withdraw his license. The Laker saga was to continue and it will be taken up again later as it was one of the main catalysts in the liberalisation of fare structures on the Atlantic and had a major impact upon Anglo-American aviation relations in the 1980s.[11]

Secondly, the CAA nurtured competition by implementing the policy guidance of 1972. It gave preference to B.Cal. - at least until 1974 - and it was also prepared to substitute independents for BA on routes that that airline under used, or on which it failed to achieve a high enough standard. By 1974 the CAA felt that B.Cal. had used up all its 'preference' in acquiring routes such as Toronto, Singapore, Boston, Atlanta, Houston, Brussels and Algiers. It was felt within the CAA that the job of nurturing B.Cal. was then completed. To some it might have appeared that the drive for a more competitive industry was slowing down. The CAA was taking less of a pro-active policy regarding reallocation of routes and the government had expressed the view towards the end of 1973 that it believed that the scope for double designation was only small. However, the job of nurturing competition within the reference of the 1971 act, and under the guidelines given in 1972, had really been achieved. So, in one sense, it could not be described as a slowing down, but more as a completion of the limited goals set. There was no inclination in the CAA to reverse policy. Increased competition within the framework that had been achieved would now proceed according to the extent that market forces had been allowed to come to bear through the second force airline, more competitive fares, the licensing of Laker, and reallocation of routes. Having created a more competitive structure, there would follow the commercial experience of more competition.[12] However, even before the Labour Government that came into power in 1974 tried to turn much of this on its head, British policy suffered from the same kind of economic difficulties that affected and modified the US drive for more competition. Also, as has already been mentioned, the British had to come to terms with their fears of being swamped by, what appeared to be, ever increasing US capacity and in 1972 that had resulted in a very illiberal interpretation by the Heath government of the Bermuda 1 capacity provisions.[13]

The adverse economic circumstances that emerged in the early seventies undermined much of the potential that the British Government had created for swift developments in aviation liberalisation. Some of the routes awarded to B.Cal. remained without traffic rights and the routes which did come into operation on the north Atlantic soon had to be abandoned because they were not economically viable. Over-capacity in the 1973 recession prompted multilateral capacity reductions and added to the growing concern about the overall health of the airline market and seemed to indicate, to some at least, that a highly regulatory system was still necessary.

In the broader political context, enthusiasm for the free market also appeared to be on the wane. After coming to power with a clarion call for more reliance on the market and its discipline, the Heath Administration found itself being pushed into more and more intervention. Rolls Royce was only one of many examples of the 'u-turn'. By 1974 the Conservatives had introduced a statutory prices and incomes policy. Ironically, this interventionism provoked a militant reaction by the unions, and in particular a strike by the National Union of Mineworkers, which forced Heath to call an election on the issue of free collective bargaining and on the wider question of who ruled the country - the unions or the elected government.

The result of the March election was the return of Harold Wilson to 10 Downing Street at the head of a minority Labour Government. In September of 1974 the shortest Parliament of the century was ended when Wilson called the second General Election of the year in an attempt to get a working majority. This time Labour won by an overall margin of three seats and held on to power until 1979, at the end with support from the Liberals. Their precarious position during these years did not, however, inhibit them from pursuing some radical changes of policy and civil aviation was not unaffected.

The return of Labour to power meant that there was more inclination to regulate and protect the nationalised airline. As Colegate put it: 'Things began to change when there was a change of personnel in the Departments and a change of government.'[14] At the official level one of the key players was George Rogers, who was in charge of international transport matters in the Department of Trade and 'who was personally devoted to the idea of 50/50 passenger sharing [and] single designation on all routes.'[15] The two successive Secretaries of State at the Department of Trade were Peter Shore and Edmund Dell: the latter came in when Callaghan succeeded Harold Wilson in 1976. Colegate who was at the CAA at the time described their aims as wanting 'to undo as far as they could the work of the Heath government.'[16] That judgement is a little harsh with regard to Dell, as will become clear when the Bermuda 2 Talks are examined, nevertheless, things took a definite turn towards reregulation. The CAA found itself under pressure from the time Labour returned to power until a High Court decision of late 1976 about Laker's transatlantic license, which will be considered shortly. But during that three year period, from early 1974 until late 1976, 'the CAA was digging its heels in and trying every way of preserving such liberalisation as had been achieved.'[17] It was a testing time for the CAA and liberalisation and Peter Shore generated most of the testing.

During 1974 and the first half of 1975, Shore set in motion a review of Britain's civil aviation policy. At first, many feared that there would be a complete reversal of the policies of nurturing a second force and of whittling away of the prerogatives of the nationalised airline. In the event that did not happen. The CAA, despite its short life, had already accumulated a great deal of experience and expertise by 1974 and outclassed the Department of Trade in specialised knowledge. As a result, much of its advice, and hence its pro-competition philosophy, was to be effective in the review and it helped to moderate some of the more reactionary inclinations of the Shore team.

The CAA, along with BA and B.Cal. submitted reports to Shore in May 1975. Two months later Shore spoke in the House of Commons and while an extreme 'u-turn' had been averted, there was still a very definite change of direction. Shore's reasoning was that the competitive dispensation outlined in the Edwards Report had assumed an expanding market and this had not happened. Consequently, Shore decided that it was necessary to modify existing policies. Laker's Skytrain license would be revoked, double designation on long-haul routes would be abandoned, and the second force airline, instead of competing directly with BA, was to be given a sphere of interest within which to operate. In effect, Shore was proposing the return to regional chosen instruments similar to the old BEA/BOAC system, except now one was an independent and one a nationalised company.[18]

Over the following months these stated aims were developed within the Department of Trade and George Rogers 'was one of the architects of the ... policy guidance' which was issued for the CAA in February 1976.[19] In anticipation of the new policy, the government asked BA and B.Cal. to sit down together and sort out a rational route structure that would realise the government's aim of creating two non-competing spheres of influence. The airlines were reluctant to do that and considerable pressure had to be exerted. Eventually in January 1976, with Sir Frank McFadzean succeeding Henry Marking as chairman of BA, things began to move. B.Cal. was strengthened in its existing spheres of operations in Africa and in South America, but it lost routes elsewhere, notably those to North America where its double designation routes were withdrawn leaving it with only licences to serve Houston and Atlanta when they became available for international services. By 11 February all was set for the publication of the new policy guidance.[20]

Market conditions and international constraints were used to justify the retreat from the freer market that the Heath Government had promoted. Shore referred to the failure of B.Cal. to establish itself on the North Atlantic. He noted the restrictions imposed by states which effectively meant that they kept 50 per cent of any market for themselves and thus double designation would simply be a carve-up of the remaining 50 per cent between two British carriers and not an expansion of Britain's market share.

Such a dividing up would only weaken both British carriers. He pointed to the fact that even the pro-competition USA had agreed to capacity controls on the Atlantic to try to cope with the difficult circumstances of recent years. He wrote:

> There is now virtually no major long-haul route on which it would be possible to introduce a second British airline on terms that would leave any scope for the British share of the total earnings from the route to be increased.[21]

The double designation experiment on long-haul routes was at an end. Paragraph 7 of the guidance began: 'In the case of long-haul services ... the Authority should not, except as provided for in paragraph 8, license more than one British airline to serve the same route.'[22] The exception in paragraph 8 was where BA might wish to mount a Concorde supersonic route. If one were to be developed in B.Cal.'s sphere of interest then the CAA was to ensure that it was adequately compensated for any loss of traffic that that might involve. Not only was long-haul double designation out, but, apart from Concorde, no airline was to be allowed into either BA's or B.Cal.'s sphere of interest without their consent. The guidance stipulated that:

> It is the intention that, even in the case of long-haul routes not already being operated by the preferred airline, the Authority should only in quite exceptional circumstances grant to another airline, against the objection of the preferred airline, a licence to provide a long-haul scheduled service.[23]

The policy for the domestic and short-haul markets was slightly more permissive. Some double designation on routes to and from London was considered to be viable though only if various criteria were met. The impact of diversion of traffic upon an airline, especially on its feeder operations for international services, would have to be considered. Also the CAA was to satisfy itself that:

> a) the traffic is likely to be sufficient to support competing services by British airlines profitably within a reasonable period of time; and
> b) the choice and standard of service available to the public are likely to be improved, particularly as regards the choice of airport in the London area; and also in the case of an international route that:

c)   satisfactory arrangements have been made or are likely to be made with the country or countries concerned for the introduction of a second British airline on the route.[24]

Shore's review had had to try to come to terms with a number of unpalatable facts which had become more acute because of the downturn in the economic fortunes of the industry in the early 1970s. Firstly, without greater access to the international market and/or a larger home operating base, to what extent could Britain sustain a multi-carrier strategy? Connected with this difficulty was the British fear of the USA continuing to overload the Atlantic with excess capacity from an ever increasing number of scheduled airlines and from its charter operators. How could Britain counter the USA on this and seek multiple designation itself? Commitment to competition was one thing, but when there were difficulties of sustaining it even in healthy economic circumstances, then, with a Labour Government in power, its viability was almost certain to be brought into question. When Labour coincided with a depression in the industry then the questioning became ever more searching.

Secondly, there was the problem of airlines operating in an environment that was not under the control of the British Government. Even if the Labour Government had been wholeheartedly behind a competitive strategy, it would have been forced to take account of the international framework and economic practices of other states in working out its policies. Of course, it had little doctrinal commitment to pursuing freer market policies and, in some ways, one might say that given the pressures that existed for re-introducing or strengthening protective controls, the Shore response to the situation was fairly moderate.

Finally, a point that appears to be of minor importance in the guidance, but which was subsequently to develop and to play a major role in the future, was the matter of choice of airport in the London area. This was the beginning of worries about congestion at Heathrow and attempts by the government to redistribute traffic to Gatwick. Edmund Dell, Shore's successor, was to make important decisions on this matter.

The policy guidance, though more moderate than many in the pro-competition camp had thought likely and with much evidence in it of the CAA's influence, was still unacceptable in part to the CAA. Shortly after the guidance appeared Lord Boyd-Carpenter, the Chairman of the CAA, wrote to Shore:

The Authority, dissents from the provision of paragraph 7 of the draft of the new guidance insofar as they are intended to and would have the effect of inhibiting the Authority from granting, even in the most exceptional circumstances, an air transport licence to more than one British airline on the same route.[25]

The issue that Boyd-Carpenter raised here concerned the independent status of the CAA and its regulatory role under the provisions of the 1971 Civil Aviation Act. In that act the minister was required to give 'guidance' from time to time. However, Shore's 'guidance' in February 1976 amounted to more than just guidance with regard to double designation: it was a direction that the CAA should not double designate, with the exception of supersonic services. It was on the basis of this that Freddie Laker alleged that Shore was acting *ultra vires* and so took him to court to try to retain the right to mount a transatlantic Skytrain. The results of that action were to have important consequences for the British negotiating hand with the USA in late 1976 and during the first half of 1977.[26]

In April 1976 James Callaghan became Prime Minister after the resignation of Harold Wilson. The new Secretary of State for Trade was Edmund Dell, who was one of the more 'economically dry' members of the government.[27] Dell arrived in office at a particularly difficult time for the economy in general and for civil aviation in particular.

By June 1976 the pound was suffering from yet another of its recurrent crises. It threatened to undermine the whole economic strategy of the Labour Government, which involved a commitment to high spending on education, health, welfare, and pensions in return for wage restraint by the unions: this was called the Social Contract. When the economic crisis broke at the beginning of June, it looked as if the Americans would be helpful, but it transpired that assistance arranged by them through the Bank for International Settlements (BIS) only provided a very temporary respite because of its conditions. Unlike normal rescue operations, the loan had to be repaid in full within six months. As things transpired that forced Britain to go to the IMF as a last resort. In return for assistance, it required the Labour Government to reduce its public sector borrowing right, which in turn torpedoed the, admittedly already floundering, Social Contract. Dell maintains that he and his department made no direct connection between the behaviour of the USA in the sterling crisis and the development of policy toward the Bermuda Agreement, and Callaghan maintains that the IMF conditions were little different to the remedial measures that he and Chancellor of the Exchequer Denis Healey had independently decided were necessary. Nevertheless, it was against the backcloth of considerable resentment towards the USA and with a sense of desperation about Britain's economic plight, and especially her balance of payments problem, that Dell undertook his review of the Bermuda Bilateral.[28]

The balance of payment problem focused attention on the fact that the reciprocal exchange of air service rights under Bermuda 1 yielded approximately £120 million and £350 million respectively to British and American carriers (that is according to Department of Transport figures; *The Economist* reported figures of £120 million and £300 million on 26 June 1976) [29]. That had to be changed so far as Dell was concerned and he instigated discussions between his department, the CAA, B.Cal. and BA. He became convinced that drastic action was necessary. In one sense this was simply the continuation of Shore's policy and an attempt to put the ideas of George Rogers about division of traffic, capacity controls and single designation into operation. However, there were disadvantages for Britain if it did that unilaterally on the Atlantic without trying to get the same kind of regime accepted by the USA.[30]

The likelihood of the Americans accepting increased regulation looked distinctly unlikely because the Administration of Gerald Ford had publicly set its heart on, at the very least, some degree of deregulation. During the summer of 1976 the American CAB, by then under the Chairmanship of a reformer, John Robson, recommended that NWA and Delta should be allowed to join TWA, Pan Am and National on the Atlantic routes. Competition from US airlines in terms of both increased capacity and pricing looked as if it might deteriorate into predatory practices.[31]

Dell and his advisers came to the conclusion that they should aim to achieve a 50/50 split of traffic with the USA, single designation, a predetermined capacity control agreement to replace the existing system of *ex post facto* adjustment, more gateways in the USA, and the withdrawal of fifth freedom rights, so that both countries would operate solely on a point to point city pair basis from their respective territories. The British also wanted to maintain the double approval fares regime which the USA disliked. The Americans wanted to change the present system which set standard fares relatively highly and used the profit to cross subsidise discount operations. They wanted standard fares to reflect costs plus a reasonable profit margin and then base discounts around that level of pricing. They felt that such a system would reflect the workings of the market better and would avoid undesirable levels of subsidisation and maintain a distinction between charter and scheduled markets. They were also concerned to ensure that the new APEX fares did not damage charter operations, which they now felt also had to be liberalised to enable them to continue to compete with the scheduled carriers.[32]

Quite clearly, Dell's goals were extremely ambitious and they came at a time when Britain was vulnerable because of her weak economic state and a time when the US was seeking less not more regulation in civil aviation. The Ford Administration's record on this was not without regulatory blemishes, or at least policies that were not entirely compatible with the principles of the free market, but nevertheless, any move to restrict the market, particularly when the restrictions would be so self serving for Britain, would not be well received in Washington.

Having decided what he wanted to achieve, Dell then had to decide what would be the best way of achieving his goals. His decision was to denounce the Bermuda 1 Agreement with twelve months notice as provided for in the bilateral. Before doing so, he consulted the FO and the Embassy in Washington. Both advised against. In Washington he was cautioned by the DOT and the State Department not to act rashly. If Bermuda were to be denounced, the Americans told him that the result at the end of the day would be less favourable for Britain than the existing agreement. The Americans were furious at the prospect of denunciation and particularly incensed because they were on the verge of a presidential election.[33]

However, Dell remained resolute. Even when the FO 'said, more or less, we think this is most ill advised, but it's your departmental business, if you want to do it, get on with it.'[34] Dell decided that he would. As the FO had not forbidden him to act, the matter did not go to Cabinet and on 22 June 1976 Dell denounced the Bermuda 1 Agreement.

Between 1970 and June 1976 the fortunes of civil aviation liberalisation in the UK had taken two steps forward and then one step back, with the possibility of further backtracking in Britain's relationship with the USA in the Bermuda 2 Talks. However, the CAA, the courts in the Laker case, and Dell himself, as the diplomatic wrangle over Bermuda 2 developed, all acted to salvage something of the competitive elements that the Heath Government had nurtured at the start of the decade. The CAA continued to favour more competition than the Labour Government, but they moved closer to each other during the 1976-77 talks with the Americans. The courts ruled in favour of Laker, which drove a cart and horses through the Shore policy guidance, and Dell turned out to be not unhappy about that. In fact, Dell's position was generally more pro-competition than Shore's despite the fact that he took the highly confrontational approach to the Americans and initially advocated a highly regulatory regime on the Atlantic.

So, in the summer of 1976, a contest was about to take place between the UK on the one hand and the USA on the other. The UK had moved towards liberalisation in the early 1970s and then put that sharply into reverse in 1974-76. Later it began to edge back again under pressures from the CAA, Laker, the courts, and Dell. In the USA the pressure for deregulation of the domestic aviation industry and liberalisation of the international sphere had mounted steadily during the seventies with some departures from that line of policy in order to cope with the economic difficulties that US airlines suffered in the early 1970s. Both presidential candidates, Ford and Carter, were personally devoted to deregulation and the crisis occasioned by Dell's denunciation of the Bermuda Bilateral came at a time when the USA believed that the worst of the over-capacity problem was over and it was therefore in no mood to tolerate increased restrictions upon its international civil aviation industry, which would reduce its market share. Even when the slight shift away from the Shore attitude on international policy is taken into account, the British and the Americans were still miles and miles apart.[35] Just how far will become clearer after the development of policy in the Ford Administration is examined.

Notes and References

1. Interview with Alan Boyd, sometime Chairman of the CAB, US Secretary of Transport, and Special Ambassador in charge of the US delegation to negotiate the Bermuda 2 Agreement, 9 April 1991, conducted by the author; British official sources.

2. Baldwin (1985). I have drawn liberally on Baldwin's work for much of my account of the CAA.

3. Cmd. 4899, 1972, 'Civil Aviation Policy Guidance', which quotes the relevant part of the 1971 Civil Aviation Act.

4. Baldwin (1985), pp. 92-3; *Flight*, 2 July, 1970, editorial.

5. Ibid.

6. Cmd. 4899, 1972, introduction.

7. Ibid.

8. Ibid.

9. Colegate Interview.

10. Gunston (1988), pp. 60-1; Lowenfeld (1975); Shaw (1985), pp. 110-11; *Flight*, 20 July 1972, p. 76; Baldwin (1985), pp. 180-86.

11. Gerald Ford Library, Papers of William Seidman, box 53, folder: CIEP (4), J. M. Dunn memo. for Seidman, 30 July 1975; *House of Commons Debs.* 896 col. 1502, 29 July 1975.

12. Baldwin (1985), p. 103 and pp. 167-70.

13. See ch. 2.

14. Colegate Interview.

15. Ibid.

16. Ibid.

17. Ibid.

18. *House of Commons Debs.* 896 col. 1502, 29 July 1975.

19. Ebdon Interview.

20. Baldwin (1985), pp. 104-11; Ebdon Interview.

21. Cmd. 6400, 1976, 'Future Civil Aviation Policy [including, 'The Policy Guidance']'.

22. Ibid.

23. Ibid.

24. Ibid.

25. Quoted in Baldwin (1985), pp. 109-110, source House of Commons Debs. 905/6 col. 107, 23 Feb. 1976.

26. Ebdon Interview; Colegate Interview; Shane Interview; Dell (1985).

27. Interview with the Rt. Hon. Edmund Dell, Secretary of State for Trade, 1976-78, 8 Dec. 1989, conducted by the author.

28. Interview with the Rt. Hon. Sir James [now Lord] Callaghan, 26 February 1987, conducted by the author; Dell Interview; James Callaghan(1987), ch. 14; *Sunday Times*, 14 May 1978, 'How the Hard Men Took Over Britain', by S. Fay and H. Young; '1976 IMF Crisis Symposium', *Contemporary Record*, 3 (1989), 39-45; Dell (1991); Dobson (1991 B).

29. *Flight*, 3 July 1976, p. 4; *The Economist*, 26 June 1976, 'New Rules or Else, Britain tells America'.

30. Dell Interview.

31. *Flight*, 8 Jan. 1977, p. 52.

32. Dell Interview; *The Economist*, 26 June 1976, 'New Rules'.

33. Dell Interview.

34. Ibid.

35. Ebdon Interview.

Chapter 5
Gathering Pace

My Administration has made the reform of government regulation one of its highest priorities. We have initiated a national debate on the role that government regulation should play in our economy. (Gerald Ford) [1]

Compared with its predecessor, the Ford Administration was more unified on economic policy. It was more doctrinally committed to, and placed more emphasis on, regulatory reform and it devoted more political and administrative energy in the seeking of that goal. There was also increasing demand from the Congress and from economists for at least some degree of deregulation, especially in aviation. As one analyst has noted:

[economists argued that] regulation simply prevented firms from competing in price, thereby leading them to compete instead by scheduling an excessive number of flights with excessively empty airplanes while charging higher fares. In the early 1970s, the Senate Judiciary Committee, together with the Department of Transportation and the White House, examined the industry in detail, and basically accepted the critics' arguments.[2]

Nevertheless, in 1977 Edward Schmults, chairman of the President's taskforce on regulatory reform, could only wistfully conclude that:

Thirty to forty years of government regulation cannot be changed in a few months or even a few years .... Much remains to be done.

93

We hope that the efforts of the past two and a half years provide a beginning.[3]

Even with determination and an administration bent on regulatory reform things did not move smoothly. Opposition from the industry, complications arising from international airline operations, adverse economic conditions, and potential damage to Ford's re-election chances in trying to reform in an area that had as 'much political sex appeal as a sick alligator' all acted as a drag on the drive for reform.[4] Some important steps were taken in other sectors of the economy, but reform in the airline industry was rather piecemeal and, with regard to the international policy of the USA, at least one branch of the Ford Administration believed that policy became more not less regulatory in tone and content.[5]

Many in the Ford Administration had little time intellectually for economic interventionism. Ford, himself, was economically literate and a strong advocate of the free market. He favoured deregulation. His opinions had been formed partly by Schmults' predecessor in charge of the taskforce on regulatory reform, Roderick Hills, and by Paul MacAvoy of the CEA. Even more committed to reform, were two highly influential men - William Simon and Alan Greenspan. Simon was a flamboyant economic right-winger who was Secretary of the Treasury and Chairman of the Cabinet level Economic Policy Board (EPB), which overlooked much of policy development. Alan Greenspan was more subdued and intellectual, but no less of a right wing economist and political theorist. He was chairman of the president's CEA. James Lynn was Director of the OMB and slightly more liberal, as was Arthur Burns at the Federal Reserve Board. Secretary of Labor, John Dunlop and Elliot Richardson, Secretary of Commerce from November 1975, were just about as liberal as any in the Ford team, but they were definitely in the minority and did not have great influence. Policy tended to be dominated by Ford, Simon, Greenspan, and also by the White House economic adviser William Seidman.[6]

Seidman was a keep fit enthusiast and he needed the stamina that provided him in order to maintain momentum for regulatory reform. He was a key figure in the administration and played an invaluable co-ordinating role. His influence was derived ultimately from the close relationship that he had with Ford: administratively it was manifested most effectively through his executive directorship of the EPB. Seidman was more of a political animal than either Simon or Greenspan and he gave more weight than they did to the impact on the fortunes of the administration that regulatory reform proposals would have. Like Vice President Nelson Rockefeller, who likened the appeal of regulatory

reform to that of ailing alligators, Seidman became troubled by the reaction against reform from many influential quarters and, consequently, he
tempered his support to fit with the political realities of the situation.

The development of deregulatory policies during Ford's term of office
brought forth a number of problems, particularly in terms of inconsisten-
cies between domestic and international reform proposals and tensions
between policies devised to protect the interests of US airlines at a time of
great economic difficulty and those that were intended to craft a more
liberal operating regime for them. At the heart of many problems was
excess capacity in the industry. This was a particularly difficult issue for
the USA because its industry, both domestic and international, had traditionally used capacity to compete as price competition was not allowed.
Capacity competition now came under review because of subsidised capacity from state owned airlines, and over-capacity provided by charter
lines and wide bodied jets. In its domestic market, where the Administration had more control over matters and, for example, could guarantee that
anti-competitive subsidies would not operate to distort things, the USA
shied away from capacity controls. In the international sphere policy was
more equivocal.

The Administration came to condone capacity agreements on overseas routes
in the short-term as a way of dealing with an excess of seats which reduced load
factors to uneconomic levels. Foreign subsidised capacity and unacceptably
large amounts of sixth freedom traffic, carried in particular by the Dutch carrier
KLM, were targeted for reduction by the USA. However, the avid pro-competition faction in the Ford Administration repeatedly emphasised that if such
capacity agreements were to be pursued by the USA, above all things, they
should not be used as a means of dividing the market share artificially between
national carriers. That approach was generally approved by the Administration,
but its principle was compromised in talks with the Soviets when the CAB
proposed a pooling arrangement. In the end it never came about, but US policy
could be seen as uncertain and lacking the kind of consistency that made arguments of principle, often favoured by US negotiators, difficult to deploy
effectively.[7]

The problem of dealing with excess capacity caused the Ford Administration
to agonise over its policy. In essence, the problem was the inclination to pursue
free market solutions for the problems of operating airlines in a situation that
was not wholly under the control of the US Government. As it was not in full
control, it could not ensure that other nations' carriers would abide by free
market rules. If they did not, then they could gain advantages over American

carriers: hence the equivocation about how to deal with over-capacity. Self-interest and the pursuit of the free market were not always compatible for the Americans.

When Ford took over from Nixon, the matter of most immediate concern was that of the serious economic problem afflicting the USA's two main foreign flag carriers, TWA and Pan Am. Their situation was so serious that a Federal Action Plan had to be undertaken as an overriding priority. US airline losses had to be stemmed but, while the action taken by the Ford Administration in the autumn of 1974 looked protectionist to some, an editorial of the influential *Flight* magazine acknowledged that TWA and Pan Am were more efficient than many of the state owned airlines in Europe and yet they had difficulty competing with them because of various factors such as subsidised capacity and discriminatory landing charges: TWA paid $1.9 million in 1973 at Rome airport while Alitalia paid none.[8]

Capacity, after providing the USA with a competitive means of exploiting the early postwar international market, was now posing a threat to US interests. The airlines of the USA were not government owned and, although they received some small subsidies on uneconomic domestic routes, the international carriers had to succeed or fail through competition. However, in the face of state owned airlines with subsidised operations, they were now finding it more difficult to survive and excess capacity was undermining their economic viability.

It was not only subsidised capacity, discrimination and illegally discounted fares alone that were to blame for TWA and Pan Am's difficulties, there was also another problem illustrated most vividly by the operations of KLM. The Dutch airline's exploitation of sixth freedom traffic brought to light some of the different circumstances of European and US airlines and their abilities and potential for competition.

KLM, rather like BA was to do in the early 1990s, looked at its own tiny domestic market and realised that to be able to gain any comparable competitive position to the USA with its huge domestic market, it would have to broaden the area over which it garnered passengers. The result by 1974 was that 55 per cent of passengers flown by KLM to the USA were sixth freedom traffic fed into Holland from other countries for flights across the Atlantic. KLM thus managed to command a much higher percentage of the transatlantic traffic between the USA and Holland than US airlines. So, not only did the reduction 'of excess capacity ... [become] a key element of the President's action plan for international aviation', but also the CAB and the State Department wanted to renegotiate traffic rights, for example with the Netherlands, because 'the

United States can no longer tolerate the overall imbalance of benefits in the bilateral Air Transport Agreement.' If challenged, the Americans would have argued that renegotiating such agreements was not with the intention of artificially dividing the market (though as has been noted they could not argue this entirely on principle as they had proposed a pooling arrangement with the Soviets), however, maintaining that position came to rest on making ever finer distinctions and rather byzantine arguments. If imbalances in benefits could be used to justify the USA demanding the right to renegotiate an air service agreement, then it could also be used by others in the same way. The Americans were to learn this to their cost in the Bermuda 2 Talks when the British pointed to the imbalance of benefits reaped by the two sides. Of its bilaterals with European states, only the one with Portugal yielded a greater proportionate benefit for the USA than the one with Britain. The USA generated 59 per cent and carried 58 per cent of the passenger traffic in the US/UK market.[9]

In order to deal with the problems afflicting US foreign carriers, Ford issued a directive to the relevant government departments on 18 September calling for proposals that would give substantial help to US international operators. Claude Brinegar, the Transportation Secretary, had turned down a request for a $10.2 million monthly subsidy for Pan Am, which had lost $174 million since 1968, but he was prepared to take other measures to help. On 1 October he announced the Federal Action Plan, which was carried forward with the necessary legislative back-up in the International Air Transportation Fair Competitive Practices Act of 1975. The action plan made seven points: fare structures should be simplified and made more compensatory; capacity on international routes was to be reduced; measures against illegal discounting and rebating should be enforced; postal rates should be made more remunerative; Americans were to be encouraged to fly in US airlines; foreign discrimination was to be reduced; and uneconomic routes should be merged with others or closed down. On 3 January 1975 Ford signed the International Air Transportation Fair Competitive Practices Act into law which gave the US Government more power for effective remedial action.[10]

US policy had some successes, but there was also resentment among foreign governments at US action and resistance regarding the reduction of capacity and the elimination of the use of heavily discounted fares. The President's Council for International Economic Policy (CIEP) summarised the achievements of the Action Program in March 1976 as follows:

> Positive results... in the areas of route restructuring, service suspensions, unilateral capacity reductions, and capacity agreements; also mail rates are more compensatory and the "Fly U.S. Flag" program has made a contribution. However, DOT is concerned that progress has been slow in other areas such as compensatory fares, tariff enforcement, and reduction of excess foreign carrier capacity.[11]

Another positive side to the Action Program was that it helped to reassure the financial backers in the airline business and, in particular, helped sustain financial support for TWA and Pan Am. Certainly, so far as TWA was concerned, that support was still desperately needed. A memorandum for Seidman reported in December 1975 that TWA, unlike Pan Am and Eastern, had not taken necessary remedial steps and that it would lose an estimated $142 million in 1975. Another problem that persisted, which the Action Plan forced out into the open, was the conflict between the principles of free enterprise, that the Ford Administration generally favoured for the airlines, and the difficulty of squaring them with the perceived need to prevent the US flag carriers from going bankrupt, especially when foreign competitors were not playing the free market game themselves. This conflict began to tell within the Administration and manifested itself in different views about how to develop US aviation policy.[12]

In August 1975 the Administration considered requests from US international carriers that it should reaffirm its commitment to the Action Plan in order to help strengthen the financial standing of the airlines. It responded positively, but there were differences about what further action to take. The DOT and the CAB wanted to suspend below cost fares. The CAB had tussled with this problem for months. At the turn of the year it had followed the UK and recommended a fare floor for charters, but then withdrew it under pressure from the scheduled airlines who thought the floor had been laid too low. The CAB had then urged the acceptance of a criterion based upon direct operating costs for setting a minimum fare, but now it was the charter companies who cried foul. Their direct operating costs were much larger than their indirect, whereas with the scheduled airlines the reverse was the case. So, the criterion advocated by the CAB would result in a higher minimum fare than the charter companies wanted and would in effect give a measure of protection to the scheduled airlines, which were already reaping some benefits from APEX fares introduced on the Atlantic in April. The CEA opposed the CAB criterion and the Department of Justice was also dubious about its appropriateness. There

98

were similar pro and anti-competition splits on capacity controls, the reduction of foreign flag capacity, and tariff enforcement. However, the context of the Federal Action Plan is not the best for an examination of the way the Ford Administration's aviation policy debate developed: its legislative initiatives for deregulation and its evolution of a new international aviation policy statement (IAPS) provide richer material and a better picture.[13]

Although considerable emphasis has been given to the facts that the Ford Administration was more strongly committed to a free market creed than Nixon's, and that it was more unified and purposeful in its attempt to achieve regulatory reform, it is also important to bear in mind the intractability of the problem that it confronted, which accounts in part for the failure to achieve radical change. Though in danger of being repetitive, it is important that the problems of regulatory reform are kept in focus, otherwise the characterisation of the Ford Administration that has been given will appear implausible in the light of the relatively modest changes that it achieved.

During its lifetime, opinions were changing and becoming more supportive of reform, but the industry itself, the unions, small communities, and powerful factions in the Congress and in the Administration remained opposed or lukewarm. In addition, the job of juggling with two different policies for the domestic and the international spheres of aviation became more and more difficult to perform. The economic ailments of the airline industry made reform a more dangerous gamble than it might otherwise have been, and the diffusion of power in the US Government, including the independence granted to regulatory agencies, all made the task of reform difficult and slow. And finally, Ford did not have a popular mandate to wield in support of controversial policy developments.

His administration was unique in that neither he nor his Vice President had been elected. Ford had been drafted in as Nixon's Vice President when Spiro Agnew was forced to resign because of financial shenanigans stemming from his time as Governor of Maryland. When Nixon went because of Watergate, Ford became President and Nelson Rockefeller was brought in as the new Vice President: the world's greatest democracy had a President and a Vice President neither of whom had been elected. That situation, combined with the whole unsavoury inheritance of Watergate, did not give Ford a strong base. As President, he had severe political handicaps.[14]

While the Federal Action Plan was a rather *ad hoc* response to serious economic problems that beset US airlines in the early 1970s, the Administration also tried to shift policy development in a more carefully planned and well considered way towards reform. The debate on regulatory reform was developed and some legislative initiatives, in addition to the International Airline Fair Competitive Practices Act, were introduced to the Congress. In fact, considerable momentum for reform developed from 1975 onwards within Congress itself.

Democratic Senators Howard W. Cannon of Nevada and Edward Kennedy of Massachusetts, both did a great deal to advance the cause of regulatory reform, in particular in the airline industry. Cannon was later to become the floor manager in the Senate of the 1978 Air Transportation Regulatory Reform Bill, and in 1976 he chaired hearings on airline regulatory reform. But it was the year before that in 1975 that Kennedy took the first important initiative as head of a Judiciary Committee subcommittee investigation into the practices and procedures of the CAB. His report found the CAB guilty of pursuing incoherent route policies and unnecessarily anti-competitive practices such as upholding high fares by restricting charters and concentrating on nurturing profits at the expense of competition.[15]

Criticisms like this were not without effect in building up support for reform and the Kennedy Report actually came at a time when the CAB was beginning to take stock of itself and initiate some changes. In 1973 the CAB began to alter its policy on rate regulation and allow some changes to its inflexible system of regulation. Under Timm generally, however, the emphasis had been on sustaining profit margins for the airlines and it looked as if the CAB were going to dig in its traditionally protectionist heels. With Ford's appointment of John Robson things looked better for the reformers. Robson was troubled by the problems that afflicted the USA's international carriers and that made him cautious about reforms in that sphere, but he was sympathetic to calls for change in the domestic market. In the summer of 1975 he proposed the introduction of a limited deregulation experiment in 1976 on some selected domestic routes to try to evaluate what the effects of such reforms would be. The response to that was unfavourable: the reformers thought that it was too timid; the supporters of the *status quo* thought that it might establish a dangerous precedent. Nevertheless, Robson persevered and carried out a short lived experiment. He believed that reform was necessary and in particular the unconscionable delays within the CAB on cases brought to it had to be stopped. On one occasion he said: 'My objective can be stated rather simply: Let's give people answers more quickly.' Robson thus brought about some changes within the existing administrative framework. The CAB began to relax its stranglehold on the airline industry. It speeded up its bureaucratic procedures and relaxed restrictions on charter operators, but it was not seen by other agencies within the Ford Administration as the best medium through which to channel regulatory reform proposals. In fact, the main legislative initiative of the Ford years was drawn up without any consultation with the CAB.[16]

The development of the political debate on deregulation within the Administration and the way forces gathered around the pro and the less pro-competition positions will be considered in some detail when the review of international aviation policy is examined. For the present, in considering the legislative initiatives that the Administration took, the main emphasis will be on the resulting proposals that emerged from the bureaucracy rather than on how they were formulated.

In March 1975 Brinegar was replaced at the Department of Transportation by William T. Coleman, a black Republican who had some liberal inclinations, in particular he was involved in the National Association for the Advancement of Colored People. In economic policy he was a moderate conservative, who favoured reducing government controls in the transportation industry. He had some measure of success, most notably with the enactment of the Railroad Revitalisation and Reform Act of 1976, but he also had a major input into trucking and airline industry deregulation. During his first six months of office he had the opportunity to express his general ideas in the preparation of a Statement of National Transportation Policy, which he delivered on 17 September.

The Statement said nothing revolutionary. It reaffirmed the commitment of the USA to competitive policies, but noted that fare discounting and over-capacity continued to trouble US overseas airline operators. It also pointed out that different policies were being deployed in the domestic and international sphere.

> The pursuit of capacity agreements in the international transportation field, while the Department has generally opposed them in the domestic field, is merely recognition that the international transportation policy must consider the economic and political views of the foreign countries.[17]

The differences between the two marketplaces raised problems for those who argued for deregulation and a free market in terms of doctrinaire principles. That difficulty was in danger of being compounded if one of the possible routes for development mentioned in the statement were to be adopted. Coleman wondered whether to continue with the existing policy of having two or three international US operators, or to liberalise entry for domestic into international operations and *vice versa*. If the latter were adopted after there had been regulatory reform in the domestic sphere then there would be a number of airlines operating within two different frameworks: a deregulated market domestically, and a regulated market internationally. From such a situation there would inevitably arise a struggle between the forces of regulation and the forces of deregulation in an effort to increase their respective domains. The more deregulated the domestic US market became, the less easily would it operate alongside the regulated international environment and that would cause difficulties for the formulation and implementation of US international policy.[18]

At the same time as the policy statement was being prepared, so was the 1975 Airline Regulatory Reform Bill and proposals for other measures of liberalisation within the US transportation industry. The proposals for the 1975 Airline Regulatory Reform Bill were drawn up by the DOT and the President's staff: the CAB was not consulted.[19] The bill involved quite radical departures from existing policy, but they were only arrived at after considerable compromise and accommodation between those who favoured moderate and those who wanted more drastic reform. The moderates won.

The main change in the bill was a switch of emphasis from the importance of protecting an 'infant industry' to stressing competition. Entry of new companies and of charter operators onto the main trunk lines was to be made easier and rules governing charter services were to be relaxed further. CAB procedures were to be speeded up; abandonment of uneconomic routes was to be made easier; price competition was to be developed except where it became predatory (i.e. fares fell below direct operating costs); and merger rules were to be made more permissive. Pooling, capacity, scheduling and equipment agreements were to be prohibited, but other anti-competitive agreements were to be given antitrust immunity providing that they met a serious transport need and that a more competitive solution was not available.[20]

The reforms proposed would change the general character of the domestic airline industry by putting what, until now, had been largely competition rhetoric into practice. The old principle of 'public convenience and necessity' which had been used to regulate entry and exit from routes was to be replaced by a more liberal and competitive dispensation. Thus the aims of the CAB were changed from 'providing for competition only to the extent necessary' to 'encourage development of the industry with maximum reliance on competitive market forces and on actual and potential competition.' The demands for price competition were also becoming irresistible, especially when the examples of deregulated intrastate airline operations (outside the federal authority of the CAB) could be held up as models of efficiency and cheap travel. Mergers, which might increase efficiency were also to be made easier, though they would be subject to scrutiny under antitrust legislation. Ford emphasised the new direction that the bill was intended to take the airline industry in his message to the Congress: 'the focus of the new regulatory system will be to protect consumer interests, rather than those of the industry.'[21]

Even Greenspan, with a little reluctance, acknowledged that the bill was about as radical as existing circumstances permitted.

> While there are portions of the draft bill that require less reform than needed in the long run (e.g. in permitting new airlines to enter the industry), this draft legislation represents a reasonable compromise among conflicting points of view .... For these reasons, the CEA strongly urges the expeditious submission of this draft legislation to Congress.[22]

The very fact that the bill was acceptable to Greenspan meant that it would be unacceptable to many others. By mid October, the bill was regarded as 'controversial' and had 'already aroused vigorous comment.' Ford was somewhat taken aback by the furore that was unleashed by what he saw as a bill that embodied compromise and accommodation by contending members of his Administration. The compromises, however, while acceptable within the Administration, clearly were insufficient to appease many outside. As the temperature of the debate increased members of the Administration began to have doubts about the political wisdom of the proposals as presidential election year came upon them and those less keen on regulatory reform, who had made compromises with the radicals, began to have doubts about the wisdom of having done that.[23]

Even the six foot eight Secretary of Commerce, Rogers Morton, was unable to rise above this. He noted how the bill was jeopardising traditional support from the transport industry and its unions for the Republican Party. Vice President Rockefeller and Seidman were also worried by the political implications of regulatory reform. In early 1976 a number of concessions were made in order to assuage some of the criticism and, in particular, the Republican small town constituencies were given reassurance that they would not be deprived of air services. Amendments were made to the bill so that subsidies could be provided for commuter airlines until 1986, which would help to keep air services to small communities going during the difficult period of transition to a free market domestic airline system.[24]

Despite the changes that the Ford Administration made, Congress did not enact the 1975 Bill, though it did receive thorough hearings. However, rather courageously, Ford continued to press for regulatory reform even though it was controversial and being pressed for in an election year. He had success with the railroad bill going through and in May he emphasised once again the importance of regulatory reform and proposed a structured timetable for legislative action. 'We cannot untangle 40 year's worth of bureaucratic red tape overnight, but we can at least set the process in motion.' He proposed a programme stretching out until 1981, which was intended to supplement, not replace, the legislative proposals that he had already sent to Congress. During 1976 the Administration abandoned the 1975 bill in favour of a simplified and amended alternative, which Ford submitted to Congress as the 1977 Aviation Act. Its basic purpose and content were the same as its predecessor, but in November the American electorate had spoken and it did not allow Ford the opportunity of seeing through all these plans for regulatory reform. It was left to his successor Jimmy Carter to make the real breakthrough in airline deregulation.[25]

During the early years of the Nixon Administration, US policy-makers had addressed the problems of international aviation within two broad guidelines: the need to counter acts of international terrorism involving airlines, which is of little interest to the present narrative; and the need to respond to growth in the industry. By 1974, the concerns of the USA had changed somewhat, largely because passenger growth had not met expectations, and it was deemed that a new international aviation policy statement was desirable. It was also thought that it would have a good chance of a reasonable hearing from foreign governments, whose airlines were suffering under the present regime just as US ones were. A memorandum for the EPB, some way into the review that was set in motion, summarised the issues which needed addressing as:

> economic efficiency of operations, adjusting to rising costs, capacity flexibility needed to meet traffic fluctuations, restraints on U.S. carriers by foreign governments/competitors, the expansion of low cost transportation services, and the viability of U.S. carriers.[26]

The process of reviewing the international aviation regime was put under way during Nixon's time with the commissioning of a report from an independent consultancy agency Harbridge House. It was jointly funded by the State Department, the DOT and the CIEP. The two volume study that it produced was considered by a conference sponsored by the State Department at the end of April 1975. It acted as a stimulant for thought, setting out five possible avenues for development ranging from a regulatory to a free market system, but failed to be in any way a determinant of subsequent policy developments. It did not take political trends into account adequately and, after the conference, the rather bland and predictable conclusion was that 'the basic question of policy alternatives came down to whether we should have more or alternatively less regulation.' The majority thought that in the international sphere more deregulation was not feasible, but a determined minority took the contrary view. It was left to agencies and departments within the Administration to hammer out new policy.[27]

The international aviation policy review (IAPR) began in January 1975, but there were problems from the start. Even between the State Department and the DOT, which were close on policy matters, there were difficulties about jurisdiction. Which department should direct the IAPR? Its management and direction throughout its eighteen months of work were troublesome. Most of the work was done by a steering committee which embodied a compromise within the bureaucracy as it was chaired jointly by Assistant Secretaries Robert Binder and Thomas Enders of DOT and the State Department respectively. Enders was later succeeded by Assistant Secretary Katz. The CIEP also had a co-ordinating role and the EPB had final say on what was to go to Ford for approval. As Executive Director of the EPB, Seidman and his office thus had a major input into the policy review, especially as a broker between contending factions in 1976, when positions had hardened and there was conflict between the moderate and radical reformers.[28]

The Steering Committee tussled with its task in the spring and early summer. A division of opinion within it began to raise questions as to just what the review should seek to achieve. It became questionable whether or not a new policy statement should be made. Some thought that it would be easier and less politically controversial simply to make piecemeal reforms. By August 1975 the Steering Committee had produced a preliminary draft statement, but there was little consensus on new policy. There was support for a large US presence in the international network provided it could be sustained without subsidies: exceptions to that were to be permitted on routes of national interest such as New York-Moscow. It favoured the liberalisation of charter rules and price flexibility generally, though the State Department observed that: 'This may have to go hand-in-hand with capacity controls in some markets to reduce excess capacity, a major change from past U.S. policy.' Agreement on these matters was tentative and severe problems of principle remained. 'An underlying conceptual issue is the extent to which "deregulation" should be applied internationally.' The State Department thought that any attempt to pursue the domestic goal of aviation deregulation through international action should be delayed until the IAPR was completed 'and all agencies have a better understanding of the implications and the costs, political and otherwise, of that attempt.'[29]

Some on the steering committee favoured making the preliminary proposals public in order to receive opinion from outside the Administration, but 'given the "philosophical" nature of the division' within the Steering Committee, others doubted if that would do much good.[30] The question of to publish or not to publish came before the EPB Executive Committee on 27 August. It decided against and returned the draft paper to the Steering Committee for further development.[31] Bill Gorog, Seidman's deputy, in a memorandum for his boss, clearly showed why the committee decided as it did.

> This paper is really "preliminary" since it presents more options than conclusions...
> ... the options split on the question of moving aggressively towards a more competitive environment consistent with new domestic initiatives versus fence-straddling and perpetual tinkering with an anticompetitive and anticonsumer oriented regulatory system. I feel that this is a dangerous paper which should be re-worked.[32]

Because wide interagency differences remained unresolved, the draft was returned to the assistant secretary level in order for it to be sorted out. The Steering Committee failed to do that. There were two problems: one was the difficulty of getting people to attend meetings; the other was the difference between the radicals and the moderates. By mid December 1975/early January 1976 matters were coming to a head. It looked as if the radical reformers led by MacAvoy of the CEA might make concessions. He believed that he could persuade Thomas Kauper, Assistant Secretary in the Justice Department in charge of the Antitrust Division, and Collier from OMB to concede ground if the Steering Committee were to be chaired by Seidman. The committee had done some redrafting, but had failed to resolve the differences. Co-chairman Binder was now pressing for an EPB decision for the statement to go ahead, though there was still the possibility that instead only piecemeal reforms would be undertaken.[33]

On 28 January a new draft was produced with the CEA, OMB and the Justice Department expressing their dissent on a lengthy series of issues. They believed that only supply and demand should determine minimum levels of service. They wanted the Public Convenience and Necessity requirement for entry to be abandoned. They opposed capacity and scheduling agreements. On pricing they wanted the market to rule, with the US pulling out of IATA in the future and abandoning its policy of opposing rate rebating and discounting. The USA should penalise foreign carriers for discrimination, but should not use that as a means of artificially dividing the market. By early February matters were in the hands of the EPB.[34]

In the papers brought before the EPB by the DOT, State Department, CIEP, the National Security Council (NSC), and CAB, it was felt that the need to meet the new circumstances of international aviation required 'a Presidential policy statement that is strong and specific in its support of increased operating efficiency and preservation of a major role for America's private carriers.' The CEA, OMB and Justice Department on the other hand emphasised 'freer competition and opposition to anti-competitive agreements or practices.' The result of the continuing differences between theses two groups meant that four questions still remained unresolved. Firstly, should excess capacity be eliminated by temporary inter-carrier agreements or by market forces? Secondly, should the USA take action against a state that offered excess capacity in violation of its bilateral with the USA? Thirdly, should there be substantial increases in penalties for tariff violations? And fourthly, should there be a public necessity and convenience requirement for new supplemental carriers?[35]

The objections of the radical reformers to the January draft of the new policy statement were spelt out by Kauper of the Antitrust Division.

> The new International Aviation Statement is significantly more anticompetitive than the 1970 statement. Although less restrictive charter regulation is endorsed almost every other is anticompetitive and pro the two largest U.S. flag carriers.[36]

Even the charter liberalisation proposals were not as radical as those recently proposed by the CAB, which would place the Administration in the rather invidious position of being led in the field of reform by the industry's own regulatory body. Kauper listed the three areas where the statement appeared to be more reactionary than progressive. These were: capacity regulation in the international sphere; a move away from the 1970 endorsement of discounted fares; and a shift away from point to point competition by two or more US airlines. There were other minor anti-competitive proposals intended to restrict cheap fares, but these were Kauper's main worries.[37]

Kauper's observations were accurate and the flaws in the statement as he saw them were not remedied before the statement was issued, but that might give an erroneous impression of what the new policy did and of what the general intent of the Administration actually was. The intent was not to move towards protection and reregulation so much as to attempt to sustain the fortunes of competition and hopes for liberalisation in the future in the face of both economic conditions in the industry that had deteriorated since the 1970 statement and determined movements by other states to adopt more regulation. It was a more anti-competitive policy document than the 1970 one and it was to cause difficulties for the USA in subsequent talks when it tried to push a liberal policy line in international negotiations. However, it represented what appeared to be politically feasible to most people in the Ford Administration, given the facts that it was an election year, the economics of the industry were difficult, and that they had to take into account that US policy had to work alongside the policies of other countries which were moving toward more not less protection.

The EPB decided that a statement should indeed be made, but, on the request of various members of the EPB, including Coleman and Secretary of Commerce Richardson, not until amendments were made.[38] While they were under consideration within the Administration developments were taking place outside that were also to bear on the form of the final statement.

Like the USA, foreign countries were having to respond to the problems of over-capacity, low returns on investment and unprofitable operations on international routes. The policies that they adopted would inevitably have some impact on US policy and on the condition of US airlines. In a CIEP report of March 1976, it was noted, with some alarm, that both Britain and Japan had moved towards more predetermination of airline services and capacity controls. It added that: 'These moves challenge basic long-standing US policies on the essential role of competition.'[39] With such developments there was a difficult question for American policy makers to answer: To what extent could the USA buck the trend toward more rather than less regulation in the international airline market through its own unilateral policy? There could be serious costs to pay if the USA adopted a more liberal policy at a time when others were becoming more protectionist.

At the same time as the CIEP report was circulated, the Director General of IATA, Knut Hammarskjold, made a speech in which he passed some highly critical comments about US policy. The degree to which he commented on internal US affairs was quite unprecedented. He was dismayed by the lack of US leadership during a difficult period for the world's airlines and believed that strong action was required. Above all, the three component parts of the industry needed to be brought into a balanced relationship: namely, routes, capacity and rates. In calling for such action, he clearly viewed regulation rather than the free market as the means to achieve that balance. Some of these arguments appear to have impressed, or at least reinforced views already held by members of the DOT and the State Department.[40]

The concern about Britain moving toward a more restrictive international aviation policy was given dramatic substance in June when the Secretary of State for Industry Edmund Dell denounced the Bermuda Air Service Agreement. That highlighted the difficulties that the US had in trying to uphold its traditional view concerning the value of competition and its attempt to spread the deregulation creed abroad.

John Robson saw the crisis in relations with Britain as an obstacle to the final formulation of the US international policy statement. He emphasised the practical problems that confronted the USA in the forthcoming renegotiation of the air services agreement with Britain: 'The point is that there exists a fundamental and visible relationship between a new international aviation policy statement and the resolution of ... pending "real world" matters.'[41] He opposed issuing the statement because he felt that it would either have to be too elastic, in order not to pre-empt possibilities of compromise with the British, or else it would be too specific and fall foul of contradiction by the new bilateral agreement which would then undermine its credibility.

Robson's argument was not persuasive for members of the Administration. In fact the contrary argument put by the State Department that 'a clear and forward-looking policy statement would strengthen the U.S. negotiating position' became the favoured course of action.[42] Allied to that belief was the fear that a failure to come forward with a new statement, when the public knew that a review had been under way for some time, would be seen as a lack of resolve and evidence of division in Ford's team. But the Administration also had another positive reason for issuing a statement. It had begun the review with the conviction that the mid 1970s required new policies. Criticism of US lack of leadership in international aviation from people like Hammarskjold had rankled feelings in Washington and reinforced the belief that the USA should come forward with a new statement of policy to impress the international community.

As a memorandum from Coleman to Seidman urging that the statement be issued put it: 'These nations must know that we continue to be firm in our preferences for the play of competitive forces in, rather than government control of, the international aviation market-place.'[43]

The Administration might have had to modify its initial hopes for regulatory reform in the face of the economic, political and international realities of the day, but the spirit remained committed to a competitive airline industry where market forces predominated. Unfortunately for the Americans, their compromises, in the international policy statement that was issued, gave ambiguous signals to countries like Britain. For the compromises made it appear that the USA was modifying its competitive philosophy for its international airline industry. In some ways it was, but its overriding goal was still to promote competition and rely on market forces as much as possible and that brought it into direct conflict with the British and their desire for more not less regulation. If the CEA, OMB and the Antitrust Division had got their way, it would have made the US position more straightforward and easier to defend in principle: but, it may have meant that agreement with Britain would have been impossible to achieve for, as will be seen, even with the compromises on competition policy in the September statement, the British and the USA were miles and miles apart on policy at the outset of the Bermuda 2 negotiations.

By 26 July the final draft (with only minor subsequent amendments), of what was to be the International Air Transportation Policy Statement of 8 September, was completed. It had accommodated the views of those agencies 'most involved on a daily basis with international aviation', which in effect meant that the consumer interest/radical reform group composed of the CEA, the OMB and the Antitrust Division had had to give ground.[44] The thinking that determined the statement had four fundamental concerns. Firstly, the USA wanted low cost and readily available air travel. Secondly, it wanted to ensure the financial viability of US international carriers and that they had a fair and equal opportunity for competition as free enterprise companies. Thirdly, the USA sought regulatory reform that would enable these first two concerns to be catered for and achieve sufficient flexibility to meet changing market conditions. Fourthly, the USA recognised the role that foreign airlines played in the international system and took that into account in formulating its policy.

While this Policy Statement calls for a large measure of regulatory reform, consistent with our domestic aviation policy, differences between the

110

approaches taken here and those in the proposed Aviation act of 1975 reflect awareness of substantial differences that exist between the international and domestic operating environments: ... [45]

In particular, American policy had to take into account the problems that arose for their privately owned airlines competing against subsidised, state owned, foreign carriers that were often afforded protection by their governments against competition. Also, there was a capacity problem. Wide bodied jets might operate in the US domestic market on densely populated routes without any serious problems, but it was a different story on less dense international routes. The Ford Administration was confessing that it could not immediately pursue the kind of competitive policy that it favoured in principle because of the realities of the existing international aviation marketplace.

> The United States cannot dominate the world aviation community, but it can endeavour to lead - with policies that reconcile the interests of the aviation consumer and the profit-oriented carrier, the interests of the privately-owned, competitive aviation companies we favor and the government-controlled and subsidized carriers found elsewhere.[46]

Thus, although the policy statement sought air transport at as low a price as possible and relied on competition to achieve American goals, there were a number of acknowledgements that non-commercial considerations would also play a part in the new dispensation. Competition was to be pursued to the greatest extent feasible, but only after taking into account the views of other countries and the need to reach agreement for bilateral air service agreements. Other influential factors in determining US policy were: the need to support the nation's airlines where they were efficient and competitive; safety and environmental considerations; and aspects of US defence, foreign policy and international commerce.[47]

The danger of exposing US airlines to unfair competition from airlines of countries which did not share the US commitment to the free market, the need to compromise in order to achieve bilateral agreements with foreign states, and the continuing concern about the economic situation of the airline industry were all factors which appeared, in one way or another, in the statement and explained why it was not as radical as some in the Ford Administration would have liked. Another, but unspoken consideration, was the political difficulty of coming forward with controversial and radical proposals on the eve of a presidential election.

Despite the misgivings of someone like Assistant Secretary Kauper, which on the whole were justified given his free market position, there were some liberalisation aspects to the new statement. There were some measures which were consciously more liberal, such as the relaxation of the rules governing charter operations. There were also some recommendations, the full implications of which did not become apparent for some time, which facilitated future liberalisation. Particularly important in this respect were proposals to restructure the relationship between the domestic and the international airline markets by allowing all US international operators to have domestic feed systems and by moving away from reliance on traditional international gateways and opening new ones in the interior of the USA. When these aims were realised, they, along with the policy of licensing more domestic operators for international routes, laid the basis for the hub and spoke systems to spread out from a variety of points within the USA and reach directly into the international system. Those developments encouraged competition among US carriers both for feed into the hubs of the new international gateways and for transatlantic, transpacific and Latin American international traffic departing from those hubs. The ability to have a large number of gateways in the USA designated in a bilateral also provided some air service agreements with their only redeemingly liberal feature, or so at least one American official believed in 1991 regarding Bermuda 2.[48]

In the three most important component parts of the statement, namely: rates; capacity and routes, the policy was either unchanged or edged away from the liberal principles of the 1970 policy statement. On fares, the USA again condoned IATA procedures, but expressed reservations and wanted more flexibility for individual carriers. At the same time, the Ford Administration did not like heavy discounting and talked of taking action against such practices. It was generally held that fares should not dip below a reasonable return on investment and that the difference between promotional and normal fares should be diminished, thus reducing the element of cross-subsidisation. Greater flexibility in pricing would be allowed for charters and where other states insisted on market share capacity agreements that threatened to extinguish capacity competition.[49]

The most significant changes in route policy de-emphasised competition on a point to point basis, but tried to nurture competition in a wider context created by increasing the number of US international gateways.

The policy endorses a movement away from head-to-head competition between U.S. carriers in city-pair markets, and supports improved services in present coterminals and expansion into new cities, if it can be supported economically. The U.S. seeks an improved competitive posture for U.S. carriers vis-a-vis foreign carriers and elimination of discriminatory practices.[50]

The move away from head to head competition had much to do with concern about capacity and the dangers of US airlines flying too many empty seats to be profitable. The specific proposals on capacity policy made 'explicit the U.S. view that capacity levels should be set individually by carriers, although because of the importance of economically viable operations, ... [the USA] would support temporary carrier agreements under certain carefully prescribed conditions.'[51] Those conditions should not be such that capacity was predetermined for market share reasons because that would involve 'restraints unrelated to carrier efficiency or traffic demand.'[52] In American eyes much of the excess capacity was created by foreign airlines which were subsidised and less efficient than US carriers or who, like KLM, breached air service agreements (again, according to the USA) by over-exploitation of sixth freedom traffic.

From a foreign perspective it looked as if the USA wanted multiple designation, but only on routes which it decided could sustain both foreign and at least two American competitors; it was against market share capacity agreements because they would discriminate against the multi-airline American industry, but they favoured temporary agreements to sustain American carriers where there was over-capacity; they wanted the reduction of sixth freedom traffic carried by foreign airlines, but never gave passing thought to the opening up of the American domestic feeder market to foreign airlines, though the increase in gateways within the USA did something to reduce the advantage that US airlines had with their immense domestic market. In short, many of these provisions were conveniently self serving for US airlines, which was understandable enough, but when the US negotiators berated their foreign counterparts in moralistic and principled terms about the superiority of a freer market it aggravated already irritated sensibilities.

Before the Policy Statement was issued, the Americans were already trying to assess the impact that the Bermuda 2 negotiations might have on subsequent developments. Despite its dramatic denunciation by the British, the Americans hoped that there might be room for actual improvement on some of the provisions in the original Bermuda Agreement. That was important because they anticipated that 'a new agreement will represent for the future of aviation what the Bermuda Agreement has represented for the past 25 years.'[53] The Americans were to be disappointed on both counts. In most American eyes Bermuda 2 produced a less favourable environment for American airlines and the new agreement was only ever regarded as a model in the sense of what not to do in other US bilaterals. Although the Ford Administration managed to encourage the dynamics of regulatory reform within the internal transport sector and in other areas of US domestic industry and commerce, it found that the international marketplace was a much more recalcitrant beast.

Notes and References

1. *Congressional Quarterly*, May 1976, Text of President's Message on Regulatory Reform, 13 May 1976.

2. Beyer, in Majone (1990), p. 15.

3. Reichley (1981), p. 400.

4. Ibid.

5. Ford Lib., CEA (Greenspan Files) box 87, folder: Aviation International, undated response to 28 Jan. 1976 IAPS draft, attached to Kauper to Seidman.

6. Ford (1979), pp. 263-4; Reichley (1981), pp. 399-400; Richardson (1976).

7. Seidman Papers, box 113, folder: 8/76-9/76, text of 'Statement of International Air Transportation Policy of the United States', 8 Sept. 1976; ibid., Coleman to Seidman, received 13 Aug. 1976 with summary of 26 July draft IAPS; ibid., box 319, folder: USSR 29-30 Nov. 1976 (3), undated 'Civil Aviation - Background Paper', in Briefing Book for Secretary Simon's visit to the USSR.

8. *Flight*, 10 Oct. 1974, editorial, and 11 Jan. 1974, p. 31; Seidman Papers, box 53, folder: CIEP (3), memo. Dunn to Seidman, 30 May 1975, the financial difficulties of the airlines were dealt with by a special taskforce under Deputy Secretary Barnum of the DOT; ibid., folder: CIEP (8), CIEP Summary Status Report - International Economic Policy Issues, 7.7, Federal Action Plan, 12 March 1976.

9. Ibid., box 113, folder: Airlines 9/74-7/75, CIEP memo. US - Dutch Negotiations on Airline Capacity, Oct. 1974; ibid., R.J. O'Melia, acting CAB chairman, to Ford, 11 April 1975; Ford Papers, WHCF, CA 1/ 24/76-1/20/77, box 2, folder CA 8/1/76-9/8/76, memo. R. Porter to R. Nessen, 'Briefing on U.S. International Aviation Policy Statement', 8 Sept. 1976.

10. Seidman Papers, box 38, folder: Airlines International Aviation Policy Group, Barnum to Seidman, 23 Sept. 1976 and attached, 'U.S. Government Statement Reaffirming its Support of the 1974 Federal Action Plan for Improved Profitability in International Airline Operations'; Ford Lib., Papers of Philip W. Buchen, box 2, folder: CAB (1), Lazarus to Buchen, 1 Nov. 1974, 'International Air Transportation Fair Practices Act of 1974', enacted as PL 93-623, 3 Jan. 1975, 88 stat. 2102. Ford had taken executive action, effective from 27 August 1974, to enable the CAB to retaliate against countries mounting capacity levels which the CAB believed impaired the right of US airlines to fair and equal opportunity to compete: included in such unfair practices was the CAB's controversial judgement on excessive 6th freedom traffic.

11. Ibid., box 53, folder: CIEP (8), CIEP Survey Status Report - International Economic Policy Issues, 12 March 1976.

12. Ibid., folder: CIEP (6), Dunn to Seidman, 'Financial Situation of Eastern, American and TWA: a Status Report', 9 Dec. 1975.

13. Ibid., box 13, folder: Airlines 8/75-12/75, memo. 'Implementation of Administration's Action Plan', 12 Aug. 1975, attached paper 'Prospective Actions'; *Flight*, 27 Feb. 1975, p. 321, also 10 April 1975 and 17 July 1975. During the period 1970-74, the CAB had created a fare regime in the course of what was known as the 'Domestic Passenger Fare Investigation': the goals were to relate fares to costs, eliminate discrimination and abolish cross-subsidisation, see Haanappel (1984) and Lowenfeld (1975).

14. Nixon (1978); Ford (1979).

15. Breyer, in Majone (1990), p. 22 and footnote 21; *Congressional Digest*, June - July 1978, 172-4, extracts from Senate debate 19 April 1978 on proposed Air Transportation Regulation Reform Act of 1978, Senator Cannon. Kennedy Hearings, 'Oversight of Civil Aeronautics Board

Practices and Procedures: Hearings before the Subcommittee on Administrative Practice and Procedure of the Senate Judiciary Committee, 94th Cong. 1st session, 1976.

16. Breyer, in Majone (1990), p. 16; *Flight*, 17 July 1975, p. 72, also 20 Nov. 1975, p. 743.

17. Ford Lib., Papers of J.M. Cannon, box 35, folder: Transportation April to October 1975, 'A Statement of National Transportation Policy', by Secretary of Transportation 17 Sept. 1975.

18. Ibid.

19. *Flight*, 20 Nov. 1975, p. 743, interview with John Robson.

20. Cannon Papers, box 3, folder: Aviation March 1975 - July 1976, 'Aviation Act of 1975', US DOT Publication, which compared existing with proposed new law; ibid., folder: Airline Regulatory Reform, Connor to Cannon, 8 Oct. 1975, attachment tab B, Aviation Act 1975, 'Summary of Provisions/Analysis of Need'.

21. Ibid.; *Flight*, 16 Oct. 1975; *Congressional Quarterly Almanac*, 1975, 28-a, Ford Message to Congress: 'Airline Deregulation', 8 Oct. 1975; for an interesting discussion of the merits and demerits of mergers, monopolies, consumer interests and antitrust laws see Adams and Brock, (1991).

22. CEA Papers (Greenspan Files), folder: Airline Regulatory Reform Legislation, Greenspan to Cannon, 7 Oct. 1975.

23. *Flight*, 16 Oct. 1975; Reichley (1981), pp. 399-400.

24. Ibid.; Cannon Papers, box 54, folder: EPB 3/26/76, P. O'Neil to EPB, 24 March 1976 re amendments to 1975 act. Proposed amendments approved by EPB, 26 March 1976.

25. *Congressional Quarterly*, May 1976, 'Regulatory Reform: Timetables Proposed', 1309-10; Ford Papers, WHCF, box 2, CA 1/24/76-1/30/77 (Gen), folder: 9/9/76-1/20/77, Ford to Congress, 13 Jan. 1977.

26. Seidman Papers, box 38, folder: Airlines International Aviation (2), draft memo. for EPB Exec. Cmte., subject IAPS, 12 Feb. 1976.

27. CEA Papers (Greenspan Files), box 87, folder: Aviation Conference on International Aviation Policy, Proceedings of the Conference Sponsored by Dept. of State, 29-30 April 1975, to discuss Harbridge

House Report; Harbridge House, (1975) *US International Aviation Policy at the Crossroads: a Study of Alternative Policies and their Consequences 2 vols.* (Boston).

28. Seidman Papers, box 38, folder: Airlines International Aviation (1), CIEP memo. for EPB, 13 Jan. 1975; ibid., Porter to Seidman, 26 Jan. 1976; ibid., folder: Airlines International Aviation (2), Seidman to Sec. of State and Sec. of DOT, 8 Sept. 1976.

29. Ibid., box 53, folder: CIEP (3), Dunn to Seidman, 30 May 1975; ibid., box 113, folder: Airlines 8/75-12/75, State Dept. Briefing Paper, Aug. 1975.

30. Ibid., Discussion Paper, 15 Aug. 1975.

31. Ibid., box 38, folder: International Aviation Policy Group (1), Porter to seidman, 26 Jan. 1976.

32. Ibid., Gorog to Seidman, 27 Aug. 1975.

33. Ibid., Porter to Seidman, 26 Jan. 1976.

34. Ibid., 'Statement of International Aviation Policy of the U.S.', Draft, 28 Jan. 1976.

35. Ibid., folder: Airlines International Aviation (2), DRAFT memo. for EPB Exec. Cmte., subject IAPS, 13 Feb. 1976.

36. CEA (Greenspan Files), box 87, folder: Aviation International, response to 28 Jan. 1976 IAPS draft attached to Kauper to Seidman, undated.

37. Ibid.

38. Seidman Papers, box 113, folder: airlines 8/76-9/76, Coleman to Seidman, received 13 Aug. 1976 with summary of draft IAPS of 26 July 1976.

39. Ibid., box 53, folder CIEP (8), CIEP Summary Status Report - International Economic Policy Issues, 12 March 1976.

40. Ibid., box 38, folder: Airlines International Aviation Policy Group (2), Piper to Dunn, 15 March 1976, subject: address by Hammarskjold 10 March 1976.

41. Ford Papers WHCF, CA box 2, 1/24/76-1/20/76, folder: 9/8/76, Robson to Seidman, 24 May 1976.

42. Ibid., folder: CA 8/1/76-7/8/76, Porter to Nessen, 8 Sept. 1976.

43. Seidman Papers, box 113, folder: airlines 8/76-9/76, Coleman to Seidman with summary of policy statement draft of 28 July, received 13 Aug. 1976.

44. Ibid.

45. Ibid., text of 'Statement of International Air Transportation Policy of the United States', 8 Sept. 1976.

46. Ibid., Coleman to Seidman, received 13 Aug. 1976.

47. Ibid., 8 Sept. 1976 Statement.

48. Shane Interview.

49. Seidman Papers, box 13, folder: airlines 8/76-9/76, text of 'Statement', 8 Sept. 1976.

50. Ibid., Coleman to Seidman, received 13 Aug. 1976, summary of Policy Statement, 26 July draft.

51. Ibid.

52. Ibid.

53. Ibid.

Chapter 6
Re-regulating Air Services:
Bermuda 2

Britain secured more of its objectives than a cool assessment of
the relative strength of the two contenders made probable.
(Edmund Dell) [1]

At the outset of the Bermuda 2 Talks the general consensus was that the
two sides were miles and miles apart on all three of the major components
of air service agreements: routes; rates; and capacity. For the sake of dramatic contrast, one could characterise the two positions in the following
terms. The British wanted universal single designation, provisions that
would control capacity, fares, and the number of gateways in the USA, and
point to point city pair third and fourth freedom services with no beyond
rights or behind feed. "The US wanted multiple designation, free determination of capacity, and no control over prices [or] over route schedules."[2]
It also wanted agreement on charters as well as on scheduled operations to
protect what it still tried to maintain were their respective markets.

As with all characterisations some over-simplification is involved here. Particularly on the American side, there were differences of opinion about policy
which meant that things were somewhat more fluid than the impression just
given and both sides, while unhappy with the existing fares regime, had no
settled view on how it might be reformed . There was also willingness to compromise, though that quality was not always very apparent. At the same time,
there was a deep policy divide between the two countries. That divide was

between policies desiring more and less regulated competition. It was between the USA, which since 1946 had used capacity as a means of competition, and the British who thought that uncontrolled capacity damaged the economy of already beleaguered airlines. It was between Americans wanting equal opportunity to compete and the British who placed more emphasis on equality of benefit and objected to the USA gaining over twice as much as they did from Bermuda 1. It was between the Americans who had much to gain from beyond rights and behind feed and the British who had little. Whichever way one looks at it, they were indeed miles and miles apart at the outset of the talks.

If the USA were unable to get the British to make substantial changes to their position then either there would be no agreement, or else the USA would become saddled with a highly regulatory bilateral in its most important international airline market. That in itself would be bad enough, given the desire of the Ford and Carter administrations for a competitive airline industry, but it would also set a dangerous example that other countries might wish to emulate in their dealings with the USA.

The situation was fraught with difficulties. Americans feared that their airlines could be badly damaged if the British were to realise their aims. Only a week after Dell's denunciation of Bermuda 1, Pan Am Vice President William Waltrip spoke to government agencies concerned with civil aviation and told them that he thought it would be 'difficult to negotiate a new agreement which will satisfy British Airways and still prove profitable for U.S. flag carriers.' He spoke in the lurid language of being prepared to 'go to the mat' and of stopping air services completely between the two countries with Pan Am re-routing its London flights through Amsterdam.[3]

Government officials agreed that the talks were going to be very difficult and of high priority. Joel Biller of the State Department, who initially led the US delegation, while seeing great difficulties ahead was also perceptive enough to identify a likely means of making progress. He said: 'considering the serious nature of the problem, senior political officials in the U.K. and the U.S. will be probably involved in the negotiating process, and the final decision will not be made on narrow financial grounds, as the British Airways people might prefer.' Robert Hormats of the NSC agreed with Biller, at least to the extent of pledging that his agency would follow developments to ensure that 'our broader policy concerns are reflected in the U.S. negotiation position.'[4] Elevation of talks to a higher level soon became a major goal of US tactics, but the intrusion of broader political considerations were to be as much a hindrance as a help to the USA in its attempts to reach a satisfactory agreement.

The Americans were angered, not just by the denunciation itself, but also by its timing. The Presidential election was only weeks away and the outcome hung in the balance. In the meantime, the Ford Administration did its best to deal with the situation that the British had created. It was not easy. Departments were still struggling to produce a new international aviation policy statement and reconcile calls for radical with more moderate policy proposals. However, in early August there was one development that had an immediate bearing on things. The CAB gave a long awaited decision on transatlantic route proceedings. It proposed that NWA and Delta should join Pan Am, TWA and National on Atlantic routes. British fears of American capacity being used to prey competitively on BA were thus further increased. In January Ford alleviated those worries somewhat by rejecting the CAB recommendation, but it was only a tactic to bring pressure to bear in a different way. He suggested that the CAB should think about 'using more European destinations rather than concentrating on services from US cities to British gateways.'[5] In saying this he was emphasising the possibility of by-passing Britain which was something that had already come under consideration in relation to the Bermuda 2 Talks.

The atmosphere was oppressive before talks began because of denunciation. It was then made even worse because of a capacity dispute. This prompted Elliot Richardson, US Secretary of Commerce, to report in early September that US airlines had been asked to draw up contingency plans in case of a cessation of air services. At the end of August Britain and the USA had been unable to resolve disagreement over appropriate capacities for the Miami and Chicago routes to London. On 7 August *Flight* commented about US policy that: 'For all the academic talk of "deregulation" there have been remarkable US compromises with hitherto inviolable anti-trust ideology.' That was true and was to be in evidence some weeks later in the new international policy statement, but as Ross Stainton of BA more tellingly observed, the US Government 'recognises need to rationalise capacity only as an exception, and regulation would not be needed when business picks up.'[6] In the cases of Miami and Chicago, it would have no truck with regulation. So, when the British imposed unilateral capacity limits on the routes, the American reaction was swift. They declared the controls to be contrary to the Bermuda 1 Agreement and retaliated with threats to restrict BA's route to Los Angeles and by demanding that all British airline schedules be filed with the CAB for approval. Under this pressure the British Government backed down. It accepted the capacity levels called for by US airlines and by early October the matter had been resolved.[7] Nevertheless, it illustrated the state of relations between the two countries and did not augur well for negotiations about replacing the denounced air service agreement.

Talks between Britain and the USA began in September 1976. The British side was led by George Rogers, Under Secretary at the DTI, and the American by Joel Biller, Assistant Secretary of State for Transportation. As noted before, Rogers was one of the architects of the regulatory policy that had been developed by the Labour Government and he saw it as part of his job to implement that policy in the international sphere. According to a BA official he was 'a tough grinding old cookie who would not let anything out of his sight', but others on the British side had a somewhat more critical view of him. For his part, Alan Boyd, who took over the leadership of the US delegation in 1977, thought him 'waspish' and 'anti-American', at least in the aviation sphere.[8]

Biller was a highly competent man, but was not as experienced in aviation negotiations as some would have liked on the US side and he had neither the status nor the presence to impose order on his delegation.[9] Nevertheless, in the first meeting with Rogers, he made his mark.

Rogers was blunt and uncompromising. He laid down British demands: for capacity controls through airline consultations and through single designation; for the abolition of fifth freedom rights; for a more equal division of spoils from the routes designated under the bilateral; and for a limited number of gateways in the USA. Biller's riposte was to ask what economic studies the British had done to show that this tightly regulated market would be a better option, not only for the airlines, but for the travelling public.[10] The Americans were also concerned by the fact that the British did not want to include charters in the new agreement. The British argued that there was insufficient time, but there was an anomaly in insisting on a more regulated market while leaving charters outside of the overall system.[11]

Rogers had nothing of substance to offer in reply to Biller except that the British had taken it as self evident that their scheme would be beneficial. According to Raymond Colegate, the senior CAA official on the British delegation, 'Biller sustained his point and at the end of the first morning it became apparent that Rogers was very wrong-footed.'[12] The outcome of this was that both sides undertook to produce economic analyses of their respective proposals. The British one was placed under the auspices of Colegate and the CAA; the Americans did two: one by the CAB, the other by the Department of Transport under the guidance of Raymond A. Young III, an acting Deputy Assistant.

Awaiting the outcome of these analyses, plus the disruption caused by the US presidential election and Carter's victory over Ford, delayed progress for several months. There were further talks in October and December but little progress was made. In particular, Rogers, despite being wrong-footed by Biller in the first meeting, could not be persuaded to shift ground at all or be more accommodating in his manner. Gradually this was to become of concern not only to the Americans, but to the British as well.

The US position had serious problems. In addition to the uncertainties about the future because of the presidential election, there was also a lack of unity within the US delegation and dangerous ambiguities in US policy. Despite their rejection of the principle of controlling capacity in order to divide markets, the US had agreed to temporary capacity controls in the international sphere in the recent past and the September policy statement indicated a willingness to move away from US multiple designation in cases where it was deemed to be economically unviable. The new policy had been promulgated in an attempt to give foreign countries a clear indication that the USA intended to uphold its competitive airline policy, but it also made some concessions to the need for regulation. Not surprisingly among foreign officials who, like the British, were looking to increase regulation, those parts of the declaration that were compatible with that goal were highlighted in their minds. Ford's rejection of the CAB recommendation for Delta and NWA in January further reinforced the hope that the USA would moderate its stance on multiple designation.

In the second round of talks in late October, the British, believing that there was some flexibility in the US position on capacity issues, tabled proposals that would have allowed governments to set a base level of capacity which could then be added to by agreement between carriers as and when required. However, there was little give in the US position at this time, and apart from some progress on technical and non-controversial matters nothing else was achieved. The outcome of both the economic analyses and the presidential election prevented any advance.

By the time of the third round of talks in December, the presidential contest had been decided in Jimmy Carter's favour and the only option for the US delegation was to adopt the lowest of profiles in the talks. Little could be done until Carter had settled in and decided on his transportation team. Meanwhile, there was an important development in the UK. In December, the Appeal Court ruled that Peter Shore, when Secretary of State for Trade and Industry, had acted *ultra vires* when he decided to abandon double designation and order the CAA not to license two British carriers on the same route. Under the 1971 Civil Aviation Act the Minister could give policy guidance, but the court ruled that Shore had gone beyond guidance and had issued a directive which he did not have the authority to do. In short, requiring single designation was illegal. That put a new perspective on things, but as it turned out one that was not uncongenial to Shore's successor Edmund Dell.[13]

Dell has described himself as one of the economically 'drier' members of the Callaghan government. While he regarded it as imperative to alter the balance of benefits garnered from the Bermuda 1 bilateral in order to help both BA and the British balance of payments, he was not averse to encouraging elements of competition. Thus when the High Court decision was handed down, although he disagreed with some of the reasoning, he welcomed the judgement. He opposed colleagues in Cabinet Committee who believed that Laker should be taken to the Lords for an appeal and he won the argument.[14] Laker would thus be allowed to fly scheduled services across the Atlantic and if there were to be some double designation then Laker could be a competitor for Britain as well as BA. This gave the British more flexibility. Single designation was now no longer a principle to be attained, but one of several means by which the problem of over-capacity could be tackled. Dell believed that the ability to play the Laker card strengthened his hand and helped him to regain some of the moral high ground lost to the Americans because of Britain's apparent desire to avoid competition between British and American airlines. Now he could argue that he was not against competition, but only against its disruptive and destructive forms. He could also tweak the conscience of Americans by pointing to their past opposition to scheduled services by Laker and their reluctance to grant operating rights to Concorde as evidence that they too were not always in favour of competition.[15] In fact the environmental objections to Concorde of the New York Port Authority soon added further complications to the Anglo-American negotiations.

Developments on either side in late 1976 and early 1977 - the illegality of HMG requiring single designation and the Laker decision, the US international aviation policy statement and the Ford decision on the transatlantic route cases - tended to ease the tension on the fraught question of multiple designation. Such changes created potential for progress in the fourth round of talks which had been rescheduled to February from January in order to give time for the Carter Administration to find its feet. However, the Americans still doubted that progress could be made while Rogers remained in charge of the British delegation and at least one senior British official had similar doubts.

The Carter Administration had an even more determined commitment to deregulation than its predecessor. Some of the key actors here were to be Carter's Chairman of the CAB, Alfred Kahn, and the President's Domestic Policy Adviser, Stu Eizenstat.[16] But, the credentials of Brock Adams, the new Secretary of Transport, were somewhat suspect regarding deregulation. Of course that did not mean that he was a weak exponent of the interests of US airlines: he just conceived of their interests in a somewhat different way. In the past he had been unhappy about deregulation and as the Carter programme developed there was concern about Adams' desire for strong statutory protection for labour in the deregulated marketplace. His views on this were far more regulatory than those professed by the President, the CEA, the Justice Department's Antitrust Division and the OMB. Nevertheless, in his confirmation hearing in the Senate, Adams said: 'I support legislation to reduce CAB regulation and increase competition in the domestic airlines.' On international deregulation he was more reticent and cautious, but that did not lead him into sympathy with the regulatory stance of the British in the Bermuda 2 Talks. Quite the contrary happened for he took a very aggressive stance in order to gain concessions from the British and was prepared, unlike Alan Boyd, to see a suspension of air services between the two countries if he did not get what he wanted.[17] Nevertheless, the bilateral eventually negotiated was the most restrictive that the USA was to make in many a long year and rightly or wrongly some Americans laid the blame for this at the feet not just of Alan Boyd, but also at those of Brock Adams and the US DOT.[18]

Within days of Carter being sworn in as President, Adams wrote to him concerning the Bermuda 2 Talks. He reported that US airlines were so disturbed by what had happened so far that they had petitioned the CAB for permission to plan a co-ordinated cessation of services to the UK in the event of such action becoming necessary. Adams thought that the British delegation was tightly controlled by a skilful negotiator who was very knowledgeable about aviation, whereas the US delegation was divided and lacked sufficiently strong leadership. The US DOT, the Commerce Department, the CIEP and the CAB were all represented on the delegation and were supposed to be given leadership by the State Department, but it 'cannot devote full time to this one effort, as important as it is.' Adams suggested the appointment of a special ambassador to lead the US delegation in order to reinvigorate it and give strong leadership.[19]

As this suggestion made the departmental rounds it was not unanimously popular, but Secretary of State Cyrus Vance and his department, perhaps rather surprisingly, came down in its favour. But, State had no intention of losing control over the talks. Policy and tactics would still have to be cleared through an inter-agency committee chaired by R.N. Cooper, Under Secretary of State for Economic Affairs, and the new ambassador would be attached to the State

Department. In addition to this there were positive advantages, which were identified in a letter from the department to Carter's National Security Adviser, Zbigniew Brzezinski:

> We endorse the appointment of a high level negotiator, provided it is matched by a similar upgrading on the British side, because it will benefit U.S. interests by lifting the negotiations out of the very narrow aviation context to which the British have attempted to limit them.[20]

In short, it would get rid of George Rogers. By this time there is evidence that such an upgrading was not unpalatable to the British. Raymond Colegate has suggested that by early 1977 FO officials were probably receptive to the idea of sidelining Rogers to prevent having a fiasco on their hands if the talks deadlocked and air services were stopped.[21] When Dell originally mooted the possibility of a denunciation, the FO had cautioned against such a course of action. They thought it unwise.[22] It is doubtful if the lack of progress by February 1977 had disabused them of their original judgement and more than likely that Rogers' performance had made them even more pessimistic. After the Americans announced that Boyd was to take over the US delegation, the British, who had been consulted beforehand, replaced Rogers with his immediate senior, Deputy Secretary, Patrick Shovelton. This decision was made by Dell after full consultation with his Permanent Secretary, Sir Peter Thornton.[23]

Judgement about the wisdom of elevating the talks to a higher level varies on both sides of the Atlantic. BA was not pleased and officials there thought that it was a poor tactic to change one's chief negotiator midway through. Some officials at BA believed that if Rogers had stayed in charge fewer concessions would have been made and more advantages would have been gained. But this was perhaps based on the inaccurate supposition that Rogers' intransigence would not provoke the USA to suspend services between the two countries. One BA official thought that such an eventuality was inconceivable given what the Americans stood to lose, but documentary and oral evidence points to the fact that the Americans were indeed prepared to suspend services. Even with Shovelton and Boyd leading the talks, and after there had been considerable concessions on both sides, the possibility of breaking off aviation services was still seriously contemplated until the eleventh hour.[24]

In the USA, there was widespread dissatisfaction with the final Bermuda 2 Agreement. In retrospect some would have preferred a more dramatic show-down to see if the British Government were bluffing or not. If they were then more concessions might have been gained. The irony was that, by elevating the talks through the appointment of Boyd, the USA did indeed manage to introduce wider considerations than just airline economics, but the assumption that that would necessarily benefit the USA was not correct. Overriding considerations for Boyd were to succeed in getting an agreement and to avoid a breach in Anglo-American civil aviation relations. He regarded the latter as such a high priority because he feared that the breach could not be limited to aviation matters alone. He did not want a crisis arising in Anglo-American relations because of failure to negotiate a Bermuda 2. In addition, with his broader view of things, he also came to appreciate some of the points that the British side had to make. For example, he found it difficult to defend all the American fifth freedom rights out of London when Britain had nothing of commensurate commercial value out of the USA.[25] And finally, there was also undoubtedly an egotistical side to all this. No-one likes to invest their prestige in trying to make an enterprise succeed and then see it fail.

By the time the fourth round of talks got under way in late February both sides had replaced their delegation leaders and had had time to digest the economic analyses that had been done. The economic facts made interesting reading, but did not resolve matters of disagreement. The USA derived 70 per cent of the benefit from the bilateral, but it also generated 60-70 per cent of the market. On that reading the agreement was not one-sided. The Americans responded to British criticism of US capacity competition by saying that there was nothing to stop Britain mounting more capacity itself through double designation. If it objected to doing that on the grounds of unnecessary damage both to load factors and to the environment because of flying more empty seats, there was always the case of the 'flying kerosene tank' - Concorde - which the Americans could point to. How did the British justify that? It also seemed strange to the Americans that the British Government was demanding a larger proportion of the market on the Atlantic at the very time when, on BA's own admission, it had a larger percentage than ever before. The American analysis showed that all airlines on the Atlantic could make a profit. It was just a matter of how much. And finally, regarding worries about capacity, the problem was already beginning to recede with an upturn in the airline market.

In the British camp they still wanted to divide the market more equitably and gain more gateways into the USA, though BA had a limit to the number it wanted. On capacity no-one, according to Dell, 'seriously expected to achieve single designation on the New York-London route'. That 'would have been a miracle'. However, Dell and his new delegation chief Shovelton, still sought to control capacity through getting as much single designation as possible as well as through screening of airline capacity proposals and the reduction of fifth freedom rights.[26] This latter matter was troublesome not only because there was an incommensurability between the value of fifth freedoms to Britain out of the USA and fifths for the USA out of the UK and out of Hong Kong, but there was also a capacity aspect to it.

The problem with fifths was symptomatic of difficulties that were to become greater as the market effects of deregulation developed. At the heart of the matter were population and geography. During the stage of development that had been reached in the transatlantic market by 1977, the immediate problem was that the geographical position of the USA did not provide any lucrative beyond rights for BA to exploit. On the other hand, with Europe on Britain's doorstep, beyond rights for US carriers were useful and also, because of the wording of Bermuda 1, they could be used to justify capacity levels for US carriers. Bermuda 1 specifically stated that there should be 'provision of capacity adequate to the traffic demands between the country of which such air carrier is a national and the country of ultimate destination.'[27] This allowed the USA to add traffic for destinations beyond London to its capacity calculations on the routes to the UK, and thus schedule more flights, and top them up in London with fifth freedom traffic. In contrast, Britain had no commercially viable destinations beyond the USA and thus found itself at a disadvantage. In the light of all this, it is understandable that British concerns about over-capacity and US capacity competition resulted in their wish to abandon fifth freedoms and adopt straightforward city pair arrangements on the basis of third and fourth freedoms.

Before the fourth round of talks began on 28 February Dell spoke to the London Chamber of Commerce saying:

> We need capacity control to avoid waste. We need balanced routes, which give similar opportunities to both sides. We need competition as a guarantee to the consumer and we need a better opportunity for British airlines within the international air transport system.[28]

Despite the reasonable tone, the Americans still saw the British position as very threatening and even Boyd, who was so determined to get agreement, decided, within the first few hours of direct negotiation, to advise Washington that it was 'essential to make contingent plans for possible cessation of U.S. airline services.'[29] At the end of two weeks of talks Boyd wryly commented that the only thing that 'Patrick Shovelton had given away was kind words.'[30] Actually even that was an improvement on what had happened previously. Before Boyd appeared on the scene the tone of the talks had been very discordant. Dell recalled some years later that one of his most vivid memories of the Bermuda 2 affair was the ill-temper on the U.S. side. At one point matters deteriorated to the point where a State Department official threatened that all trade relations would be broken off if the British did not become more accommodating about an air service agreement. Dell knew that this was an idle threat, but it was indicative of how badly the talks were going for such extravagant claims to be made. Boyd's comment on the US delegation that he took over from Biller was that 'they were not a bunch of happy campers'.[31]

Boyd managed to improve the tone of the talks, though there were still angry moments on both sides. He also proposed substantial concessions by offering to reduce drastically the number of routes on which there were to be double designation and by agreeing to screen US airline capacity proposals.[32] In spite of these moves the British remained dissatisfied and towards the end of the fourth round of talks there was a new development through which they tried to force the American hand even further.

The 10-11 of March saw the first visit of Prime Minister Callaghan to the new President. Callaghan had got on extremely well with Ford at the personal level though there were serious political differences between their administrations, particularly about economic affairs. With Carter personal relations were also to be good (though not as intimate as with Ford) and, notwithstanding the dispute over the air service agreement, policy differences were generally of a lower order. Nevertheless, Callaghan gave Carter some stiff words about both Concorde and Bermuda 2. He told the President that the latter 'could generate "a great deal of heat and division between us", especially with Concorde in the background.'[33] It is difficult to assess the impact that Callaghan had on Carter and vice versa. Subsequently they talked about Bermuda 2 matters over the transatlantic telephone, twice according to Dell[34], and they may also have exchanged views during Carter's May 1977 visit to the UK. Exactly what was said and when will have to await archival disclosure, but some aspects of these exchanges are known, if rather inferentially, and will be considered later.

By the end of the fourth round essentially all cards were on the table and there had been considerable movement on the US side.[35] Boyd felt that agreement was possible, but it would now depend on reciprocity by Britain. That need produced discussions in Washington involving Vice President Mondale, Adams, Boyd, Cooper, Tim Deal the NSC civil aviation adviser and Eizenstat's Domestic Policy Staff, in particular his assistant William Johnston who had been given the task of liaising between the US negotiating team and the White House.[36]

On 18 March, Boyd explained to Carter:

> While making concessions, the U.S. has stated in the strongest terms it will not agree to a regulated market split, will not agree to a U.K. veto of U.S. airline capacity increases, and will not agree to limit the right of U.S. airlines to pick up and discharge passengers beyond London.[37]

There was also a further complication, namely the difficulty over landing rights for Concorde and the British had made it clear that 'denial of Concorde access to New York will have an extremely adverse impact on aviation negotiations.' Just how much more difficult that could make the British was difficult to see, for at the end of round four they were still insisting on a 50/50 split of revenue contrived through single designation, capacity controls and the denial of fifths freedoms. In the light of this Boyd spelt out the rather gloomy alternatives that confronted the USA.[38]

He observed that if the British did not become more accommodating then on 21 June the USA could: agree with the UK and create a non-competitive market; it could propose a one year extension to Bermuda 1, but that would probably be unacceptable to the UK; it could operate on a permit basis, but that would play into UK hands by allowing them to divide the market; it could order a cessation of scheduled services - that would leave charter services intact and the UK would probably feel constrained to push for an early settlement. The last option would involve continuing preparations for alternative European destinations to allow US carriers temporarily to by-pass Britain and fly directly into Europe.[39]

Carter, after hearing reports about the fourth round, made it clear that the USA should 'not yield on the competition issue.' There was more at stake than just airline economics. There was the need both to promote US policies of airline competition and avoid the danger of setting bad precedents for imminent talks with the Japanese and the Italians. There were also the needs of the travelling public and finally: 'Failure to reach agreement would have an adverse impact on overall relations and possibly undermine Western co-operation in other economic areas.'[40]

At a meeting on 23 March, Mondale, Adams, Boyd and Cooper considered what the USA might do in the light of all this to try to persuade the British to make some concessions. Out of it came a proposal for more Presidential involvement and specifically that Carter should telephone Callaghan with suggestions for moving things forward. At the same time contingency plans were to be developed in order to make the threat of a termination of air services credible.[41]

Some time during early to mid April and again towards either the end of the month or early May, Carter spoke to Callaghan over the telephone about the difficulties arising from the Bermuda 2 Talks and in particular the dangerous repercussions that would hit Anglo-American relations if air services between the two countries were to break down. Apart from this general issue, at least two more specific matters look as if they were raised: the problem of fifth freedom rights; and Concorde landing rights in New York.[42]

On 4 May, in response to a request from Carter, Boyd explained British allegations about US unrequited fifths out of London:

The U.K. does not exercise its rights to serve Hong Kong-U.S. and Bermuda-U.S. markets or to operate beyond the U.S. on routes it now has. We should not feel obliged to compensate the U.K. for routes on which it has chosen not to compete. In the particular case of beyond rights, the British argument is simplistic. They do not seek routes beyond the U.S. and adopt the position that hence the U.S. should not be able to carry traffic via London to Europe.[43]

While Boyd appears to have adopted a hard line on fifths here, and indeed he was determined to preserve substantial beyond rights for U.S. carriers, he did believe that the position on fifths was one-sided and found it difficult to defend all the fifth freedoms that the USA had had under Bermuda 1.[44]

On the second issue, that of Concorde landing rights, the Americans, through the President, wanted to assure the British that they were trying to persuade Governor Carey of New York to allow Concorde to operate into Kennedy Airport, but that problems arising out of federal principles of autonomy prevented a diktat from the White House to the New York Port Authority.[45]

The main message that Carter had to send Callaghan, however, was the danger of the talks failing and the adverse repercussions that that would have, not just on aviation, but on relations generally between the two countries. This prompted Callaghan to call in Dell and ask him exactly what was going on and what the dangers were. Dell's cool response was that he did not believe that there would be a breakdown and termination of scheduled air services. With that judgement Callaghan appears to have been satisfied. He was a Prime Minister who had the courage to have faith in his ministers and the matter was left to Dell and was never taken to the Cabinet. This is not to say that Carter's intervention had no effect. In fact both Carter and Callaghan 'told their representatives that the talks must not be allowed to fail.'[46] Also, Dell and Shovelton were well aware of the dangers of failing to reach agreement. Carter's personal intervention must have made them wary of pushing Boyd too far, and as we shall see the British did make concessions as the 21 June deadline approached.

While Shovelton and Boyd strove to reach agreement, their respective governments continued to pursue policies in other settings that were very different in character. In February, US Senators Cannon and Kennedy wrote to Carter seeking his support for their bill to deregulate the domestic US aviation market and Carter responded enthusiastically. The bill made considerable progress and signalled the Administration's intentions to move quickly to improve the competitiveness of the airline industry. Later, in the face of opposition, there was some backtracking and the only significant measure that was passed in 1977 was the liberalisation of air cargo services, but more was to follow in 1978.[47] Meanwhile, in Britain, an agreement was reached with Japan in the spring of 1977, which controlled the airline market between them and ensured balanced earnings and that capacity would match demand.[48]

Clearly, from policy developments elsewhere, as well as from the course taken by the Bermuda 2 Talks, there was still much to be bridged if the British and the Americans were to come together. In the fifth round of discussions, begun at the end of March and which ran into April, only minor progress was achieved. Both sides came closer together on capacity and route designation matters, but there was little else to report. However, as we have seen, it was at about this time that political pressures from on high were brought into play to try to move things along. The stakes had been raised, but, as the negotiators entered the final month of talks, things still looked unpromising.

By mid May the British had abandoned their demand for a 50/50 split of the benefits from a new bilateral and the Americans had agreed to limit double designation to two gateways with a trigger mechanism for additional double designation once traffic on a route exceeded prescribed limits. From any perspective that was progress, but difficulties still remained. The Americans wanted more beyond rights than the British were prepared to countenance; they were

132

set firmly against vetoes of capacity increases; they wanted more opportunity to operate from Hong Kong; they wanted to open more gateways in the USA; and on the 11 May Boyd had been informed in no uncertain terms from Washington that British commitment to a liberal charter regime had to be gained.[49] Much of what remained as goals for the British were couched in the negative. They did not want the USA to continue to enjoy beyond rights out of London; they did not want over-capacity to re-emerge because of lack of controls; they did not want to enter into charter arrangements at this stage for various reasons to do with timing and commitments in Europe. On the positive side they wanted routes to the American south west and to Seattle; they wanted a more flexible pricing arrangement; and they wanted landing rights for Concorde and were reported as having threatened to refuse to sign a new bilateral until approval was forthcoming.[50]

It was at this point that the tone of the negotiations began to deteriorate once again, largely because of interventions by Brock Adams. The timing of the Bermuda 2 Talks had been a sore point from the moment of Dell's denunciation. The Americans did not take kindly either to being forced to re-negotiate the bilateral or to do so at an unsettled moment politically, namely, the eve of a presidential election. Dell's argument was that the timing of the pursuit of British interests should not be dictated by America's election timetable. Nevertheless, there was a certain British insensitivity evident and one cannot help but wonder whether American action over the IMF affair in 1976 diminished British inclination to defer to American sensibilities. In the event, Dell thought that the timing only yielded Britain advantages on the margin and, ironically, once the talks had been set in motion, it was the Americans who made a great fuss over completing them by the deadline of 21 June. Dell was willing to continue to talk after then with Bermuda 1 rules continuing to operate, but the Americans publicly refused to countenance that, although in private it was considered as an option. Thus in May 1977 Adams began to use the deadline to threaten the British with imminent and dire consequences if agreement were not reached.[51]

On 23 May Adams said that he would stop the talks if agreement were not in sight by the beginning of June. On the 28 May his provocative statement was confirmed in Washington. To Dell it seemed as if Adams were making a speech every day 'saying if the UK doesn't come off this we will suspend civil aviation New York-London.'[52] Certainly both sides were now looking seriously at the possibility of air services being stopped. The British believed that their contingency plans were more advanced than the Americans' and hoped to service North America via Canada. The Americans for their part had approached European countries about increasing services in the event of being denied operations into Britain. They had mixed results. The French refused, but the Dutch were only too pleased to oblige. In addition, the Americans had conferred with the Canadians and it was unlikely that services from Canada to the USA would be increased to distribute USA bound passengers from Britain. In fact, it seems that both sides thought that they had the advantage over the other. The British thought that they could service the USA via third parties better than the USA could service Britain, but the Americans doubted that. The British thought that the suspension of services would badly damage American airlines, whereas the Americans thought that the loss of tourist income from the USA would not be acceptable to the British with their delicate balance of payments problem.[53]

The fact that both sides felt that they had strong cards to play resulted in intransigence which made final agreement difficult to reach. The talks did not fail at the beginning of June, but agreement was still elusive. On the 13 June new American proposals were rejected by the British as they appeared to provide less control of capacity than they thought had previously been agreed. For a short time negotiations stopped. Three days later in Washington Adams repeated what was now a well known refrain: 'We'll call a halt [to air services between Britain and the USA]. We have reached the bottom line; the President has reached the bottom line .... Sure this is a tough time between our countries.'[54]

In London Dell was determined to sit it out. He and Shovelton tenaciously held to their basic position (though that does not mean that they were to make no substantial concessions). There was a degree of bluff involved in this. As Dell was later to recount, the Americans may have assumed that the British Government was wholeheartedly behind their delegation's bargaining position, whereas, in fact, things never got that far. Matters were never discussed in Cabinet. The only resolve to be tested was that of Dell and Shovelton, and, indirectly, Callaghan's in the sense that he had the courage to allow matters to remain in Dell's hands.[55] The collective nerve of the British Government was never tested and in that sense the American tactic of upgrading the talks in February failed to achieve its main aim, namely, raising negotiations above the narrow confines of aviation diplomacy and bringing wider political considerations to bear that would help the US negotiating position.

In Washington things were rather different: there was more direct high level political interventionism. One of Boyd's fears was that the State Department might try to tie his hands too tightly in the final stages of the talks and prevent him from making cosmetic concessions upon which final agreement could be dependent.[56] Feelings in the Administration were hardening against Britain and generally there was a determination to show resolve and avoid losing what was considered to be the basic competitive character of air services between the two countries. The question was just how could this be done.

US Ambassador to London, Kingman Brewster, was keen not to inflame Anglo-American relations generally and he advised that if no agreement were reached that the US should not initiate anything unless the British took unacceptable action. Tim Deal of the NSC took a much stronger line.[57] He knew that the President did not want confrontation with Britain, indeed as Eizenstat was to record later, Carter worked closely with Cooper's inter-departmental committee ' to get a fair agreement with the UK in such a way as to prevent political embarrassment to Prime Minister Callaghan,'[58] nevertheless, Deal thought that the deadline could not pass by without firm US action.

Deal thus disagreed with Brewster. He thought that: 'The threat to cut off services during the high tourist season is our strongest bargaining tool.' He wanted an agreement and thought that some further concessions might be in order, but the threat to cut services had to be made credible. He wrote to his chief, Brzezinski, that the USA 'must be prepared to take the ultimate step though we all hope this will not prove necessary.'[59]

By 19 June, Boyd was guardedly optimistic. The Americans had revised their proposals on capacity, which were now more acceptable to the British. He thought that it might be possible to salvage a basic competitive structure for the bilateral. He did not want Washington to prevent him making last minute concessions if they could produce agreement. And, most importantly, as Johnston reported to Eizenstat: 'Bringing about cessation of services should be avoided except over matters of the most fundamental principle.'[60] The President went along with that, thus, effectively, limiting the amount of leverage that was possible via the threat of suspending air services.

After elevating the talks so that broader political consideration was given to the Bermuda 2 negotiations, it was that type of consideration that limited the leverage the USA could bring to bear on the British. As a result, though probably unknown to the Americans at the time, this meant that matters never reached the British Cabinet and so they never became exposed to the kind of broader consideration the Americans had wanted and, rather ironically, had given matters themselves.

The struggle to reach agreement went on until, and technically over, the deadline. Carter held back from issuing dire threats, which some of the American hard-liners wanted him to make, and Boyd was allowed some flexibility to make more concessions.[61] In the end, the British were also prepared to concede points. Capacity problems had been solved before the final sessions. Perhaps inevitably there was some compromise involved, but the British had more or less got what they wanted. On a fares regime there had been universal agreement that the present system was far from ideal. Finding a solution, however, was not easy. The situation was very volatile. On 12 June Carter had formally given his approval of Laker's Skytrain and had added in longhand 'with pleasure J.C.'[62] On both sides of the Atlantic there were those who favoured more price competition, but there were also opponents and an uncertainty about how things would develop because of Laker's new operations and the fact that the Americans failed to get British commitment to a liberal charter agreement. As a result there was little movement on the issue of fares. Bermuda 2 established a committee to examine things, but it produced nothing of note and according to one British official's recollection only met once.[63]

The issues that continued to cause difficulty as Shovelton and Boyd went into the last round of talks were: a number of lower order matters such as baggage handling rights in Hong Kong; some remaining doubts about multiple designation; serious difficulties over British demands for a route to Seattle and also their route to Texas still had problems; lack of a British commitment to a liberal charter regime; and, most seriously of all, beyond rights. Beyond rights was the one remaining issue that Boyd feared might prevent reaching overall agreement. After considering Boyd's latest assessment, Brzezinski and Eizenstat wrote to Carter on the 20 June that there was consensus that:

> one outstanding issue - the so-called note 1, the right of our airlines to transfer U.S. passengers in London onto other U.S. flights - involves a fundamental principle. If the British will not accept this principle we must be prepared to cease service on Wednesday. [but] ... *we believe that Boyd* should be given some flexibility in the closing hours to make additional compromises he feels are necessary, as long as they do not violate our basic commitments to competition or *undermine our world operating rights.*[64]

The final talks continued gruellingly into the early hours of 22 June. The British conceded to Boyd on the demand for US airlines to have unrestricted rights to change of gauge and to mix and match passengers with tickets for onward destinations and to carry them beyond London after a stop-over in the UK of upto one year. This provided a possibility for US airlines to establish hubbing operations out of London if traffic flows were large enough to make them profitable. It did not include an extension of fifth freedom rights: under the provision passengers could not originate from Britain. In fact,

Bermuda 2 involved a severe cutback in fifths out of London and a failure to achieve more commercial beyond rights out of Hong Kong, which the USA had had high on its agenda, especially after granting routes across the Pacific into the USA for Britain. Out of London, the American fifths to Brussels, Vienna, Sweden and the Netherlands were to be phased out leaving only Frankfurt and Pan Am's round the world route (a fifth right to Oslo was also kept, but after 1982 it had to be via Prestwick!). At the time, these fifths were very important to the USA, but in retrospect Boyd commented: 'God help us, one of our key requirements was to maintain the round the world operation of Pan American, which, as I look back, what we paid for that - incredible!'[65]

It is probable, because before the final talks they had considered this as a trade that they would be prepared to make, that the agreement on beyond rights for the Americans was connected with British route demands. Britain got its route to Seattle and a route to Houston for B.Cal., but the latter was not what had been hoped for because of conditions that were attached. B.Cal.'s service was to be a one stop flight to Houston for the first three years and it would have to compete against a direct non-stop passenger service by an American airline from Dallas and an all-cargo service from Houston. On other matters concerning routes, the British had more success. They managed to gain greater access to the US market by opening six new gateways, to which they believed that British airlines could operate profitably. The Americans actually wanted a more liberal arrangement with more gateways, but all that they could achieve at this time was the right to a 'wild card' gateway option: they could choose an additional gateway to be opened in three years time.[66]

The Americans failed to get a British commitment to a liberal charter agreement and the problem of a new structure for fares was fudged with the creation of what turned out to be an ineffective fares working group. The capacity arrangements largely agreed to before the final session embodied more of the British initial position than the American. There was to be pre-screening. If agreement could not be reached then existing capacity levels plus modest increases per season were to be allowed. This was not a very flexible arrangement and it was a very interventionist system. It worked with minor liberalisation over the next few years, but only because Pan Am and TWA continued to decline and never really mounted a major effort to compete through capacity in the 1980s. America lost six out of its eight previous double designation routes. There was a mechanism to trigger a right to double designation on new routes once passenger density exceeded prescribed limits, but this was not acceptable to many in the USA.[67] In particular, the loss of double designation on the Boston to London route was to prove a major political problem for Carter and its solution was to have long-term consequences. Alan Boyd himself thought that on this he had made a mistake: 'If I had to do it over again, I would be intransigent on that point.'[68]

Both sides had stepped back from the danger of suspending air services and the wider and unpleasant consequences that might have flowed from that: but it had been a close run thing. The atmosphere in the discussions of the early hours of 22 June was tense as the negotiators struggled to find agreement and get the text onto the cumbersome, but at that time state of the art, word processor. As the final paragraphs fell into place one of the negotiators wearily asked if there were anything else to be sorted out. An equally weary reply came that: 'Well, there was the matter of handling oneself at Hong Kong.'[69] The amusement that this caused, one participant later recalled, was the kind of thing that helped everyone keep their sanity and their will to bring the task of reaching agreement to final fruition. The following day in *The Times* readers were informed: 'Britain and the United States initialled a new North Atlantic air services agreement yesterday, but only after one of the most tense "cliffhangers" in the recent history of international relations.'[70]

Was there more reregulation or deregulation in all this? Whose interests were enhanced? Dell and Shovelton felt that they had crafted an agreement that substantially improved the prospects for British airlines and a subsequent increase in their proportion of benefit arising from the bilateral seems to support that. There was now more control over capacity, fewer fifths for the Americans, less double designation and more routes into the USA. The fares regime remained a double approval system and agreement on charters still had to be negotiated. However, there were some in London who disliked aspects of the new bilateral.

The restrictions on B.Cal's route to Houston were unfortunate and were heavily criticised by Conservative spokespeople in the Commons. There was no guarantee that the outcome of further discussions on charters and fares would be beneficial for Britain. BA was unhappy about provisions for behind feed and some aspects of those to do with beyond rights. Section 5, note 5 provided that:

> a designated airline may serve points behind any homeland gateways shown in column "a" with or without change in aircraft and flight number and hold out and advertise such services to the public as through services.[71]

American airlines' ability to draw upon their home market was thereby enhanced and British airlines' ability to compete for American passengers away from the gateways was reduced. Regarding beyond rights, although the Americans had failed to gain what they wanted out of Hong Kong and had lost fifths out of London, they had achieved what they had come to regard as a fundamental right by the end of the negotiations, namely, licence to mix and match passengers in London from American airlines for onward flights. Some in BA saw this (as well as retaining fifths to Frankfurt and for Pan Am's round-the-world route) as a significant victory for the USA. However, Shovelton does not recall it as a matter of any great significance in the talks and the DOT currently doubts that it has been of much value.[72]

The reservations nursed by some in London paled to insignificance when compared to the fears about the likely consequences of Bermuda 2 in Washington. Michael Egan of the Justice Department complained to Carter on 15 July that Boyd had failed to get a British commitment to a liberal charter agreement despite undertaking to do so. He said that he thought the British had intended to diminish the scope for competition and 'in all candour, I believe that the British have gained a good deal in pursuit of this objective, and but for your public endorsement of the general outline of the agreement I would recommend that you consider rejecting it.'[73] Criticism was so strong that on 22 July, the eve of the formal signing of Bermuda 2, Eizenstat and Johnston prepared a lengthy paper for the President setting out the criticisms and weighing up the pros and cons of delaying signature and trying to get changes to what had been agreed.

It was not just Egan who was disturbed by what Boyd had agreed to. One of Carter's main allies in the Senate for pushing through deregulation policies was Edward Kennedy and he thought that Bermuda 2 would have a 'profoundly negative impact on competition ... [and is] substantially more anticompetitive than Bermuda 1.'[74] From the various comments made, Johnston and Eizenstat identified four main criticisms: a damaging reduction of double designation from eight routes to two; an over-restricted number of US gateways; over-controlled capacity; and no commitment from Britain to a liberal charter arrangement. These criticisms came from those who were genuinely concerned with the USA's competitive posture and from airlines and other parties who felt that their interests had been slighted.

To be weighed against these criticisms were doubts that the capacity provisions would be restrictive of growth, and beliefs that nothing else could have been squeezed out of the British on double designation and gateways.

Alan Boyd believed that the agreement protected the rights of American carriers to operate in all major markets with flexibility and without undue restriction.

Johnston and Eizenstat summed up things for Carter thus:

> In the light of these realities, it might be a mistake to postpone signing to give Congress and other critics of the agreement time to generate opposition. Prolonged negotiations and cessation of service to Britain might be able to produce an agreement that is marginally better than this one. But there will be criticism of *any* agreement that does not grant unlimited service to all cities by all carriers at unrestricted prices.[75]

Carter wrote on the memorandum: 'Stu - I'm not going to postpone.'[76] On 23 July 1977 the Bermuda 2 Agreement was duly signed. But, it was never regarded in the way Bermuda 1 had been. The Americans never did a Bermuda 2 with other countries. Unlike Bermuda 1, it was never held up as a model to follow. Quite the contrary, if it were ever regarded as a model by the Americans, it was of what not to do in bilateral air service agreements. Although the British were to develop their own ambitions for liberalisation and competition from 1979 onwards, their views were by no means as one with the Americans'. Because of that, Bermuda 2 proved to be of great bargaining use to Britain. It enabled the British to trade restrictions that were either initially in Bermuda 2, or subsequently arose from it, for concessions from the USA, which allowed Britain to influence significantly the way and at what speed liberalisation was to be pursued and much of its substantive character. In short, the reregulation aspects of Bermuda 2 posed problems for the USA for many years and in relation to many aspects of the developing world airline system. But, given the political considerations that weighed upon the minds of Boyd, Carter and his immediate advisers, it is rather difficult to see how matters could have been brought to a different conclusion. As Eizenstat and Johnston had put it, there would have been great risks involved if Carter had not signed the agreement and little chance of getting a bilateral that was anything more than marginally better.[77]

Notes and References

1. Dell (1985), p. 358.

2. Ebdon Interview.

3. Ford Library, WHCF, CA 1/24/76-1/20/70, box 2, folder: 6/1/76 - 7/31/76, Hormats to Scowcroft, 30 June 1976.

4. Ibid.

5. *Flight*, 8 Jan. 1977, p. 52.

6. Ibid., 7 Aug. 1976, p. 305, 28 Aug. 1976, p. 479, 4 Sept. 1976, p. 578, 4 Dec. 1976, p. 1621.

7. Ford Papers, WHCF, box 21, CA 7, folder: UK 5, Kearney to Ford and Biller to Kearney, 8 Oct. 1976.

8. Ebdon Interview; Colegate Interview; Boyd Interview.

9. Ibid.; see also *Flight*, 25 Sept. 1976, pp. 960-1; Carter Library, WHCF, Subject File, box CA-1, folder: 6/30/77-2/28/78, Adams to Carter, 3 Feb. 1977.

10. Colegate Interview; *Flight*, 25 Sept. 1976, pp. 960-1.

11. Colegate Interview; Shovelton to the author 18 Jan. 1993.

12. Colegate Interview.

13. Dell Interview; Baldwin (1985), pp. 112-15.

14. Dell Interview.

15. Ibid.

16. For commentary on economic policy-making in the Carter Administration see Hargrove (1988), ch. 4.

17. Carter Library, Staff Offices, Domestic Policy Staff, Eizenstat, box 148, folder: Aviation - Airline Regulatory Reform 1, Mary Schuman to Eizenstat, Eizenstat to Carter, Carter to Eizenstat and Eizenstat to Carter, 23 and 25 March 1977, also Adams' answers to supplementary written questions from the Senate Commerce Committee, 18 Jan. 1977.

18. Ibid., WHCF, Subject File, box CA-1, folder: 10/1/77-8/31/78, Schuman to Eizenstat, 15 May 1978, subject: International Aviation Leadership Meeting.

19. Ibid., folder: 6/30/77-2/28/77, Adams to Carter, 3 Feb. 1977.

20. Ibid., C. Arthur Borg to Brzezinski, 10 Feb. 1977.

21. Colegate Interview.

22. Dell Interview.

23. Boyd Interview; correspondence, Dell to the author, 2 Nov. 1993; Carter Library, WHCF, Subject File, box CA-2, folder: 1/20/77-9/20/81, Adams to Vance, 11 Feb. 1977, subject: meeting with British Ambassador Ramsbotham.

24. Ibid.; Ebdon Interview; also see below e.g. Carter Library, WHCF, Subject File, box CA-1, folder: 1/20/77-2/28/78, R.N. Cooper to Carter, 20 June 1977.

25. Boyd Interview.

26. Dell Interview; Colegate Interview; *The Economist*, 26 June 1976, p. 70.

27. Cmd. 6747, 1946, 'US, UK Civil Air Services Agreement, Bermuda', para. 6.

28. *Flight*, 5 March 1977, p. 508.

29. Carter Library, WHCF, Subject File, box CA-1, folder: 6/30/77-2/28/78, Adams to Carter, 4 March 1977, conveying views of Boyd.

30. *Flight*, 19 March 1977, p. 690.

31. Dell Interview; Boyd Interview.

32. Carter Library, WHCF, Subject File, box CA-1, folder: 6/30/77-2/28/78, Boyd to Carter, 18 March 1977.

33. *Flight*, 19 March 1977, p. 687; Callaghan Interview.

34. Dell Interview.

35. Boyd Interview.

36. Carter Library, WHCF, Subject File, box CO-64, folder: CO 167, 3/1/77-3/31/77, Brzezinski to Hormats, 29 March 1977 and NSC memo. Hormats to Clift, 23 March 1977; ibid., box CA-1, folder: 6/30/77-2/28/78, Hormats to Clift, 23 March 1977 and enclosed brief by Tim Deal for meeting with Vice President Mondale.

37. Ibid., Boyd to Carter, 18 March 1977.

38. Ibid.; *Flight*, 21 May 1977, 'Concorde Could Block Bermuda 2'.

39. Carter Library, WHCF, Subject File, box CA-1, folder: 6/30/77-2/28/78, Boyd to Carter, 18 March 1977.

40. Ibid.; ibid., box CO 64, folder: CO 167 3/1/77-3/31/77, Brzezinski to Hormats, 29 March 1977.

42. Actual dates of the telephone calls are unclear. The suggestions in the text are based on documents from the Carter Library and comments by Dell, Boyd and Colegate.

43. Carter Library, Staff Offices, Domestic Policy Staff, Eizenstat, box, 299, folder: US-UK civil aviation negotiations 2, Boyd to Carter via Jack Watson, 4 May 1977.

44. Boyd Interview.

45. Carter Library, WHCF, Subject File, folder: CO 167, 4/1/77-4/30/77, Eizenstat to Carter, 11 April 1977.

46. *The Times*, 15 June 1977.

47. Carter Library, WHCF, Subject File, folder: CA 1/20/77-2/28/78, Kennedy and Cannon to Carter, 22 Feb. 1977; ibid., Staff Offices, Domestic Policy Staff, Eizenstat, box 148, folder: Aviation - General Issues, memo., subject: signing ceremony for HR 6010, 3 Nov. 1977.

48. *Flight*, 9 April, 1977, p. 886.

49. Carter Library, Staff Offices, Domestic Policy Staff, Eizenstat, box 299, folder: US-UK Civil Aviation Negotiations 1, Associate Attorney General Egan to Carter, 15 July 1977.

50. *Flight*, 21 May 1977, 'Concorde Could Block Bermuda 2'. In fact, it did not. While there was no agreement on landing rights by 21 June, the signs augured well and Concorde began operations to New York on 22 Nov. 1977.

51. Dell Interview; Dell (1991); Callaghan (1987); *Sunday Times*, 14 May 1978, 'How the Hard Men Took Over Britain'; 'IMF Crisis Symposium', *Contemporary Record*, 3 (1989), 39-45.

52. Dell Interview; *Flight*, 28 May 1977, p. 1468 and 4 June 1977, p. 1632.

53. Dell Interview; Boyd Interview; *The Times*, 15 and 17 June 1977; Carter Library, WHCF, Subject File, box CA-1, folder: CA 1/20/77-6/30/77, Deal to Brzezinski, 17 June 1977.

54. *The Times*, 17 June 1977.

55. Dell Interview.

56. Carter Library, WHCF, Subject File, box CO 64, folder: CO 167, Brzezinski and Eizenstat to Carter, 20 June 1977.

57. Ibid., box CA-1, folder: CA 1/20/77-6/30/77, Deal to Brzezinski, 17 June 1977.

58. Ibid., folder: 10/1/77-8/31/78, Eizenstat and McIntyre to Carter, 18 May 1978.

59. Ibid., folder: CA 1/20/77-6/30/77, Deal to Brzezinski, 17 June 1977.

60. Ibid., Staff Offices, Domestic Policy Staff, Eizenstat, box 299, folder: US-UK Civil Aviation Negotiations, Johnston to Eizenstat, 19 June 1977.

61. American attitudes covered a spectrum, from Boyd who along with Brewster, Eizenstat, Carter and Brzezinski wanted to be flexible, to the moderate hard-liners which included Deal from the NSC and Cooper and others from the State Department. Fluctuating rather erratically between the moderate and real hard-liners was Adams and others at the DOT. Finally there were the hard-liners which included Egan from the Antitrust Division, Kahn of the CAB, representatives of the airline industry and politicians such as Edward Kennedy. See ibid., Eizenstat and Johnston to Carter, 22 July 1977; ibid., WHCF, Subject File, box CA-1, folder: CA 1/20/77-6/30/77, Deal to Brzezinski, 17 June 1977.

62. Ibid., Staff Offices, Counsel - Robert Jerome Lipshutz, box 8, folder: CAB Foreign Routes Final Action, 3-6/77, Laker Airways Docket, 25427 and 25457, 12 June 1977.

63. Colegate Interview; Shovelton's recollection is that it had a rather more useful life: correspondence, Shovelton to the author, 18 Jan. 1993.

64. Carter Library, WHCF, Subject File, box CO 64, folder: CO 167, Brzezinski and Eizenstat to Carter, 20 June 1977.

65. Boyd Interview; Cmd. 7016, 1977, Agreement Concerning Air Services [Bermuda 2], Annex 1, section 1, US routes 1 and 2, and Annex 1 section 5.

66. Ibid., Annex 1, section 3, UK routes 1 and 6, and Annex 1 section 6.

67. Ibid., Annex 2.

68. Boyd Interview.

69. This was to do with airlines gaining the option of providing their own ground services rather than having to buy them in.

70. *The Times*, 23 June 1977.

71. Cmd. 7016, 1977; criticism came from John Nott and Norman Tebbit, *Hansard*, 23 June 1977, cols. 1754-65.

72. Ebdon Interview; Shovelton to the author, 18 Jan. 1993; British official source.

73. Carter Library, Staff Offices, Domestic Policy Staff, Eizenstat, box 299, folder: US-UK Civil Aviation Negotiations 1, Egan to Carter, 15 July 1977.

74. Ibid., Eizenstat and Johnston to Carter, 22 July 1977.

75. Ibid.

76. Ibid.

77. Ibid.

Chapter 7
President Carter and the Airline Deregulation Revolution

It is time to return this industry to the free enterprise system.[1]
(Alfred Kahn: CAB Chairman 1977-78)

Carter acted boldly on deregulation. He wanted to change what he saw as the over-interventionism of the federal bureaucracy and, more than either Nixon or Ford, he was prepared to invest political capital in deregulating the airlines as part of that wider programme.[2] In 1976 he wrote:

> There is rarely any public interest in a subject when it is technically or narrowly defined. The special interests almost invariably prevail. But if political leaders can understand what is right and fair, devise a comprehensive plan for improvement, and describe to the public clearly what should be done, then even the most far-reaching reforms are possible.[3]

Within weeks of entering office he set about doing just that with reform of the domestic airline system.

Although Carter belonged to the Democrats, who are better disposed to welfare and economic intervention by government than Republicans, he was a fiscal conservative with a populist streak that made him dislike large conglomerates and economic power blocks. He felt that they undermined the public good for their own narrow economic interests. In the airlines, he saw a stark example of both the abuse of consumer interests and of economic inefficiency. Furthermore, by the time he came to office, the public and Congress were critical of regulated industries and the airlines in particular. Carter and his advisers believed that this provided them with potential to gain a rapid deregulation victory, which would benefit not only the economy and consumers, but their own popularity rating as well. Thus, Carter took up the issue of airline regulatory reform with gusto and with more determination than his two Republican predecessors.[4]

During the reviews of airline policy by the Nixon and Ford administrations a distinction had been drawn between what could be done in the domestic and international marketplaces. Clearly, the USA was more constrained in what it could do in the latter than the former. Declaring US policy to be in favour of competition in the international sphere was one thing, actually achieving it in the face of recalcitrant bilateral partners was another. Nixon and Ford had made no great progress in the international system and, indeed, the Ford policy statement was seen by many to be a retreat from previous pronouncements. Perhaps more surprisingly, despite lengthy internal debates and ideological commitment to the free market, neither of the Republican administrations achieved any notable liberalisation in the domestic sphere. Overall, in the eight years from 1968, there had been much debate, but many obstacles to reform were encountered and many compromises required and thus little change took place. From 1977 onwards things were to alter.

Carter made a difference, but it was by no means a straightforward affair. As the story of Bermuda 2 illustrates, achieving a more liberal environment in the international sphere was not easy. Bermuda 2 was a major obstacle to the creation of a more market oriented international airline system. Although the Americans had recognised for some time that there were limits to what they could achieve abroad, no-one would have imagined that a president entering the White House committed to deregulation would have accepted such a restrictive agreement as Bermuda 2 for the largest US overseas market. In fact, in a sense, he did not. As will become apparent later, the Carter Administration was never at ease with itself over Bermuda 2 and pressures soon arose for a reconsideration of things. Before the main consequences of that were felt, however, Carter managed to deregulate the domestic US airline industry.

Carter's commitment to deregulation was strong from the beginning. The suggestion, made by at least one academic, that he was not fully aware of what he was doing is out of character and contrary to the evidence.[5] One of the failings of Carter as President was that he immersed himself in too much policy detail. For example, Alan Boyd, when he took over as special ambassador to conduct the Bermuda negotiations, was astonished by the policy minutiae that Carter was aware of.[6] He also had a clear policy vision and intervened on several occasions to push deregulation along when others saw reason for caution.

The Administration developed its position during the transition period after the election and within weeks of coming into office Carter informed Congress: 'One of my Administration's major goals is to free the American people from the burden of over-regulation.' And thus: 'As a first step toward our shared goal of a more efficient less burdensome Federal government, I urge the Congress to reduce Federal regulation of the domestic commercial airline industry.'[7]

The message spelt out precisely what this entailed for the airlines. The industry was to be moulded by competition rather than by regulation. There were to be less demanding establishment rules and easier entry onto routes, which should be allowed to develop in response to consumer requirements. There should be freedom to leave routes, though there were to be safeguards for community services. And prices were to be decided competitively with safeguards against predatory behaviour.[8] This did not come from a man who was not fully apprised of what he was doing.

The message to Congress made it abundantly clear what Carter's vision was for the future of the airlines and what kind of legislation he would promote. The Administration thought that it would be tactically better to offer support for proposals already before the Congress rather than to introduce a bill of its own. Carter had already been approached by Senators Cannon and Kennedy in early 1977 to see if he would support their airline reform bill. Carter responded favourably and co-operated with those Senators and later with Senator Pearson as well, to promote their bill for airline deregulation during 1977 and 1978.[9] The President also worked with pro-deregulation colleagues such as Blumenthal at the Treasury and Schultze, Chairman of the Council of Economic Advisers, as well as with Eizenstat and Mary Schuman from his White House staff to resist dilution of deregulation proposals, in particular, in the early days, demands for the protection of labour that came from Brock Adams the Secretary of Transport and then later wide-ranging modifications proposed by the OMB.[10] However, opposition from most of the major airlines, from labour organisations and from Congress delayed any major legislative progress in 1977. The only achievement was the 'grab bag' Air Cargo Reform Act. Eizenstat observed to Frank Moore, a Congressional liaison assistant, that the bill had been a tactical move to ensure at least some kind of regulatory reform success in 1977.[11]

There were still influential power groups opposed to deregulation, nevertheless, political and popular opinion were moving toward favouring reform.

Evidence about the possible benefits of deregulation was also mounting. In early 1977 the US General Accounting Office estimated that competitive pricing in the airline industry could save $2 billion a year. There were also examples like Pacific Southwestern Airlines operating within states, and hence outside the jurisdiction of the CAB, which created competitive low fare routes like the one between Los Angeles and San Francisco. They operated efficiently and were responsive to consumer demands. It was examples like this which were praised by economics professors Alfred Kahn of Cornell and Michael Levine of California and they respectively became Chairman and Chief of Staff at the CAB under Carter.[12]

The appointment of Kahn to the chairmanship of the CAB was an important development in the story of the deregulation of the airline industry both within and without the USA. Kahn acted as a catalyst for long-term change. Those words are chosen carefully, for, although he did much by administrative action as chairman of the CAB, the long-term future of domestic US airline deregulation could only be secured by legislation. What Kahn did by executive action was to set things in motion and create a more competitive environment, which demonstrated the benefits of deregulation. Kahn was a man of conviction. One gets a sense of moral unease with regulated markets from the title of his paper: 'Deregulation and Vested Interests: the Case of the Airlines'. But the cosseting of vested interests was not his only concern, he also believed that airlines would be more efficient and serve consumer and the national economic interest better if they were deregulated.[13]

The arguments marshalled against deregulation might have intimidated a less adventurous soul. There were fears of inefficiency and low load factors if too many airlines entered the market to chase too few passengers. Instead of fares being lowered they would have to be raised to cover costs. Not entirely compatible with this first criticism was the fear of consolidation and a few mega carriers dominating the industry. Once that had been achieved competition would become a chimera and again fares would be raised. Accompanying these changes would be unpalatable symptoms such as: job insecurity for labour; a decline in safety standards; the demise of low volume passenger routes; and a growing inability of the airlines to re-equip with modern aeroplanes as their profit margins were squeezed. Kahn was aware of these arguments, but had faith in the ability of airline management to cope with a deregulated market. Furthermore, he believed that, so long as competitive fares and freedom to operate routes were accompanied by free entry and exit from the market, the dire consequences predicted by those wishing to conserve the existing system would not materialise. Confronting Kahn was a choice: to let the present system continue, which had steadily reduced prices over time, had allowed the airlines to acquire ever more modern equipment and had sustained a truly national air transportation system, or, to embark upon policies which would deregulate the airlines in the speculative hope that what would emerge would be something qualitatively better. As we now know, he chose the latter route and raced along it.[14]

Since the discussion about deregulation began within US government circles in the late 1960s, one of the most intractable problems had been what to do about pricing. In particular, there was the problem of scheduled and charter or supplemental operators, which had different costs. While policy still remained within the confines of incremental change, one thing the reformers did not want to do was inadvertently to remove the competition provided by these two different types of players by reforming fare structures in such a way that scheduled would put charter operators out of business or *vice versa*. One way the Nixon and Ford administrations had tried to deal with this was the CAB Domestic Passenger Fare Investigation which tried to relate fares to costs. In 1977 and early 1978 Kahn's approach, partly prompted by Carter, turned out to be very different.[15]

Perhaps Kahn's most important innovation was to encourage flexible pricing by the airlines, first of all in the domestic and then in the international market. Fares were to be set by the airlines. Experimental and low fares were now accepted and indeed encouraged by the CAB. Maintaining the indirect competitive forces provided by the relationship between scheduled and charter carriers would now no longer be of great moment if the radical commitment to creating a thoroughgoing competitive market in the international sphere could actually be achieved. This was gradually to make its mark on US charter policy.[16]

In the domestic market, to accompany the liberalisation of pricing, the CAB also began to grant routes to, more or less, all applicants including new airlines, or airlines which had not operated scheduled routes before. The CAB also encouraged operations from underused airports. In short, there was more market pricing, freer entry, and the licensing of new players and new routes, often from new airports. However, there were three things that the CAB could not do. Firstly, it could not ensure these changes of policy would not be reversed in the future; secondly, it could not allow automatic entry onto routes because it was legally charged with the job of processing all applications; and thirdly, it could not dismantle the basic framework of the regulatory system itself.

Kahn was the first to recognise the limitations of executive action as a debate that went on within the administration in May 1978 demonstrates. On the 19 April the Senate, by 83 votes to 9, had passed the Air Transportation Regulatory Reform bill, sponsored by Senators Cannon, Kennedy and Pearson.

151

However, with inflation and government spending causing severe problems, Jim McIntyre, head of the OMB, felt that its deregulation proposals could involve the government in substantial extra spending and he thus wanted to modify a number of its measures. Schultze, Brock Adams, Eizenstat and his assistant Mary Schuman strongly opposed this. The latter two wrote to Carter: 'A compromise would merely weaken the prospects for lasting competition in the industry, and would give us nothing in return with respect to the spending programs.' They acknowledged that great progress had been made by the CAB, but they emphasised that Kahn himself was 'perhaps the most forceful advocate of strong legislation.'[17] Kahn feared that a future CAB might reverse his policies. Privately, he also expressed fears that the liberal interpretation that the CAB had given to existing regulations might be successfully challenged if taken to the courts. And finally, although executive action could liberalise the way things were done, it could not remove the basic regulatory structure because that would require legislation. The CAB could not commit suicide: only Congress could arrange its demise.

After passage of the bill in the Senate the Administration concentrated its efforts on gathering support in the House of Representatives. The issue of airline deregulation was still controversial, especially regarding labour and the problem of rural areas which feared that they would lose their air services in a free market. In fact, provisions were made for direct subsidies for community routes and also safety measures were provided for labour in cases of job losses. These measures took much of the sting out of the criticisms of the bill, but nevertheless things were still difficult.

Handling the House is never easy for a President, even with his own party in the majority there. In a midterm congressional election year, it is even more difficult as Representatives look first and foremost to their constituents and the needs of re-election: the limited demands party loyalty might make upon a Representative are thus even further constrained. However, Carter had some strong and influential allies in the House. Most notable of them was Bizz Johnson, Chairman of the Public Works and Transportation Committee, who had promised to get an airline regulatory reform bill through in 1978. Glenn Anderson, Chairman of the Subcommittee on Aviation to which the bill had been referred, was more of a problem. His support was lukewarm, but the Administration was able to bring pressure to bear by offering support for a noise regulation bill, strongly desired by Anderson, in return for his help with the Airline Regulatory Reform Bill.[18] With continuing efforts by Carter and its supporters in the Congress, the bill made its way through and was signed into law by the President on 24 October 1978.

The act ensured that the US domestic airline market would continue in the direction it had been led by Kahn. The market was to develop through a short transition period to almost complete deregulation. There were automatic entry and liberal exit provisions: an airline had to give a limited period of notice before abandoning a route. Where community routes were required, the government would give direct subsidies and, where there was a loss of jobs because of deregulation, the government would provide relief. There was virtual pricing freedom and essentially the job of running the commercial side of the airline business was to be left to the airlines. Perhaps most importantly of all, the danger of policy being changed by executive action, as Kahn had done at the CAB in 1977 and 1978, would no longer be possible. Kahn had explained in a submission to the House Subcommittee on Aviation that there was a danger of rapid changes in policy from regulation to deregulation and possibly back again: 'Only Congress can say which of these it prefers, and make sure this whirling dervish ends up facing in the direction you want it to face.'[19] By October Congress had decided and the dervish was pointing down the road of deregulation that led to a competitive, market-run airline industry.

Within a few years domestic deregulation in the USA was to have an effect in the international system. It created pressures there for reform and it also eroded the line, often drawn by governments and operators alike, between the domestic and international marketplaces. But, in the short term, it still seemed sensible to observe that there were major differences between the two. Indeed, at first, deregulation at home made the contrast with what went on in the international marketplace more stark than ever. The Carter Administration found that difficult to tolerate and took several initiatives in order to try to introduce more competition to the international airline system.

The Administration drew up a new international policy statement and acquired stronger powers to promote its competitive policy in the international sphere through the 1979 International Air Transportation Competition Act. It also proceeded to try to implement its new policy through renegotiating a substantial number of its bilateral agreements, including Bermuda 2. The Administration's other main tactic was to try to destroy international price fixing. Strictly speaking, this initiative came from the CAB rather than the Administration. Furthermore, there was no prior consultation between the CAB and the State and Transportation departments, but the CAB initiative was quite clearly in line with what Carter and his close advisers wanted. There was little daylight between the policies favoured by Carter and those of Kahn. If Carter had disapproved in any way of Kahn, it is doubtful that he would have appointed him on 25 October 1978 to the key post of President's Counsel on Anti-inflation at a time when the control of inflation was the President's top economic priority. Before looking at the new policy statement and attempts to revise US bilaterals, this initiative of the CAB will be analysed.

Ever since the Bermuda 1 Agreement of 1946 fares agreed at IATA tariff conferences had been adopted by over 80 per cent of the world's scheduled international airlines. If IATA rates were approved by US authorities, then the airlines were routinely granted immunity from US antitrust laws. But, on 9 June 1978, the CAB decided to try to change all that by suggesting that IATA fare setting was not in the public interest. Both American and foreign airlines could thus become subject to antitrust prosecution and if that succeeded they would then be liable for punitive damage claims. The CAB issued a 'show cause order' (SCO) requiring IATA to show cause in proceedings before the CAB why this new interpretation of IATA's role should not be accepted within the USA. The SCO was correctly perceived as a manoeuvre by the CAB to try to destroy not only inter-carrier fare agreements but also IATA itself.[20]

It elicited a spirited response from IATA and in particular from Director General Knut Hammarskjold, which blunted the thrust of the show cause weapon and in doing so also exposed some of the lingering doubts and differences within even the Carter Administration toward radical deregulation, especially in so far as to how and to what extent it should be implemented in the international sphere.[21]

The SCO was issued at the same time that a bureaucratic review was going on in Washington over which department should take charge of developing long range international airline policy: at the time no-one had clear responsibility for it. In the course of the review two other issues arose. Firstly, the DOT made a bid to take over the chairmanship of the tripartite inter-agency group, composed of itself, the CAB and the State Department, which decided on positions and strategy for specific negotiations. Currently that was chaired by the State Department and it had recently successfully negotiated pro-competition bilaterals. Those achievements contrasted rather favourably with the only time that the DOT had taken the lead in negotiations, namely the Bermuda 2 Talks. The second matter that was addressed was the question of who should conduct the face to face negotiations with foreign officials.[22]

After some discussion all departments agreed that DOT should take charge of long-term policy though this was rather moot as the new international policy statement had already been largely formulated. The only agency with reservations was the CAB which was worried that its own influence would be reduced with DOT in charge of long-term policy. The DOT was not as enthusiastic about deregulation as the CAB would have liked and this might have contributed to the decision to take the precipitate action of issuing the SCO. So far as the idea of the DOT chairing the inter-agency group was concerned, both the CAB and the State Department opposed this, as did other agencies and departments whose expertise was called upon by the group from time to time. On the question of face to face negotiations all were agreed that the State Department should continue to play this role. Clearly, from all this, there were differences between the DOT, the State Department and the CAB of both a procedural and substantive kind.[23] And once the SCO had been issued, those differences were exacerbated because the State Department was most uneasy about the reaction of foreign governments to the SCO, and both it, and the DOT, felt that the CAB was taking too abrasive a line and seeking too much deregulation too quickly, though both departments generally favoured deregulation.

The SCO put the USA unambiguously in a competitive posture that was contrary to the policy inclinations of the vast majority of foreign governments and their airlines and indeed of its own two major flag carriers Pan Am and TWA. In the spring of 1977 the most important ICAO conference since Chicago in 1944 convened in Montreal. IATA sent a large number of observers and the main pressures at the meeting were for more, not less, government intervention in the airline industry. One influential journal summed up the mood with the headline: 'More Control is the Message'.[24] In that kind of situation, it was not surprising that IATA's hostile response to the SCO garnered much support from the international community. After an extensive publicity and educational campaign, in particular about the dangers of the extraterritorial application of US antitrust laws, a large number of governments expressed concern to the State Department.[25]

At the same time that IATA sought to mobilise opposition to the SCO, it also sought to mollify its American critics by reforming itself. In fact, a review of its tariff role was underway before the SCO was issued. At the end of June and the beginning of July a special IATA conference proposed reforms which radically changed the tariff role of IATA. Carrier participation in the tariff conferences was to be optional and procedures were to become more flexible. In the autumn these proposals were accepted at IATA's annual conference and were subsequently submitted to the CAB for its consideration.[26]

At a symposium in Jamaica organised by the State Department in January 1979, Under Secretary of State, Richard Cooper, was bombarded by his foreign counterparts with criticism of the SCO.[27] In the face of this, and IATA's reform of itself, the USA began to moderate its stance. In May 1979 the CAB gave interim approval of IATA's reformed tariff procedures and it decided to restrict the SCO hearings to routes with stops in the USA. Even so, as the summer went by, the State Department became more and more sceptical about the wisdom of the SCO. In August it filed a written submission to the CAB opposing the SCO and in so doing it noted: 'the uniformity and intensity of foreign opposition to the board's procedures.' It concluded that 'the board's proceeding could be counterproductive to the goal, which this department and the board share, of promoting a more competitively-oriented international aviation environment.'[28]

Public hearings finally began at the end of October 1979, but were something of an anticlimax. IATA was now not the 'sitting duck' it might have been had not tariff reforms already been made.[29] A majority of witnesses and the State and Transportation Departments opposed the dismantling of the IATA fare regime. Such developments had impact in the US Congress where Senators Cannon and Pearson had introduced, in August 1978, what became the 1979 International Air Transportation Competition Act. Originally it had provisions prohibiting the CAB from approving inter-carrier fare agreements, but by the time the House of Representatives approved that bill in November 1979 those provisions had been deleted.[30]

The CAB itself continued to moderate its stance. As Kahn's successor, Marvin Cohen, explained in early 1980 the hearings had made a positive impression regarding the work of IATA:

The Board was impressed by the support given to the new IATA mechanism not only by many witnesses who are familiar with the industry, but also by our own Departments of Transportation and State and other foreign government leaders who support the procompetitive policies of the United States.... Diplomatic considerations are primary reasons for our decision to extend immunity to the new IATA.[31]

On 5 December 1979 the CAB issued a statement that it was terminating the SCO proceedings. However, this was not the end of the matter. The CAB's concern narrowed and the SCO was restricted to the Atlantic market, but the assault on price fixing had not been abandoned completely. Over the next two years talks continued, off and on, with the European Civil Aviation Conference (ECAC), established as a consultative body in 1954, which played a major role for European governments and their airlines. In 1980 the USA extended IATA's antitrust immunity for two years but forbade its own airlines from taking part in IATA fare-setting on the Atlantic, and Cohen continued to press for more competitive practices.[32] By this time the main line of American assault on international regulation was through the State Department's initiative to renegotiate bilaterals. Included among other things in these new bilaterals were liberal pricing arrangements, but even here the CAB Chairman would have preferred a more energetic pursuit of liberalisation. He believed that many State Department officials did not have their hearts in the enterprise and Carter appears to have sympathised with that viewpoint.[33] Rather ironically, given its ideological hue, with the Reagan Administration coming into power in 1981 a more pragmatic policy emerged in the White House and at the CAB. Reagan's CAB Chairman, Dan McKinnon, was more receptive to the initiative from the IATA for a flexible system of fare bands, optional participation in tariff conferences and for its permissive attitude toward more government, rather than IATA, inputs into pricing. The State Department and Reagan himself put pressure on the CAB to take a less abrasive line on the SCO. In August 1981, while Cohen was still Chairman, Reagan wrote advising the CAB that matters of common concern to the international aviation community should be addressed in 'a co-operative manner'.[34] He appreciated the benefits of co-operative behaviour from the international community during the 1981 US air traffic controllers' strike and there were also fears both about more gains for foreign than US airlines from deregulation and the financial status of American operators. In 1982 the death knell of the SCO was tolled when the Congress refused to vote money for implementing its findings.

In 1982 after protracted negotiations a Memorandum Of Understanding was agreed between ECAC and the USA which constituted a compromise, allowing inter-carrier agreements, or multilateral carrier fare co-ordination as it was referred to (IATA was not mentioned), in return for the acceptance of a more flexible, liberal and market-led pricing system.[35] Things had by no means returned to the *status quo ante* the SCO. The role of IATA in fare-setting had been dramatically changed, though this was not just because of the SCO, but also because of pressures for fare liberalisation exerted by the USA through its renegotiation of bilaterals and because of market dynamics released by Freddie Laker's Skytrain, which had effects upon both scheduled and charter operators.

The SCO had been a bold attempt at radical and swift change. It finally expired with the demise of the CAB at the end of 1984, but long before then it had lost its bite. However, it had achievements to its credit. It did not destroy IATA: in 1987 the organisation had more members than ever, but of its workload only 20 per cent was devoted to tariff matters.[36] The SCO had forced the IATA to reform itself and relax its scheme of fare-setting, most dramatically on the Atlantic. Government policy and bilateral agreements became more important than IATA in determining the types of fares to be allowed. The SCO helped to make a more competitive system of fares possible by reducing IATA's effectiveness and Carter's new international aviation policy, the US renegotiation of bilaterals, new operators like Freddie Laker, and the gradual development of more competitive airline philosophies in the UK, Holland and the EC made competitive fares a reality on many routes.

While the CAB developed its own strategy, albeit approved of by Carter, in order to liberalise the international market, the Administration also bent its efforts towards achieving similar results through different means. The disappointment with Bermuda 2 helped to prompt the Administration into efforts both to draft a new international policy statement and to renegotiate as many of its bilaterals as it could into more liberal form. However, the most immediate developments stemmed from unsettled Bermuda 2 matters, namely, fares and charters and from the continuingly controversial issue of multiple designation.

The latter achieved the highest profile in the USA, largely because of the political influence of Massachusetts politicians Tip O'Neil and Edward Kennedy, who complained vociferously about the loss of double designation for Boston. The resolution of this matter was to be of great consequence, but it did not come to a head for some time. In contrast, charters and fares, which were by their nature in the 1970s very much interrelated, demanded immediate action after the Bermuda Agreement had been signed.

Charters had been a major problem in the Bermuda talks. The USA had viewed charters as a distinctive and important force for competitive pricing throughout the airline industry since the 1960s when the CAB began to foster their development. But, as time went by, the USA found it increasingly difficult to deregulate scheduled operations and maintain a distinction between them and charters. In order to compete, charters found it necessary to become more flexible and more like cheap scheduled services in order to keep a substantial market. The worst possible scenario would be a liberal bilateral governing scheduled services that allowed low fares without getting the partner in the bilateral to allow liberal charter operations. In such circumstances US charter operators would not survive for long. Once charters were squeezed out there would always be the danger of a reversal to an illiberal bilateral, or, higher fares being imposed with impunity by the scheduled carriers. In the mid 1970s it thus became standard US policy to try to incorporate liberal charter agreements into bilaterals: previous practice had been that bilaterals only governed the operations of scheduled carriers.

In the Bermuda Talks the Americans had sought, but Boyd had failed to get, a liberal charter agreement as an integral part of the bilateral. Edward Driscoll, Chief Executive Officer of the National Air Carrier Association, wrote to Carter that the charter provisions of annex 4 were not approved by the US delegation and that Boyd's failure to get a liberal charter agreement was regarded by the CAB as a serious error.[37] Interestingly, Boyd recalled some years later that the British had pulled a fast one on him with regard to an important aspect of the agreement. At the time he could not recall what it was, but it looks suspiciously like US acceptance of annex 4.[38] The US was so unhappy with its provisions that talks continued on this subject right up until the moment of the formal signing ceremony in July, though to little avail. The British pointed out that they had multilateral obligations to partners in ECAC relating to charters and that it was therefore difficult to come to a separate bilateral arrangement with the USA. In fact, this was largely a ploy as Britain was the only European state at the time with a major stake in the transatlantic charter business[39]

Within three months of being confronted by what the USA considered to be the shortcomings of the Bermuda Agreement, talks were again underway with the British on the vexed questions of charters and fares. Even before the formal talks began an *ad hoc* agreement was signed with the British on 19 September, approving discount fares between London and New York. Laker's Skytrain was the market leader there, but for the time being the British did not wish to see low fares spreading beyond the London-New York route. It was cautious about the impact on airline finances of such a development and concerned about the competitiveness of BA which would be the British player on most other routes. Ironically, given the SCO a few months later, the CAB disapproved the new low fares. One concern held widely within the Administration was about the impact low fares might have on US charter operators while the restrictive regime for charters was still in place with Britain. Also, as will become clear later, Kahn had a particularly dim view of British policies altogether and resented what their negotiators had achieved in the Bermuda 2 Talks.

Carter took a more adventurous line than Kahn. On 26 September he wrote to him overruling the CAB. 'I must emphasise that my international aviation policy carries with it a commitment to low fare, competitive international air service for the benefit of American consumers.' Only if fares proved to be predatory would he agree to their suspension. Interestingly, he went on to 'suggest that the Board give serious attention to reforming present rules covering charter flights to permit these services to be more competitive with the new low fare scheduled flights.'[40] Even with the problems of the restrictive Bermuda 2 charter provisions, Carter was not prepared to sacrifice the benefits of low fares for the sake of protecting American charter operators through government regulation. The scheduled operators had responded to competition from a relatively unregulated charter industry in the past, now it was the turn of the charter industry to respond to the challenge of the scheduled airlines, though they were not to be left entirely to their own devices. The CAB soon adopted a very liberal policy for charter operations and the administration sought to negotiate liberal charter agreements with foreign governments so that this part of the industry would not be disadvantaged. What was remarkable was the insistence by Carter that liberalisation of fares in the scheduled market should not be held up, even though it might jeopardise the charter industry in those markets where restrictive arrangements were insisted upon by the USA's bilateral partners. A whole new world of negotiating airline service agreements was being opened up. Once pandora's box was opened, it had effects not fully foreseen. The talks with the British over the following seven months were to test whether the USA could put its deregulation programme into practice, or at least carry it forward to the extent that it would not result in prejudicial circumstances for major parts of its airline industry.

With low fares allowed on the London-New York route for Pan Am and TWA, it became very difficult for the CAB to resist low fares filed on transatlantic routes by other US carriers, even if it had wanted to. Within the legalistic parameters of US public administration such a denial would constitute unconscionable discrimination. An opportunity to test such matters soon arose in relation to new routes between London and Dallas and London and Houston operated respectively by Braniff and B.Cal.

Initially Braniff filed what the British considered to be predatory fares for its route and neither the CAA or the DTI would allow them. After the British objected, negotiations took place and eventually an agreement on fares was reached with Braniff in March 1978. At that point the CAB stepped in and ordered that Braniff and B.Cal. must lower those fares or stop their operations.[41] The reaction to this in London was hostile, especially as the provisions for B.Cal.'s route to the southwest were one of the few things in the Bermuda 2 Agreement that had already been heavily criticised in Parliament as being too favourable for US airlines. Even in Washington there was apprehension about the CAB's provocative move. Only the Justice Department supported the CAB. The OMB and the DOT wanted the President to allow operations to continue with the higher fares for a week to give time for compromise. The State Department felt the most unease of all departments in Washington. It wanted to 'avoid provoking the British' and thus proposed that the President disapprove the CAB order.[42]

This crisis occurred at a sensitive time politically for Carter. In a sense, Kahn had hoisted him on his own petard, though not maliciously so. After Bermuda 2 there had been a groundswell of political and popular criticism of its restrictive character. There was much dissatisfaction from regions where the administration had failed to secure agreement for new gateways.[43] The south west had not fared too badly, but what was the point of opening up new gateways for the travelling public if fares were then kept artificially high? Or so at least the critics argued. Carter was sensitive to these points and wanted to be consistent in his drive for liberalisation of the market. Also, scheduled for 6 March in Washington, were talks about charters and fares with the British, from which the USA hoped to gain concessions. By the time the Braniff/B.Cal. crisis broke those talks were underway and Carter, not wishing to be too provocative, decided to take the advice of the DOT and the OMB. He requested the CAB to withdraw its order temporarily until the end of the Anglo-US talks on 17 March in the hope that they would have solved the problem by then.[44]

The Americans were advancing on two fronts: fares and charters. With Carter's refusal to protect charters by unilateral US regulation, liberalising the market for charters in tandem with lowering scheduled fares became an even more essential goal of US policy. By March 1978 the CAB had followed Carter's lead and had adopted an extremely liberal charter policy based on 'US Public Charters'. The US tried to break the deadlock on charters with European countries in multilateral talks with ECAC in Washington in the spring of 1978, but Britain was still the main target. How to bring pressure to bear on Britain was the main task. In renegotiating their bilaterals with other countries, and in particular with the Netherlands, the USA believed that it had found at least one lever.[45]

The Dutch had shown a willingness to be helpful to the Americans during the Bermuda 2 talks and by March 1978 the two countries were all set to sign a new protocol. Both thought that they had things to gain: the Dutch wanted more access to the US market and a lifting of threats to its 6th freedom traffic; the USA wanted liberal pricing, capacity, and charter arrangements. It was in this context that Kahn was reported to have said that he would 'stick it to the Brits.' if they did not accept liberal charter rules for the Anglo-US market. His threat was that the USA would divert traffic from Britain by negotiating liberal charter rules with adjacent countries such as Holland. This type of manoeuvre put pressure on the British.[46]

When their delegation arrived in Washington for talks on 6 March it soon gained an appreciation of the political pressures on the US negotiators to achieve a low fares agreement. By the second week of the talks the British began a strategic retreat. This was partly dictated by prudence: they had completed a most favourable bilateral with the USA only months earlier and were loath to lose the benefits of that by pushing the USA into denunciation. The *New York Times* had reported in early March that the Administration was considering renouncing Bermuda 2. In fact the report was inaccurate, but the dangers of pushing the Americans too far cannot have escaped the British.[47] In any case, in the overall agreement about fares and charters, there were things that the British felt would be of benefit to them.

On fares the British gave way to American demands and allowed not only the Braniff low fare, but low fares on all routes providing that airlines could limit the number of seats involved if they wanted to. There were also safeguards against US operators offering below cost feeder fares to their gateways and the British extracted from the USA an agreement that the low fare regime would be reviewed in October 1978. Even with these defensive measures achieved by the British, the agreement was clearly an American victory and was so pleasing to Carter that he insisted on announcing it to the public himself.[48]

On charters the story was similar. Eizenstat and Schuman explained to Carter on 29 April that the charter agreement formally signed on 25 April: 'provides for multiple designation of charter carriers, eliminates unilateral restrictions on the capacity or frequency of charter flights except in one instance relating to cargo, and establishes the principle that only the country of origin may regulate charter prices or rates.' The Americans were again clearly delighted with this outcome.[49] However, the British were not unduly concerned. They expected that their charter operators, with lower costs than their US counterparts, might do well in a freer market. In the medium term the whole business of charter operations turned out to be less important than many expected. By 1981 the percentage of world airline traffic carried by charters had been halved and of that 45 per cent was carried by scheduled airlines operating split charters. Super Apex, Standby and other forms of discount fares, introduced in the wake of Laker's progress, cut deeply into the charter market, though, as we have seen, other dynamics were at work as well. Indeed it was not always possible to distinguish between the two different types of operators in terms of how they sold tickets and carried passengers.[50]

Thus within nine months of signing Bermuda 2, the USA had executed a fairly effective counter offensive and in the two areas where uncertainty had existed in July about how things would eventually develop the USA had managed to swing things to their way of thinking. Taken in conjunction with the SCO, US policy was still quite clearly continuing to advance aggressively down the path of liberalisation in the international marketplace. However, rather like the danger of a future CAB undoing the work of Kahn and Levine, so there was a danger that a subsequent administration might put liberalisation into reverse with regard to US bilateral agreements. To try to pre-empt that, and also to strengthen the liberalisation momentum, Carter's Administration began to draft a new policy statement and push legislation through Congress in support of its liberal international policy.

Carter's decision to develop a new policy statement so soon after the September 1976 statement by the Ford Administration was indicative of his determination to engineer a radical change in the international sphere. The CAB, the DOT and the State Department, as well as the White House and the NSC, all took part in drafting the new statement under the auspices of the OMB. By October 1977 Carter had approved a draft, subject to State Department revision.[51] In fact it was not until May 1978 that a document was released for comment. Thereafter the statement was revised and issued in its final form on 21 August 1978.

Although there were differences between the three main actors: the CAB, the State Department and the DOT; which caused delays and re-drafting, the problems were largely to do with tactics and timing by the spring of 1978. The State Department, in particular, was sensitive to charges of imperialistic behaviour being brought against the USA for trying to export its deregulation philosophy in a forceful fashion. It was afraid of exacerbating the problems of dealing effectively with the sensitive and difficult diplomacy of international economics in the 1970s. Nevertheless, after all the talking had been done, the outcome was a clear commitment to the fostering of a competitive, market based, international airline industry. The new negotiating principles set the tone.

> The guiding principle of United States aviation negotiating policy will be to trade competitive opportunities, rather than restrictions, with our negotiating partners. We will aggressively pursue our interests in expanding air transportation and reduced prices rather than accept the self-defeating accommodation of protectionism. Our concessions in negotiations will be given in return for progress toward competitive objectives, and those concessions themselves will be of a liberalising character.[52]

The USA wanted price competition; the elimination of restrictions on charter operators; the removal of restrictions on capacity, frequency and route operating rights; an end to discrimination and unfair practices against the USA; more gateways for non-stop flights; competitive cargo services; and multiple designations. The announcement of this policy came five days after the signing of a new agreement with Israel which embodied many of the policy statement's aims: in particular a double disapproval price regime which was the most liberal arrangement the USA had with any country. The USA was so keen to nurture price competition that it favoured the Israelis allowing KLM to compete on the US-Israel route on the same terms as TWA and El Al, in order to increase competition and downward pressure on prices. Over the following months the USA tried to follow the example set by its negotiations with the Netherlands and Israel and implement its policy statement aims with a significant number of other countries.[53]

While this executive policy was being developed, Senators Cannon and Pearson introduced a new bill on 1 August 1978 that eventually became the International Air Transportation Competition Act of 1979 (signed into law on 15 February 1980). Like the policy statement, it went through a lengthy process of debate and amendment, including the elimination of a requirement that the CAB disallow any inter-carrier fare agreements. While the legislators backed away from this extreme pro-competition stance, the final act would make it difficult for any future administration to pursue an anti-competitive airline policy in the international sphere without new legislation.

Section 17 set out the overall priority:

> In formulating United States international air transportation policy, the Congress intends that the Secretary of State, the Secretary of Transportation, and the Civil Aeronautics Board shall develop a negotiating policy which emphasizes the greatest degree of competition that is compatible with a well-functioning international air transportation system.[54]

The act reiterated the aims set out in the international policy statement in slightly different formulation, but also added some new points and gave added emphasis to some of the old. As the name of the act suggested, one priority was the nurturing of a more competitive US industry and so there was to be integration of its domestic and international parts. This was particularly important for Pan Am which had been denied any domestic routes in the past, but it was also indicative of the growing difficulty of distinguishing between domestic and international operations. Globalisation of the marketplace was already underway. The act also embodied in law a negotiating tactic that was presently being used in the State Department's attempts to negotiate liberal bilaterals. Section 17(8) stated that:

> opportunities for carriers of foreign countries to increase their access to United States points [would be allowed] if exchanged for benefits of similar magnitude for United States carriers or the travelling public with permanent linkage between rights granted and rights given away.[55]

So far as foreign countries were concerned, the act largely reiterated policies with which they were already familiar because of bilateral negotiations or the international policy statement, but for the regulatory reformers in the USA the act helped to entrench their policies for the future. There were also some new provisions in the act, namely powers that it gave to US authorities to retaliate against unfair or discriminatory policies of foreign governments which disadvantaged US airlines.

The act advanced on two fronts regarding unfair practices. Firstly, it reduced the strength of the Ford Administration's 'fly America programme', which had been embodied in the 1975 International Air Transportation Fair Competitive Practices Act, and which was seen by some foreign governments as a form of US discrimination. Secondly, and more importantly, it sought 'the elimination of discrimination and unfair competitive practices faced by United States airlines in foreign air transportation.'

This had also been an aim of the 1975 act, but now US authorities were given much broader powers. In the new act, using a criterion of public interest (which was conveniently flexible and vague), the USA could retaliate against what it judged to be unfair or discriminatory by a variety of measures including suspension of fares and revocation of operating licences.[56] An irony that emerges from all this is that in order to promote competition in the international market the USA developed powers of intervention, whereas in the domestic realm, in order to achieve the same result, it had abandoned powers of intervention and returned the industry to the free market. A statement prepared for Carter to accompany the signing of the bill summarised its intent:

> This legislation affirms and strengthens our commitment to deregulation. The bill reduces statutory barriers against the entry of individual carriers

into new international markets and authorises carriers to change their fares within a zone of reasonableness without interference from the Civil Aeronautics Board. The bill also authorises the Board and the President to take quick and effective countermeasures against a foreign government that engages in discriminatory or anti-competitive practices against American carriers or tries to impair their operating rights.[57]

By 1980 the Carter Administration had achieved an enormous amount of its policy goals for the airline industry. The power of IATA had been diminished; the domestic airline industry was well on its way to becoming deregulated; and a new international policy statement and the Competition Act of 1979 helped both to set and strengthen the agenda for US policy for years to come. The State Department had negotiated twelve liberal bilaterals using the carrot of more access to the US market and the stick of threatening to by-pass countries or divert traffic from them through liberal bilaterals with nearby states. Many of these bilaterals involved insignificant players in international aviation, but agreements with the Netherlands, Belgium and West Germany were important. The major problems left unresolved by the Bermuda 2 Agreement, charters and fares, had been resolved largely in America's favour, but restrictions embodied in the agreement that denied double designation for Boston and the opening of more gateways in the USA increasingly troubled the Americans. So far as domestic political pressures were concerned, the Administration suffered most from what the American public perceived as these two shortcomings of the Bermuda Agreement.

Soon after the fares and charter deal was reached with the British in March 1978, demands increased from important political figures in Massachusetts for action on double designation. By mid May, Carter felt that he had to do something to correct what was now seen as a serious mistake in allowing the British to reduce US double designations from 8 to 2, which included the loss to Boston.[58] Put like that the situation actually looks worse than it was because of the eight only four routes had ever had two US airlines operate on them. Nevertheless, it was a serious political problem and on 16 May Carter wrote to Prime Minister Callaghan requesting that there should be double designation for three cities and proposing a trade for the renewal of Boston's. Senator Kennedy was delighted by this and hopes were raised for a positive response, especially after the Americans learned that Laker was also seeking amendment to Bermuda 2 in order to allow his planes to service Boston.[59]

The days slipped by, but there was no substantive response from Callaghan. On 9 June Carter tried to increase the pressure. He approved a CAB recommendation that New York and Los Angeles should be the two double designated gateways in the USA. However, in addition, Boston was also licensed for double designation and Carter requested that agreement for that should be sought with the British.[60]

When Callaghan did reply the Americans were bitterly disappointed. Callaghan put forward a proposal that was later to become of great significance in Anglo-US airline diplomacy. In 1977 Edmund Dell had become concerned about the congestion problem at Heathrow (HR). In order to deal with the situation he introduced what became known as the traffic distribution rules (TDRs) to try to divert traffic away from HR to other London airports, at this time mainly Gatwick.[61] There were suspicions that these rules were also intended to give a degree of protection to BA at its main hub and they were not entirely without substance. The British, having failed to divide the market in the Bermuda 2 Talks, and having allowed double designation on two routes and new gateways to be opened bringing yet more US airlines into London, now had a way to take the edge off their competitive position by requiring them to operate into Gatwick which was a less desirable gateway than HR.

On 14 June Eizenstat and his assistant Lipshutz reported to Carter that Callaghan's response was disappointing. 'Although we proposed to trade new *opportunities* for British carriers in exchange for the designation of a third city, they have proposed further *restrictions* on our carriers in order to obtain that right.' The British wanted flights from London to Boston and Los Angeles to be restricted to 21 a week for airlines of each side and for Pan Am to send '*all* its traffic to Gatwick.'[62] The State and Transportation Departments, the CAB and the NSC all thought that these proposals were unacceptable. And as the US Ambassador to Britain, Kingman Brewster, reported that the British were sticking 'firm' to their position, it was thought inadvisable for the President to take further action.[63]

While Carter took a low profile, American officials continued to press the British on double designation in a succession of talks during 1978 and early 1979. Tip O'Neil persisted in publicising the case for a second carrier for Boston. After an article of his in the *Boston Globe*, the British Commercial Minister at the Embassy, Lord Bridges, made what O'Neil described in a letter to Carter as a 'reasonable and very responsive' reply. In return for the USA helping with the HR congestion problem, Britain would reciprocate by being helpful to Boston. In a State Department draft reply to O'Neil a much more critical view was taken of Britain's response.[64]

The State Department noted that the proposal mentioned by O'Neil had not been put on offer by the British in official talks and, even if it were, it could not be accepted. With some indignation, the letter observed that the British were trying to get the USA to solve unilaterally their problems at HR. Already the USA had two carriers operating into Gatwick: the British could not expect more to be redirected there. The letter failed to acknowledge that most countries only had one international carrier operating into London: the USA already had four. Instead, the emphasis was upon the claim that 'Gatwick remains a distinctly less attractive gateway', largely because of its lack of onward connections.[65] The USA pushed this issue yet again with the British in talks held between 27-30 March, but the British remained resolute.

Hopes rose for liberalising Bermuda 2 with the victory of the Conservatives in the May 1979 British General Election. The new Prime Minister was Margaret Thatcher, a lady who embraced the liberal economic doctrines of monetarism, trickledown and deregulation. The change of government did make some matters easier to resolve, but the Thatcher government's renewal of Britain's sense of importance and its vigorous assertion of the nation's interests meant that liberalisation of Bermuda 2 would only proceed if and when it were perceived to be in British interests. Those interests were now defined somewhat differently and more in accordance with free market ideology, but that did not lead to automatic acceptance of American-style deregulation in the international sphere because British airlines operated under different conditions and within different market parameters than their American counterparts. For example, an important factor here was the EC and the way that its airline policy began to develop from the end of the 1970s.

During the summer and early autumn, the Americans thought of how they could best broach the subject of renegotiating a substantial part of Bermuda 2 with the British. The Administration was still under pressure to revise the provisions for double designation, and lobbying, especially from Florida, for more gateways was also strong.[66] On 12 October, the inter-agency committee composed of representatives of the CAB, State and Transportation Departments, with Lazarus attending for the White House, decided that the CAB should draw up an agenda for talks with the British and that Cooper of the State Department should pass it to them on 29 October.[67]

Over the following weeks there were considerable difficulties within the

American camp. Tension between the State Department and the CAB made it difficult for the USA to proceed to decisive talks with the British. The State Department also had a whole range of tactical problems to tussle with. It wanted to postpone talks, about charter and cargo transport, scheduled for 5 November, in order to allow the British to digest US liberalisation proposals. The advantage of this was that charter and cargo agreements, which the British now wanted more than the Americans, could be used to persuade them to be forthcoming about liberalisation. The State Department was also fearful about not having the authority to make deals on specific issues. For example, the British might offer to accept more gateways, which would relieve the Administration of its most difficult political problem at home, but, if the US team were unable to accept such an offer, there could be damaging political repercussions in Washington. The Department essentially wanted to advance in piecemeal fashion. It felt that there could be a very negative reaction and accusations of imperialistic export of deregulation, rather like the SCO had occasioned, if the USA were to talk in terms of wholesale renegotiation instead of liberalisation of specific aspects of Bermuda 2.[68]

The CAB and White House officials were less than happy with the State Department and what they saw as its procrastination and lack of vigorous pursuit of US objectives. With regard to Cooper's handing of the US menu to the British on 29 October, there had been some suggestion that it should be withheld if the British reaction to the idea of liberalisation were negative. A few days before the meeting Lazarus told Eizenstat he would 'attempt to make sure that Cooper understands that he is to present the document to the British, regardless of what attitude the Minister displays in response to the suggestion that Bermuda 2 be reopened.'[69] In fact both the handing over of the menu and the 5 November talks went ahead. The Americans were still unclear how the British would react over liberalisation, but talks were scheduled for January 1980 and Lazarus advised Eizenstat that in the inter-agency meeting on 21 November he should 'impress upon the State Department in particular that the promotion of deregulation internationally is an important Presidential concern.'[70] Even with the CAB and the State Department in disagreement over policy and with personal tension between officials from both agencies, the Administration was determined to press ahead.

By January 1980 the matter of access to HR was no longer of just academic concern. Under the new dispensation, Pan Am had been allowed to take over National, which gave it some new international and, for the first time, some domestic routes. However, after the take-over, the CAB withheld National's

Miami-London route from Pan Am on the grounds of competition considerations. It then requested airlines, including Pan Am, to submit route applications for it. Among the possibilities was Air Florida, a US Laker-style operator. The idea of a cut price airline operating into HR to compete with BA was not palatable to the British. They were quick to point out that any airline, other than Pan Am, chosen to operate between Miami and London would have to fly into Gatwick rather than HR because of the TDRs.[71] In the end the gateway and double designation reforms that the Bermuda 2 liberalisation talks achieved alleviated fears of Pan Am having an anti-competitive share of the market and it was awarded National's old route. But this is to anticipate developments: even before the talks began it was clear to the Americans that access to HR was going to be a difficult discussion point.

With the talks little more than two weeks away, CAB Chairman Marvin Cohen was still uneasy about the State Department's commitment. US aims were clear enough: 'to persuade the British to accept more gateway cities, more carriers to serve designated gateways, fewer restrictions on capacity and low fare offerings.'[72] The question was: Would the State Department push for these goals vigorously enough? Carter shared Cohen's concern and offered to help. Lazarus believed that the best way of translating that offer of help into reality would be to have Carter send a letter to Thatcher 'telling her that he is interested in the Bermuda 2 negotiations, and suggesting that she ought to be sure they are resolved consistent with her own interest in free market solutions.'[73] Among other things this might raise matters above the level of the British civil servants who dealt with aviation affairs. Without doing that, or at least bringing political pressure from on high to bear upon them, Lazarus doubted that there would be a beneficial outcome to the talks. Mary Schuman 'secretly' drafted a letter to Thatcher for the President, but objections from officials at the NSC and reservations about the wisdom of sending it expressed by Richard Cooper of the State Department meant that it never reached Prime Minister Thatcher even though the President had signed it.[74]

There were two rounds of talks, 29 January to 1 February and 27 February to 5 March in London and Washington respectively. The American delegation was led by B. Boyd Hight, Deputy Assistant Secretary of State for Transportation, and the British by C. W. Roberts of the Department of Trade. The outcome was an exchange of regulation for deregulation. In return for subscribing to British policy on the restricted use of HR the Americans got more gateways and more double designation.

Twelve new gateways were agreed, with each side having the right to nominate six for its own airlines. For three years there would be only be one airline operating each route in order to give it some startup protection. Additional double designation was to be allowed for Boston and Miami. Double designation for Miami made it easy for the CAB to allow Pan Am to take over National's route as there would now be adequate competition. And there was to be virtual cargo deregulation by 1985, which simply confirmed the outcome of talks that had culminated in March 1979. All these provisions were seen to be highly beneficial for the USA and less so for Britain. In particular, regarding the new gateways, there was a limit to the number that BA could operate to profitably. Much of its traffic was of UK origin and there was a limit to the number of British people who wanted to fly to the Kansas Cities of this world. Furthermore, without feeder services in the USA, BA was at a disadvantage in trying to capture American passengers. This was to loom ever larger as a problem as the years went by.[75]

On the other hand restricting access to HR was to benefit BA, including in some ways that were not entirely foreseen. In the December 1980 exchange of notes that formalised the liberalisation of Bermuda 2 (it was referred to by some as Bermuda 2 1/2), Roberts wrote to Hight to set out the additional restrictions on access to HR. Back in April 1978, Shovelton and Atwood had agreed that charters could no longer operate into HR, now any: 'Airlines not currently operating at Heathrow Airport will not be allowed to commence operations there.'[76] Furthermore, any new routes, other than 12 gateways listed in section 7 of the Bermuda 2 Agreement as amended, would have to be serviced by an airport other than HR. So, BA benefited in a major way by having its competitors restricted in number at HR: they were namely TWA and Pan Am. But, restrictions on access to HR also meant that as it opened new routes, and especially after it took over B.Cal., that it had to split its operations between HR and Gatwick which was not the most cost efficient way of doing things.[77]

The other regulation, which was to turn out to be a very serious regulatory hostage to fortune for the USA, was the HR corporate succession clause. There is dispute as to what the motives and intentions behind this clause actually were. The most plausible explanation is that it was intended to prevent the US from substituting a discount fare operator, such as Air Florida, for TWA or Pan Am at HR to undercut BA's prices. The Thatcher Administration had already made it clear that they sought a more competitive airline industry and that part of their strategy to achieve that was the privatisation of BA, but its fortunes had to be turned around. It had to be nurtured into a competitive, profitable airline

171

attractive to investors and so, ironically, a period of gentle protection was necessary.

The succession clause stated:

> Any London airport (including Heathrow) may be served by British Airways, Pan American World Airways, and Trans World Airlines (or the corporate successor airline in any name change, merger, acquisition or consolidation in which any of the three airlines is the major airline element).[78]

For a number of years this caused no problems. It prevented the Air Floridas of the world competing with BA at its main hub and BA was happy to see TWA and Pan Am at HR as neither were strong competitors in the 1980s. The Americans saw few problems with the agreement initially. The idea of the two great American flag carriers being replaced carried little weight behind it. But, as deregulation worked its way through the US domestic and out into the international system, then TWA and Pan Am were soon disadvantaged in competing with the likes of AA, UA and Delta, which enjoyed both economies of scale and a domestic hub and spoke feeder system. As the new international US carriers appeared on the scene carrying with them the competitive advantages created by deregulation, it became of greater concern to BA to keep them from competing directly at HR. This was not just a purely defensive posture on the part of BA because it believed that the US domestic market, under the new deregulated dispensation, gave US airlines an unfair competitive advantage because they were protected from foreign competition in their home market and that went contrary to market doctrines. In this situation, the HR corporate succession clause was to take on new importance in the 1990s.

The Carter Administration had begun with a serious setback for its deregulation policies: Bermuda 2. Over the period 1977-81 some of that damage was remedied by subsequent negotiations, much helped by the domestic and international reforms pushed through by Carter, the CAB and the Congress. The last round of talks was the so-called Bermuda 2 1/2, and at first that also seemed to be primarily a liberalisation agreement, though the corporate succession clause was to cast a retrospective regulatory shadow in the 1990s. The domestic US and international scene had changed dramatically since Carter came to office. Liberalisation still had a long way to go in the international sphere, but America's main bilateral partner was itself now moving toward a more liberal policy and, equally important for the long term, so was the EC, and it is to these developments that we must now turn.

Notes and References

1. *Congressional Digest*, June-July 1978, p. 180, Alfred Kahn testimony to Aviation Subcommittee of the House Committee on Public Works and Transportation, 6 March 1978.

2. Carter (1982), p. 69.

3. Jimmy Carter, *'Why Not the Best?'* (New York, 1976), pp. 173-4.

4. Carter Lib., Staff Offices, Domestic Policy Staff, Eizenstat box 148, folder: Aviation, Airline Regulatory Reform 2, Lazarus to Eizenstat, 21 March 1977; ibid., folder: Aviation - General Issues, Eizenstat and Schuman for Frank Moore, Congressional Liaison, 3 Nov. 1977; Hargrove (1988).

5. Lowenfeld (1975), p. 26.

6. Boyd Interview.

7. Carter Lib., Staff Offices, Domestic Policy Staff, Eizenstat box 148, folder: Aviation Airline Regulatory Reform, Message to Congress 4 March 1977, attached to Eizenstat to Carter, 22 Feb. 1977.

8. Ibid.

9. Ibid., WHCF, Subject File, box CA-1, folder: CA 1/20/77-6/30/77, Kennedy and Cannon to Carter, 22 Feb. 1977.

10. Ibid., Staff Offices, Domestic Policy Staff, Eizenstat box 148, folder: Aviation - Airline Regulatory Reform 1, Schuman to Eizenstat; ibid., WHCF, Subject File, box CA-3, Schuman and Eizenstat to Carter, 11 May 1978.

11. Ibid., Staff Offices, Domestic Policy Staff, Eizenstat, box 148, folder: Aviation - General Issues, Eizenstat and Schuman for Frank Moore, 3 Nov. 1977; PL 95-163, 9 Nov. 1977, 91 Stat. 1284, Air Cargo Reform Act.

12. *New York Times*, 28 Feb. 1977, 'Making the Friendly Skies More Friendly'; Davies (1982), 'Essay on Deregulation', pp. 675-8.

13. Kahn, *Deregulation*, in Noll and Owen (1983); Lowenfeld (1975).

14. Kahn, *Deregulation* in Noll and Owen (1983); *Congressional Digest*, June-July 1978, 'Should Congress Enact Pending Legislation to Deregulate the US Airline Industry', pp. 172-189.

15. This judgement refers to Kahn's actions in the domestic sphere. As will become apparent later, in the international sphere he had to be nudged by Carter to adopt similar pricing policies.

16. For much of the detail of CAB policy and the SCO, I have drawn liberally from, and am much indebted to, the work of: Jonsson (1987), pp. 127-51 and (1978); Lowenfeld (1975); Haanappel, (1984), ch. 2 and pp. 157-67.

17. Carter Lib., WHCF, Subject File, box CA-3, Schuman and Eizenstat to Carter, 11 May 1978.

18. Ibid., memo., 7 March 1978, by Frank Moore re meeting with Anderson; ibid., folder: CA-2 10/1/77-1/20/81, Free to Eizenstat, 8 March 1978 and Anderson to Eizenstat, 13 April 1978.

19. *Congressional Digest*, June - July 1978, 186, Alfred Kahn testimony to Aviation subcommittee of the House Committee on Public Works and Transportation, 6 March 1978; PL 95-504, 24 Oct. 1978, 92 Stat. 1705, Airline Deregulation Act.

20. CAB order 78-6-78, 12 June 1978.

21. Jonsson (1987), and contemporary articles in *Flight*.

22. Carter Lib., WHCF, Subject File, box CA-1, folder: 10/1/77-8/31/78, Schuman to Eizenstat, 15 May 1978. After the May version was released for comment it was revised before the final policy statement was issued, 21 Aug. 1978.

23. Ibid.

24. *Flight*, 7 May 1977, p. 1237.

25. Jonsson (1987), pp. 127 ff.

26. Ibid., Haanappel (1984), pp. 61-63.

27. Jonsson (1987), p. 132.

28. State Department submission to the CAB, quoted from *Flight*, 1 Sept. 1979, p. 636; James R. Atwood, Deputy Assistant Secretary of State for Aviation and Maritime Affairs, Jan. 1978 - Aug. 1979, expressed

the view later that the SCO had been a tactical error: see review article by Atwood (1980), pp. 1071-72.

29. *Flight*, 3 Nov. 1979, p. 1465.

30. Jonsson (1987), p. 139.

31. Haanappel (1984), p. 160.

32. CAB order 80-4-113, 15 April 1980.

33. Carter Lib. WHCF, Subject File, box CO 65, folder: CO 167 1/1/80-1/20/81, Lazarus to Eizenstat, 16 Jan. 1980, subject: Marvin Cohen's Meeting with the President.

34. Haanappel (1984), p. 162.

35. Ibid., pp. 157-67 and appendix 4, 'US-ECAC Memorandum of Understanding on North Atlantic Air Tariffs'.

36. *Flight*, 14 Nov. 1987, p. 8; for background on the work of IATA see Chuang (1972).

37. Carter Lib., WHCF, Subject File, box CO-64, folder: CO 167 5/1/77-6/30/77, Driscoll to Carter, 22 July 1977.

38. Boyd Interview.

39. Carter Lib., Staff Offices, Domestic Policy Staff, Eizenstat, box 299, folder: US-UK Civil Aviation Negotiations 1, Eizenstat and Johnson to Carter, 22 July 1977; *Flight*, 11 March 1978, p. 683; Haanappel (1984), pp. 19-21.

40. CAB docket 31363, 16 Sept. 1977; Carter Lib., WHCF, Subject File, box CA-3, Carter to Kahn, 26 Sept. 1977; for concern about charters see for example, ibid., OMB memo. for Carter, 3 Jan. 1978, subject, KLM and Finnair economy class and budget fares, CAB docket 31915.

41. CAB docket 32183, 28 Feb. 1978; Sampson (1984), p. 145; Jonsson (1987), pp. 124-5; *Flight*, 11 March 1978, pp. 681-2.

42. Carter Lib., WHCF, Subject File, CA-3, folder: CA 2 10/1/77-1/20/81, Schuman to Eizenstat, 2 March 1978; ibid., box CO-64, folder: CO 167 1/1/78-5/31/78, Dodson, NSC, to Green, OMB, 2 March 1978.

43. Ibid., CO 167 6/1/78-12/31/78, Brock Adams to Governor Askew of Florida; ibid., box CA-3, Senator Stone to Secretary Vance, 27 Sept. 1979, concerning 13 Sept. meeting with Tampa delegation at the White House.

44. *Public Papers of the President of the United States: Jimmy Carter, Jan. - June 1978* (US Government Printing Office, Washington, 1979), p. 471, Carter to Kahn, 6 March 1978; *Flight*, 18 March 1978, p. 743.

45. Haanappel (1984), pp. 126-37; Sampson (1984), p. 145; Jonsson (1987), pp. 124-5; *Flight*, 11 March 1978, p. 683.

46. Ibid.

47. Carter Lib., WHCF, Subject File CA-3, folder: CA 2 10/1/77-1/20/81, Schuman to Eizenstat, 2 March 1978; Flight, 1 April 1978, 904.

48. *Papers of the President: Carter Jan. - June 1978*, p. 525, 'Air Services Between the United States and the United Kingdom: Statement by the President, 17 March 1978'; *Air Services Agreement Between the Government of the United States of America and the Government of the United Kingdom and Northern Ireland: including amendments thru 1980* (US Department of Transportation, Washington, 1981), Shovelton to Atwood and his reply, 17 March 1978, Letters re North Atlantic Fares. Carter Lib., WHCF, Subject File, box CO-64, folder: CO 167 1/1/78-5/31/78, Schuman to Eizenstat, 13 March 1978.

49. Ibid., box CA-1, folder: 10/1/77-8/31/78, Eizenstat and Schuman to Carter, 29 April 1978; *Air Services Agreement* (US DOT, 1981), Exchange of Notes to Confirm the Amendment of the Air Services Agreement, Ambassador Jay to Secretary of State Vance, and Katz (on behalf of Vance) to Jay, 25 April 1978: see article 14 and annex 4.

50. *Flight*, 1 April 1978, p. 904; Haanappel (1984), ch. 3.

51. Carter Lib., Staff Offices, Domestic Policy Staff, Eizenstat box 148, folder: Aviation - General Issues, Schuman to Eizenstat, 18 Oct. 1977.

52. Ibid., WHCF, Subject File, box CA-1, folder: 9/1/78-12/31/78, 'US Policy for the Conduct of International Air Transportation Negotiations', and 'Fact Sheet', 21 Aug. 1978.

53. Ibid., folder 10/1/77-8/31/78, Schuman and Bario to Rafshoon, 15 Aug. 1978; ibid., box CA-3, Schuman to Eizenstat, 14 July 1978; March 1978 to Nov. 1982, the USA re-negotiated 23 of its bilaterals to more liberal form, the first of which was with the Netherlands: see, Haanappel (1984), appendix 3.

54. PL 96-192, 15 Feb. 1980, 94 Stat. 35, 'International Air Transportation Competition Act of 1979'.

55. Ibid.

56. Ibid.

57. Carter Lib., WHCF, Subject File, box CA-2, folder: CA 1/1/80-1/20/81, Eizenstat to Carter, 15 Feb. 1980, 'Proposed Statement on signing the International Air Transportation Competition Act'.

58. Ibid., ibid., box CO-64, folder: CO 167, 1/1/78-5/31/78, Schuman and Eizenstat to Carter, subject: Senator Kennedy's letter on International Aviation, 29 April 1978; ibid., 1/1/79-6/30/79, Tip O'Neil to Carter, 20 March 1979.

59. Ibid., folder: CO 167, 6/1/78-5/31/78, Kennedy to Carter, 18 May 1978, congratulating him on his 16 May letter to Callaghan; ibid., Lipshutz and Eizenstat to Carter, 31 May 1978.

60. CAB docket 25908, approved by Carter 9 June 1978; Carter Lib., WHCF, Subject File, box CO-64, folder: CO 167 6/1/78-12/31/78, Eizenstat and Lipshutz to Carter, 8 June 1978; *Flight*, 3 June 1978, p. 1676.

61. Baldwin (1985), pp. 176-80; *Flight*, 13 March 1991, p. 6.

62. Carter Lib., WHCF, Subject File, box CO-64, folder: CO 167 6/1/78-12/31/78, Lipshutz and Eizenstat to Carter, 14 June 1978.

63. Ibid.

64. Ibid., folder: 1/1/79-6/30/79, O'Neil to Carter, 20 March 1979.

65. Ibid., box CA-3, suggested reply to O'Neil drafted by the State Department, April 1979.

66. Ibid., Senator Stone to Vance, 27 Sept. 1979.

67. Ibid., box CO 64, folder: CO 167 7/1/79-11/30/79, Lazarus to Eizenstat, 13 Oct. 1979.

68. Ibid., ibid., Lazarus to Eizenstat, 23 Oct. and 5 Nov. 1979.

69. Ibid., Lazarus to Eizenstat, 23 Oct. 1979.

70. Ibid., box CA-2, folder: 1/1/79-12/31/79, Lazarus to Eizenstat, 21 Nov. 1979.

71. Ibid., box CA-4, folder: CA-5 1/1/80-1/20/81, Eizenstat to Moynihan with the latter's memo. of 10 Jan. 1980 attached.

72. Ibid., box CA-2, folder: 1/1/80-1/20/81, memo. 12 Jan. 1980, for Oval Office meeting with Cohen, 14 Jan. 1980.

73. Ibid., box CO 65, folder: CO 167 1/1/80-1/20/81, Lazarus to Eizenstat, 16 Jan. 1980.

74. Ibid., ibid., Lazarus to Eizenstat, 29 Jan. 1980.

75. *Air Services Agreement* (US DOT, 1981), Secretary of State Muskie to Ambassador Henderson and his reply, 4 Dec. 1980; Boyd Hight to C.W. Roberts, letters re new gateways and passenger charters, and his reply, 4 Dec. 1980; amendments to annex 1 and addition of annex 5.

76. Ibid., Roberts to Hight, 4 Dec. 1980.

77. Ebdon Interview.

78. *Air Services Agreement* (US DOT, 1981).

Chapter 8
Liberalisation in Britain and the European Community 1980-93

> *We hear a good deal about what the Europeans like to call "airline liberalization", we think the real result is likely to be more along the lines of "Fortress Europe", as the European carriers consolidate their already dominant positions and band together to limit participation by U.S. carriers.*
> (Robert Crandall, Chairman, AA)[1]

The European airline industry could not be isolated from developments in the USA. US deregulation affected Europe in three ways: it created an example of what a market led airline industry could achieve; it resulted in US diplomatic pressures for a more liberal international airline system; and it released market dynamics to which European airlines would eventually have to respond. The effect of this threefold impact from the USA took time to develop. As it did, it interacted with growing indigenous movements for reform within Britain and the EC. By the 1990s, how the EC should respond to the challenges from the USA had become important not only for the development of the foreign operations of EC and US airlines, but also for the development of a common airline market in the Community with fair and equal opportunities to compete for all airlines of the Member States.

The UK and Holland were the most receptive to the idea of liberalisation. Both had developed their main international airports as gateways to and from Europe and they wanted better access to foreign passenger markets: they also had the best developed national reform programmes in the early 1980s. Indeed, Britain began to venture down a more competitive road in the early 1970s and, in any case, its domestic airline market has always been a relatively open one, with the exception of operations from Heathrow where congestion problems have required regulatory action. In 1972 the newly created CAA started to function in the licensing field and was a force for liberalisation during the life of the Conservative Government of Edward Heath. Even during the period of retrenchment under Labour, 1974-79, it fought to preserve what it could.[2] In the domestic sphere it was largely successful: in the international arena results were more equivocal. In particular, as we have seen, the need felt by Secretary of State for Trade and Industry, Edmund Dell, to readjust the Bermuda Agreement in order to get a larger market share for Britain produced a more regulatory bilateral with the USA. However, once Thatcher came to power in 1979, there was some relaxation of the Bermuda regulations and renewed impetus generally towards a freer market. The movement was co-ordinated on several fronts. Firstly, Thatcher moved to institutionalise a more competitive overall policy for British airlines. Secondly, the operation of the domestic airlines was liberalised. Thirdly, BA was to be privatised and in the wake of that there was to be a more liberal dispensation for Britain's foreign airline operations, although the need to nurture the fortunes of BA in order to ensure its success as a private company slowed the speed and restricted the extent to which this liberalisation could be pursued. At least, this was so until the 1990s when BA became a well established success. And finally, Britain began to push for liberalisation within the EC.

Thatcher wrought the most radical changes in British politics since the Attlee Administration. The emphases on market forces, self-reliance, and individual enterprise were ubiquitous. Civil aviation was to be no exception, though prudence modified ideological commitment, so far as many Americans were concerned too much so. Nevertheless, the civil aviation bill introduced immediately by the Thatcher administration indicated the way things were to go. It gave more power to the CAA, but required that the interests of users should be given equal weight to those of operators in deciding new route licenses. That may seem a trivial change, but consumer interests and their play in the marketplace were central to the dogma of the new economics.[3]

Legislative change was complemented by executive action. In 1980 John Nott, Minister for Trade, acted on his appeals authority and overruled the CAA's licensing decision for Hong Kong. The CAA had allowed BA and B.Cal. to operate the route from London to Hong Kong, but had turned down applications from Cathay Pacific and Laker. Nott ruled that all four could operate if they wished to and that the market should decide what was commercially viable. The Chairman of the Conservative Aviation Committee thought that this was 'probably the first step towards a sort of deregulated international civil aviation regime.'[4] In fact other steps were rather delayed in coming because of the exigencies of BA's privatisation. Sir Michael Bishop of BM, while pleased by Nott's action, regarded it, in retrospect, as an isolated decision.[5] It undoubtedly helped to signpost the direction in which the Thatcher Administration wished to progress: the decision embodied multiple, not just dual designation and was highly competitive in spirit, but further steps along the liberalisation road in this sphere had to be taken cautiously for both political and economic reasons. The government felt that it had to nurture BA in the short-term to enable it to make the transition successfully from a protected nationalised industry to private enterprise. BA was important both for the British economy and because of all the other things that attached to the nation's flag carrier. It was also vital that privatisation worked because this was just part of a wider programme of privatisation and the political determination to carry that forward could not be undermined by a failure in any single case. The political capital that the Labour opposition would have made out of such an eventuality could have had dire results indeed for the fortunes of the Conservative Party.

Progress in the domestic sphere was easier, but not without problems. In 1982 Lord Cockfield, the Minister for Trade and Industry, reversed one of the few restrictive licensing decisions made by the CAA and allowed BM to mount a new service on the route from Heathrow to Glasgow. This was the start of a new phase of competition. However, the independent airlines had reservations because of what might happen once Thatcher's aim of privatising BA were realised. With its dominant position in the market, BA might eat up competitors. One of the most forceful to argue this case was Richard Venables on behalf of Air UK. These factors prompted the government to ask the CAA in late 1983 to make a comprehensive study of deregulation.[6]

Its report appeared the following July and was greeted with howls of protest from defenders of BA in the House of Commons. The main thrust of the proposals was to diminish the dominant position of BA and strengthen independents by redistributing what some estimated would amount to eight per cent of BA's routes. In the face of criticism in the House, Nicholas Ridley, the new Secretary of State for Trade and Industry, tried to defend the report, but over the following months he was, according to Bishop of BM, out-lobbied by BA's Chairman Lord King who had the ear of Margaret Thatcher and the support of Norman Tebbit and Nigel Lawson in the Cabinet.[7] When the Government's White Paper was published in October it approved further deregulation in the domestic sphere, namely regarding fares, but it was less adventurous in the international realm. In fact, it decided against the CAA's main recommendations. There were to be some limited route swaps between BA and B.Cal. and help for the latter to get double designation on some of BA's routes, but there was to be no enforced reduction of BA's route system: it should not be obliged to give up its position at Gatwick, or abandon its regional routes to Europe to allow the independents more scope. Instead, the market was to be gradually developed by the CAA allowing freedom for airlines to run whatever routes they wanted and at whatever price they chose, providing it was not predatory or an abuse of a monopoly position.[8] By 1991 Air UK Managing Director Andrew Gray believed that the licensing policy was too liberal and was damaging the interests of serious carriers like his own for the benefit of opportunist players, whose only aim was to set up a route and then sell it at a profit.[9] Clearly liberalisation had made progress, but it was not a simple affair. It was not enough to remove regulation to ensure competition. Dominant positions and distortions in the marketplace could lead to abuses of the free market at the expense of consumers and operators. Some thought that radical action, as had been proposed by the CAA, to reduce the dominance of the major players was necessary if true competition were to be achieved. And as time passed it was not just dominance over routes that worried the new would-be competitors, but also landing and take-off slots, frequent flyer programmes, CRSs and, in fact, all the characteristics that had gained new importance because of, or were developed in response to, deregulation in the USA. Such considerations were not lost on those who wished to see liberalisation in Europe.

Some saw the decision not to reduce BA's dominant position by government intervention as a setback for a freer airline market: others saw it as necessary to ensure a healthy industry in the long-term and one in which Britain would have a carrier capable of competing with its foreign counterparts. The disagreements were more about means than ends. The White Paper published by the Department of Transport in October 1984 certainly spelt out a competitive manifesto for the airlines. Its aims were:

> to maintain high standards of safety...to encourage a sound and competitive multi-airline industry... to promote competition in all markets... to ensure adequate safeguards against anti-competitive behaviour... [and] to put the ownership of British Airways into the hands of private investors ....[10]

Like successive American administrations, the Thatcher government had to acknowledge that, particularly in the international realm, there were circumstances that might prevent the implementation of competitive policies. On some routes demand was too low to support more than one British operator and in some cases the policies of foreign governments might place British airlines at a disadvantage if Britain pursued liberal policies and they did not.

> Governments have to be persuaded that they do a disservice to the traveller by insisting on highly protectionist regimes. The long term goal must be to liberalise services wherever possible - where foreign competition is fair and Britain's interests are not prejudiced.[11]

Throughout the period 1979-87 a controlling factor in the government's policy was its aim of privatising BA. That aim, while in harmony with the goal of a competitive airline industry, caused short-term protectionism. In 1979-80 BA made a net profit of £11 million, the following year it plunged to a loss of £145 million. Ten years later, in world economic circumstances which were far from ideal, it made £246 million profit and £95 million the following year.[12] Ensuring that BA could get to that position in 1989-90 and 1990-91 was not easy and took skilful government action and the inspired management of Lord King and Colin Marshall. The government could not privatise BA as it stood in 1980. No-one would have bought the shares and Thatcher's whole programme of privatisation could well have collapsed. Furthermore, even when the fortunes of the airline began to improve, there were two other problems which had to be handled carefully. The first was the call to reduce BA's size and redistribute its routes for the sake of a competitive multi-airline industry. That assault was repelled in the 1984 White Paper. The second problem was Freddie Laker.

One of the most disruptive elements in the airline industry in the early 1980s was Freddie Laker and his Skytrain - its life, demise and afterlife. Disruptive should not be interpreted to mean necessarily negative things. Skytrain did much to promote low fares and a more competitive attitude in general on the north Atlantic. Skytrain's demise, however, caused much friction between the USA and Britain and severe problems for the timetable of BA's privatisation.

In 1982 Laker fell victim to the very thing that he had pioneered: low fares and low profit margins. After going bankrupt, he brought a civil action under US antitrust laws in the USA against BA, Pan Am, TWA, McDonnell Douglas and others, alleging that they had colluded to set predatory prices and had conspired to destroy a rescue package put together by McDonnell Douglas and the Midland Bank with the aim of bringing about the downfall of his company. More or less at the same time, the US Department of Justice announced that it was to investigate allegations of illegal activity by BA and others under US antitrust laws. The nature of the damage to BA that could arise from this was the claim of extraterritorial competence for US antitrust laws. If BA were found guilty and extraterritorial competence were effected then the company would be liable to punitive damage claims, namely three times the amount of damage it was assessed to have caused its victim. With privatisation high on the agenda in London this was not a good scenario because it would scare off prospective investors even though BA was now in profit to the tune of £89 million.[13]

There followed a most extraordinary episode in Anglo-American civil aviation relations and one which created a lot of ill-feeling on both sides. The British resented the American assertion that US antitrust laws could be applied extraterritorially, especially when the two parties, BA and Laker Airways, were both British companies. In the legal wrangles that followed however, the British case had difficulty in standing up in court and the government had to invoke the 1980 Protection of Trading Interests Act in 1983 in order to try to keep BA's company documents and its representatives out of American courts.

Despite these moves, the situation for BA continued to deteriorate. By 1984 Thatcher was furious and her state of mind was further aggravated by news that the US Justice Department had reached the point where it was about to charge BA with price fixing and other misdemeanours. It was a politically sensitive time in the USA because it was a presidential election year and so Thatcher kept her powder dry until after the November re-election of her friend Ronald Reagan. But then the sparks flew with a vengeance and officials in Washington began to feel the heat. As Campbell-Smith, in his history of BA's privatisation records: 'a remarkable thing happened. President Reagan gave in. There were, he said, more important fish to fry. Give the lady what she wants.'[14]

That solved one problem: the Justice Department dropped its case, but others remained. The civil suit was not resolved until August 1985, and then again only with some help from Reagan. In the end, the parties settled out of court and it cost BA £33 million. The British continued to try to get the Americans to withdraw their claim that US antitrust laws could be used extraterritorially against British companies, but they had no success.[15] Still, the main problem had been resolved and BA's privatisation could now go ahead. In 1987 it was sold by the government to private investors. A major and necessary step was thus taken to make the liberalisation of the British civil airline industry a reality. More nurturing of BA followed, but it would not last for ever. The Thatcher rhetoric about free enterprise, competition and self-reliance was not empty and eventually BA came to realise that.

Trying to nurture a competitive multi-airline industry in Britain was difficult because of the small domestic base. This disadvantage was exacerbated with the appearance of economies of scale realised by the US deregulation experience and then compounded by the success of BA, its aggressive management and desire to grow bigger in order to be able to compete on an equal basis with the US mega carriers. BM chipped away at BA's dominant position in the 1980s and never lacked the temerity to confront the market leader head on. By the early eighties BM was already the second largest operator at HR in terms of aircraft movements, but because of the TDRs it was prohibited from mounting international operations from what was now its main base. At least that was what seemed to be the case. But then BM claimed that it had grandfathered rights to operate international routes from HR on the basis that it had run a service from HR to Strasburg in the early 1970s before the restrictions on operations from HR were introduced. That argument proved persuasive and the CAA began to grant European routes to BM beginning with Amsterdam. BM flew their first scheduled flight to that destination on 29 June 1986.[16]

Such developments might seem rather insignificant, but both the willingness of British independents to compete with BA and grasp routes into Europe were to prove beneficial in the late 1980s for the new airline reform movement. After fare liberalisation in the EC, it was on routes where independents mounted competition to the two national flag carriers that saw substantial fare reductions.[17] Their success also undoubtedly encouraged Richard Branson who, with his airline Virgin Atlantic, managed to emulate the success of BM and started operations from HR to the USA and elsewhere after the 1991 HR succession rights affair, which will be considered in detail later. However, this is to anticipate the story and rather misleadingly so in some ways because the most important development in the aftermath of BA's privatisation was not the thriving of British airlines in competition with BA, but BA's taking over of B.Cal. in 1988.

The absorption of B.Cal. by BA caused some soul searching among the proponents of a freer airline market. Many felt that a competitive market could only be sustained if Britain had a multi-airline industry with at least two large strong airlines. This had been the accepted wisdom ever since the Edwards Report of 1969. If the effect of liberalisation were simply to pave the way for

BA to become even more dominant in British civil aviation then, shortly, there would be no effective British airlines to compete with it and the overall policy of nurturing competition would fail. That argument overlooked the burgeoning of globalisation in the industry and the increase in competition from foreign airlines. It also tended to discount the determination of admittedly small, but, nevertheless, able operators that remained after the demise of B.Cal. such as BM, Air UK and Virgin Atlantic. The CAA made its determination clear to uphold the importance of competition in Britain's multi-airline policy in a major review published in 1988. It was largely the work of Raymond Colegate, CAA Economic Policy Chief, and reasserted the importance of competition and made it clear that the independents would be given preferential treatment over BA if it were necessary to nurture a more competitive industry. It also declared that the CAA would keep a close watch on fares and intervene if it were deemed to be in the consumer interest to do so, which was a thinly veiled warning to BA not to abuse its dominant position and raise fares to unreasonable levels.[18] By the end of 1988 BA was operating about 90 per cent of Britain's overseas routes and an even higher percentage of long-haul routes. The only British competitor on long-haul routes was Virgin Atlantic and at that time Branson only had 5 Boeing 747s.

Liberalising domestic UK routes, trying to nurture a multi-airline industry and privatising BA were all major components of government and industry commitment to deregulation.[19] But, in addition, the British Government also began to press for liberalisation of the EC's airline industry. The ultimate goal of a single European airline market would have a number of benefits. It would provide a larger domestic base for British airlines and provide opportunities for them to grow. It would thus help British independents and encourage competition from European airlines, both of which would help to offset the dominance of BA in Britain's domestic and international route system. It would also provide BA with a larger base to negotiate from and develop its global operating plans.

In the 1984 White Paper the Government stated that: 'The European Community offers the best chance for further liberalisation.'[20] A start had already been made by striking a liberal deal with Holland that same year and others with Luxemburg, Belgium and Eire were to follow, but these moves, while beneficial in themselves, were also tactics to try to get EC-wide reform. Britain had three reasons for wanting a liberal single airline market in the EC. The first was doctrinal: the dislike by the Thatcher acolytes of industrial regulation. The second reason was that Britain, unlike other European countries, had a good string of independents - BM, Dan Air, Air UK, Air Europe, Virgin Atlantic etc.. In a freer market it was expected that these airlines, nevermind BA, would do well. And thirdly, there was an international perspective created by deregulation in the USA.

Rather ironically, given Britain's reputation as an awkward partner in the EC, in the airline industry where progress towards a single market has been so very difficult to achieve, it has been the main advocate of reform. Although progress has been painfully slow, the importance of transport to the EC is undeniable: it generates over seven per cent of its GDP and has broad economic, social and political benefits. For the Community, a common transport policy (CTP) lies at the heart of its vision. That is amply shown by its prominence in the Treaty of Rome, articles 3 and 74-84. From that basis and from an ever growing number of policy documents and decisions by both the European Court of Justice and the Council a pattern of aims has emerged since the Commission published its first memorandum on a CTP in 1961 and a programme of action in 1962.[21]

An integrated transport system would be more cost effective and it would also foster integration by facilitating the mobility of labour and by helping to develop a greater sense of unity. It would help to equalise opportunities between the industrial and commercial heartland and the outlying regions. And, finally, it would create a level playing field for transport competition throughout the EC. Yet, despite all these potential benefits, a CTP has been exceedingly difficult to achieve.

Problems have ranged across a broad spectrum from the technical to the nakedly political. In the beginning, the Treaty of Rome and the Commission made some acknowledgement of these difficulties by treating air and sea transport differently from the rest. Inland transport came immediately under the authority of article 84 and competition rules were applied in that sector in 1968, but development was plagued with difficulties. It was not easy to harmonise, nevermind integrate, the national transport systems of the Community. National railways naturally stopped at state boundaries and thus had difficulties in contributing to an integrated system. Partly in an effort to compensate for the problems of the rail network, liberalisation proposals were put forward to encourage road haulage. But, several countries immediately became concerned about the negative impact such action would have on their heavily funded railways. Problems like these stymied the growth of a CTP in the land, rail and inland waterway sectors: for air and sea transport matters were even worse. Regarding the latter two, article 84 simply stated that: 'The Council may, acting unanimously, decide whether, to what extent and by what procedure appropriate provisions may be laid down for sea and air transport.' Until 1974, because of vagueness in the Treaty of Rome and because of differences between the Member States and the Commission, these categories of transport were considered to fall outside the scope of the Treaty.[22]

In the air the EC faces four problems. Like states, it has to deal with the highly politicised airline system. Secondly, there are problems particular to both Europe and the EC with reforming existing regulations within which airlines operate. Thirdly, there are patterns of practice in the industry which could distort the market and undermine its competitiveness even after a reform of the formal framework. And finally, the EC has to meet challenges from abroad and seek some way of handling them on a Community basis. This categorisation is a simplification: one cannot actually draw lines so clearly between one problem area and another. But, as the story unfolds, the problems and the different ways that they have been dealt with should become clear. However, the general nature of the industry and the way that it operated from 1946 to 1987 requires preliminary explanation before focusing on EC-wide reform.

Until the mid 1980s, almost without exception, all European scheduled air routes were strictly regulated. Foreign routes were limited to capital cities. Capacity was restricted and often equally divided between national carriers operating under a near universal single designation regime (the only exception was out of Heathrow and Gatwick to a limited number of destinations). Revenue pooling, whereby both national carriers on a route were guaranteed returns proportional to the capacity that they offered, was commonplace. Rates were kept high by both airline collusion through IATA and the prevention of newcomers entering the marketplace through national licensing policies. Competition was virtually non-existent except from charter flights and alternative forms of high speed travel. All major operators on European routes were state owned and frequently subsidised: SAS and KLM came the closest to private enterprise with 50 per cent and 51 per cent government ownership respectively. In short, there was a cartel-type operation that was not responsive to public needs.[23] Developments both within and without Europe in the late 1970s and early 1980s, however, began to prompt change and pose challenges.

The most radical change came as a direct result of US deregulation, which eventually impacted on the character of the entire world airline system, and thus necessarily the EC and British airline industries. The reason for this was that deregulation brought into being new dynamics that were applicable to any airline. Previously, economies of scale were not thought to be applicable to the airlines, but now such shibboleths had to be abandoned. With economies of scale came the need for bigger airlines and eventually the globalisation of their operations. In order to see how these new dynamics developed it would be as well to sketch out the main contours of the post-1978 developments in the USA before proceeding further with the situation in Europe.]

[Kahn and the 1978 Reform Act let competition loose among US airlines by allowing free entry and exit to and from the marketplace, by abandoning controls over fares and by encouraging lower labour costs. A volatile period ensued, but gradually there was consolidation with mega carriers emerging to operate a new hub and spoke route configuration, which enabled airlines to enjoy economies of scale for the first time.[24]

Hub and spoke is based on as large a throughput of traffic as possible at one or a number of interconnected hubs. The results of this have been to increase efficiency in the use of equipment, raise load factors, and help airlines to capture passengers for entire journeys as they are fed into the hub on one spoke and then taken out by another. CRSs are vital for this new market, facilitating the dovetailing of arrival and departure services for vast numbers of passengers.

As the benefits of economies of scale sank home airlines began to develop as many hubs as they could and add as many spokes to them as possible. Furthermore, the domestic airlines which dominated the huge US market (approximately 40 per cent of the free world airline market), AA, UA and Delta, gradually realised two things. Firstly, that they should not be constrained by the limits of the domestic market because a spoke is a spoke, whether it goes to a US or a foreign destination: the market makes no distinctions of nationality. Secondly, they realised that they had advantages over TWA and Pan Am because, unlike the traditional flag carriers, they had domestic hub and spoke systems with which to draw passengers from the domestic market. Within a dozen years the three leading domestic carriers had also become the leading foreign carriers: while TWA and Pan Am fell into serious decline, the latter expiring in 1991.[25]]

[One may ask: What has all this to do with British policy and the creation of a single EC airline market? The answer is a great deal. First of all, the Americans stepped up their demands for liberal ASAs in order to give their carriers the opportunities of global economies of scale and an international hub and spoke system. Operating as they did from their enormous cabotage base, they had advantages over foreign airlines, which they could offer to trade as inducements to foreign governments to enter liberal agreements. The questions then arose as to what implications such agreements might have for the EC and whether or not it might be better for the Commission, rather than the individual states, to negotiate with the USA.]

Secondly, there was the problem of how European airlines were to respond to the globalisation process emanating from the USA. BA, for example, felt increasingly disadvantaged in the transatlantic market because of the huge pool of passengers in the USA located away from international gateways. While its American competitors could draw these passengers into their hubs for onward flights across the Atlantic BA was not allowed to. In early 1993 Colin Marshall, the head of BA, stated that four out of five US transatlantic passengers, who started their journey behind an international gateway, flew across the Atlantic in a US carrier. He alleged: 'That choice cannot be the result of fair competition.'[26] BA was unable to redress this situation satisfactorily because of cabotage and US ownership laws which prevented it from buying a US feeder airline (the BA/US Air deal in 1993 changed this somewhat). Prior to the emergence of hub and spoke, CRSs and mega carriers, BA did not suffer any great competitive disadvantage, but now it did. One of the imperatives of the new dispensation was large size otherwise the benefits of economies of scale would not be realised. But BA, unlike its US counterparts, had to rely on international routes to gain market volume. Its own domestic market was too small to provide it. Furthermore, BA made approximately 60-80 per cent of its profits between 1989-91 operating to the Americas, and a large proportion of that was earned on the north Atlantic. In the light of all this, BA and the British Government perceived the need to gain access to the US domestic market in order to have a more even chance of competing with US carriers, and to enlarge its market share and the overall volume of its operations. It was not just a more level, but a larger playing field that BA needed. That need dictated two things: one, that Europe should be liberalised to enable BA to expand its operations there; and two, that Europe, once formed into a single airline market, should then negotiate with the USA and it would do so on even terms for the first time. In May 1991 Lord King, then Chairman of BA, said 'We need the Community to begin to make use of its negotiating strength against the strong countries outside: ... Only then can open skies be an economic and commercial reality.'[27] Access to European and US cabotage could be exchanged enlarging the market potential for both sides. This was crucial for European airlines if they were to meet the globalisation challenge being posed by their US counterparts. Here we have powerful dynamics bearing on the drive for a single European airline market.

Thirdly, the US experience (and Britain's, though to a lesser extent) provided an example of benefits that could be got from deregulation, which further undermined support for the existing regime in Europe, but it also revealed some of the drawbacks that came with the type of full-blown deregulation that the USA had embraced. This provided food for thought about how far and how fast Europe should liberalise its market.

Faint stirrings of liberalisation began in the early 1970s. A judgement by the European Court declared that in principle the provisions of the Community's competition laws, articles 85 and 86, did apply to aviation. The opening paragraphs of those articles respectively prohibited collusion that would distort the market and the abuse of dominant positions. However, it was one thing to declare that airlines should be subject to competition laws, it was another matter to implement this. In fact means of implementation were inadequate and attempts by the Commission to develop airline policy were largely unsuccessful and a decade slipped by without significant progress being made.[28]

By 1984 things had acquired a rather different outlook. There were now calls from within the industry, from some of the Member States, most notably Britain and Holland, and from consumers for liberalisation and this was accompanied by growing assertiveness within the Commission which wanted reform. In 1984 it came forward with a second memorandum on airline policy for the Council: the first had been ineffective. While this was quite radical and far reaching, it rejected the idea of American style deregulation for Europe: 'There is scope for introducing more flexibility and competition into the existing system without destroying it or losing the benefits it has brought about.'[29] The Commission did not want to pre-empt the possibility of subsidising community routes more extensively than was the case in the USA, nor did it want carriers with dominant positions to prevent real competition which would benefit the consumer.

The memorandum proposed that pooling agreements, capacity sharing, price fixing and subsidies should gradually be phased out and that during the transitional period that there should be block exemptions from the Community's competition laws. The proposals, however, were premature. There was strong opposition from trade unions and most national carriers. The Parliament opposed the memorandum on the grounds that if the proposals were accepted then, despite the Commission's disavowals, US style deregulation would be the result. Consequently, yet again, recommendations of the Commission were unsuccessful.[30]

Despite this setback there were both political and legal moves underway that were to make it more difficult to resist regulatory reform. On the political front there had been a series of European summits calling for completion of the Single Market, and in 1985 that resulted in a White Paper known as the Cockfield Report which identified what needed to be done. In 1986 the Community passed the Single European Act (SEA) which amended the Treaty of Rome and set 1993 as the deadline for the creation of the Single Market. Article 8a clearly had implications for the airlines: 'The internal market shall comprise an area without internal frontiers in which the free movement of goods, persons, services and capital is ensured in accordance with the provisions of this treaty.' To help along the process specifically in sea and air transport article 84(2) was amended from a requirement of unanimity to read: 'The Council may, acting by a qualified majority, decide whether, to what extent and by what procedure appropriate provisions may be laid down for sea and air transport.' Furthermore, article 84 was supplemented by the application to it of article 75(1) and (3) which called for common rules for international operations within the EC, so long as they did not damage an area's economy or employment.[31] In addition to these specific measures that had direct bearing on the fortunes of the airline industry, the symbolic importance of the passage of the SEA cannot be underestimated. It reinvigorated the European movement and helped to carry forward integration in general and thus airline reform in particular.

At the same time that the SEA came into being there were two important legal developments. In 1983 the Parliament took the Council to the Court of Justice under the auspices of article 175 of the Treaty of Rome alleging that it had failed in its duty by not creating a CTP. In 1985 the Court ruled in Parliament's favour, but it also judged that the failure was not such as to warrant further proceedings. A more unequivocal ruling in favour of the need for liberalisation came with the 1986 Nouvelles Frontieres Case, which opened up a means for the Commission to implement the competition rules.[32] The Commission could now exert pressure for reform. In 1986, with new authority from the SEA and the support of the British Presidency of the Council, the Commission brought forward a liberalisation package.

In fact the Commission moved on two fronts: on the first it began proceedings against airlines under the competition laws and on the other it offered its liberalisation programme. Member States were confronted with two alternatives. Either they could accept the package, which offered a controlled move towards liberalisation and block exemption from the competition laws as an inducement to adopt this route forward, or else the Commission would force liberalisation upon the airlines through action in the Court. In December 1987, the Council opted for adoption of the liberalisation package.

It was fairly modest in its aims and its achievements by October 1989 fell short of what measured judgement might have expected. The new regulations sought to reduce capacity restrictions to 40/60 splits over a three year period and tried to open up the market by allowing multiple designations, more regional routes and more fifth freedom rights: they also created zones of fare flexibility. After twenty months the results of the first package were rather mixed. The effects on capacity regulation and fares were disappointing. The zonal fare schemes were not much used and old cartel habits died hard. It was only where new independent operators entered the field through multiple designation that the provisions for discounts on economy fares by 15 per cent were much used. The one definite success story was the encouragement of regional routes which resulted in 127 new ones opening.[33]

Within the package there was also a commitment to further reform in three years time. Momentum was now growing. In July 1989 Sir Leon Brittan, the Competition Commissioner, unveiled a second package of proposals, which was accepted by the Council in November 1990. The scope of fare discounting within zones was expanded. Market access was enhanced by allowing third, fourth and fifth freedom rights between all airports including major hubs which had previously been exempt. However, there were restrictions on fifths: they could only exploit the market to a maximum of 50 per cent of the route's seasonal capacity. There was a universal right to move from 50/50 to 60/40 capacity divisions with an additional right for either operator to add 7.5 per cent to its previous year's level. Multiple designation was made easier with the passenger threshold, at which another service could enter the market, being lowered. But there were still a number of protectionist measures. Capacity liberalisation could be delayed on routes for two years in order to allow a carrier to reorganise and there were provisions for protecting non-profitable routes because of community needs. Nevertheless, this package was a significant move towards a more liberal and competitive internal airline market. The restrictive things that now remained, apart from cabotage and government financial support for state owned airlines, were largely to do with how the new rules would be applied in practice.[34] Other restrictions were more to do with market structure and infrastructure than political regulation by the nation states, though one should add that often the distinctions are hard to make. Misuse of CRSs gave airlines discriminatory preference over their rivals, and labour relations, different licensing rules and grandfather rights, in particular the dominance at major airports of take-off and landing slots by the national carriers, posed serious obstacles to new entrants. In terms of infrastructure, a shortage of airport capacity and inadequate air traffic control were the main problems.[35] These were the things that now challenged the effectiveness of a common airline market from within. From without, the challenge came largely in the shape of the USA's desire for open skies agreements.

The USA supported the EC from its very beginnings, but as its own economy developed problems it became less willing to tolerate EC trade discrimination. By the time of the IATA Marrakesh Conference in 1989, Americans were 'paranoid' about the prospect of 'Fortress Europe' reducing commercial opportunities for their airlines.[36] Their ideal route description was: 'From the US via intermediate points to country "x" and beyond. Period. End of story.' In other words, with no restrictions on services that an airline wants to offer.[37] In fact this was not entirely accurate. The USA had a policy of restricting the number of gateways available in the USA to foreign operators and often traded gateways for liberal capacity and fare provisions in ASAs. Nevertheless, it was a much more liberal policy than prevailed in Europe even with the acceptance of the two EC packages of reform. Throughout the 1980s the USA strove to liberalise its ASAs with European countries. The main problem in Europe was Bermuda 2, for, as a senior US official explained:

> Every city pair market is restricted in terms of entry. Every city pair market is restricted in terms of capacity. Every city pair market is restricted in terms of the fares the airlines may charge the pasengers. There is no aspect of the market that is not being regulated pursuant to UK insistance.[38]

Even so, despite a variety of problems that arose in US-UK civil aviation relations in the 1980s, some progress was made in modifying Bermuda 2 and it is to those developments that attention must now be given. However, increasingly as the 1980s progressed, Anglo-American negotiations must be seen less and less as a purely bilateral affair. They also had a bearing on developments in the EC and, indeed, on the whole airline globalisation process that was gathering pace. By the end of the decade it was difficult to separate Anglo-American, EC and global airline policies and developments. In looking at issues that arose initially between Britain and the USA a perspective on the EC and, though to a lesser extent, on the global airline industry also emerges.

Notes and References

1. Remarks by Robert L. Crandall, President and Chairman AA, Duke University, North Carolina, 28 March 1991, text by courtesy of AA.
2. Colegate Interview; Baldwin (1985); Sampson (1984).

3. Civil Aviation Bill 1979/80, House of Commons Bill 68, 31/10/79 and Civil Aviation Amendment Bill 1981/82, House of Commons Bill 1, 5/11/81.

4. Colvin Interview.

5. Interview with Sir Michael Bishop, Chairman BM, 15 March 1991, conducted by the author.

6. Colegate Interview; Gunston (1988), p. 83; Bishop Interview.

7. Ibid.; *Hansard*, vol. 65, 1983-84, cols. 3-6, 30 July 1983; Campbell-Smith (1986), pp. 161 and 168.

8. Cmd. 9366, Oct. 1984, 'Airline Competition Policy'.

9. Interview with Andrew Gray, Managing Director of Air UK, 26 March 1991, conducted by the author.

10. Cmd. 9366, 1984.

11. Ibid.

12. BA Report and Accounts, 1979/80, 1980/81, 1989/90 and 1990/91.

13. Ibid. 1982/83.

14. Campbell-Smith (1986), p. 196; *Flight*, 22 March 1986, see article on postponement of BA privatisation; Sampson (1984), also covers the Laker saga; additional information came from Colegate Interview and interview with senior Foreign Office official, 8 Dec. 1989, conducted by the author.

15. Ibid.; and Campbell-Smith (1986), pp. 220 ff.

16. Colegate Interview; Gunston (1988), p. 95.

17. 'Report on the first year (1988) of implementation of the aviation policy approved in December 1987', COM(89)476, 2 Oct. 1989, 5, 12.

18. *Flight*, 6 Feb. 1988, p. 14, 'UK CAA Defined Competition Policy'.

19. Forsyth (1985); Campbell-Smith (1986).

20. Cmd. 9366, 1984.

21. 'Programme for the Implementation of the Common Transport Policy', COM(62)88, 1962; 'The European Community's Transport Policy', Periodical 3/1984, European Documentation, EC 1984; 'The Community and Transport Policy', file 10/85, DG for Information, EC, 1985; for

background see Nicholl and Salmon (1990); Swann (1992 A), (1993) and (1992 B), in particular K. Button's 'The Liberalisation of Transport Services'; McGowan and Trengove (1986).

22. For problems with CTP see Erdmenger (1983), pp. 31-37; Treaty of Rome, 25 March 1957; European Court of Justice, Law Case 167/73: it declared that provisions of the Treaty of Rome applied to civil aviation. Interview with Commission official, Brussels, 22 May 1991, conducted by the author.

23. Gialloreto (1988); Pryke, (1987); Shaw (1985); Raben in Wassenberg and Van Fenema (1981); Doganis (1985).

24. Kahn in Noll and Owen (1983).

25. Murphy Interview.

26. *Flight*, 13 Jan. 1993, p. 8.

27. 'Lord King's remarks to the Royal Aeronautical Society', 16 May 1991, text courtesy of BA; King Interview; 'British Airways Plc. Report and Accounts 1990-91', Americas' sector operating surplus was £158m and company total pre-tax profit was £130m.

28. European Court of Justice Law Case 167/73, 1974; Interview with Commission official, 22 May 1991, conducted by the author; Swann (1983).

29. McGowan (1986), pp. 83-90; 'Contributions of the EC to the development of air transport services [memo. 1]', EC Bulletin, Supplement 5/79; 'Progress Towards the Development of a Community Air Transport Policy [memo. 2]', EC COM(84)72.

30. McGowan (1986), pp. 83-90.

31. 'Single European Act', EC Bulletin, Supplement 2/86.

32. Sochor (1991), ch. 11; McGowan (1986), pp. 83-90; April 1989, the Court promoted EC airline policy further in the Ahmed Saeed Case by extending the competition laws to operations between Member and non-member states.

33. Council regs. 3975/87 and 3976/87, 14 Dec. 1987; 'Report on the first year (1988) of implementation of the aviation policy approved in December 1987, COM(89)476, 2 Oct. 1989.

34. Council regs. 2342/90, 2343/90, 2344/90, 24 July 1990 effective

1/11/90; lucid explanation of package 2 is to be found in F. Sorensen's presentation, 'European Airline Traffic After 1993', 8 April 1991, text courtesy of Sorensen; *The Independent*, 33 July 1989, David Black, 'Sharing the Pie in the Sky'.

35. A summary of problems afflicting European ATC may be found in *Flight*, 18 March 1992, p. 10, and 10 Feb. 1993, pp. 28-9: ECAC a Europe-wide inter governmental organisation set up in 1954 has played an important role in this sphere.

36. Colvin Interview.

37. Wisgerhof Interview.

38. Shane Interview.

Chapter 9
The Challenges of Liberalisation and Globalisation

> *World War Three will be started by civil aviation bureaucrats.*[1]

In the 1980s and early 1990s the deregulation movement in the USA and liberalisation in Europe had greater and greater effects on the character of the airline industry and the negotiation of bilateral ASAs. The attraction of economies of scale led the airlines to strategies that would globalise their operations.[2] Market penetration through liberal ASAs, or through alliances, mergers or take-overs, became commonplace and the need for information about these markets and how airlines operated in them also became more vital to the corporate decision makers. In Europe there was also an additional factor: the development of the single airline market and the implications that that had both for the airline strategies of Members, who each had an obligation to ensure that any agreement should be compatible with EC policy, and for non-members, who had to negotiate with them. With this development came the beginnings of something that was intended to supersede the practice of purely national bilateral agreements.

Another characteristic of the period was a new bout of financial instability in the airline industry. This was largely to do with an international economic recession, but conditions were exacerbated in the USA by the cut-throat competition of the deregulated market and because of Chapter 11 bankruptcy protection, which allowed companies to continue to trade under artificial market

199

conditions. In this recession in the airline market, a lot of airlines disappeared altogether, including great names such as Pan Am and Eastern, while others went technically bankrupt, but continued to operate under Chapter 11 protection, which helped to depress prices further and put more pressure on successful carriers. Others sought outside injections of money through investment deals, or by selling off routes or other assets to tide them over or to help strengthen themselves for when the revival in the airline market arrived. In the cases of TWA and Pan Am, the desire to sell routes was to have a major impact on the competitive relationship between Britain and the USA. There was also a renewed call from US airlines for better access to world markets from which they felt that they were unfairly excluded by protectionism and which made their already difficult trading circumstances even harder.

In Britain and the EC, there were failures such as Air Europe, take-overs such as BA's acquisition of Dan Air and B.Cal., and alliances or significant financial buy-ins such as Air France's into Sabena in 1992, but there were also cases of airlines returning to government subsidies and financial aid packages as in the cases of Sabena, Air France, Iberia, and others.

Circumstances on either side of the Atlantic were different. Despite the traumas within the US airline industry, the commitment to retaining a deregulated industry remained and, if anything, the call for a more liberal international airline industry became more strident once again. By the end of the 1980s, it was almost a return to the heady days of Kahn's show cause order and the aggressive pursuit of liberalisation under President Carter. In Britain and the EC, in contrast with the late 1970s, there was also movement towards liberalisation, but it was more pragmatic and cautious than the US movement and different market circumstances, geographical position and, perhaps most important of all, the smaller domestic cabotage base of European operators made their views about international liberalisation somewhat different from those of the Americans. These different perspectives on policy between the US and Europe became very evident in the way British and US civil aviation relations continued to develop.

During the 1980s there was something of a revival of the so-called Anglo-American Special Relationship. The two countries came to advocate similar economic doctrines and a remarkable and close relationship developed between Margaret Thatcher and Ronald Reagan. There was notable collaboration over two worrying developments of the first half of the decade: the Argentine invasion of the Falkland Islands and the increase in state sponsored terrorism in Europe the Mediterranean and the Middle East. In 1982 the USA gave invaluable assistance to Britain in the Falklands War and four years later Britain reciprocated by helping the USA to mount its punitive strike against Libya. Against this background, Reagan's helpful attitude in the Laker affair and the general improvement in civil aviation matters that gradually developed in the 1980s, after the trauma of Bermuda 2, are more understandable. Even so, in addition to the Laker saga, other problems did arise. The challenges from deregulation, in particular in terms of the pressures for globalising the market and the strain of massive costs involved in running a successful mega carrier, caused friction in various ways as the two countries readjusted to new circumstances.

The convergence of British and American political views on economic policy was helpful in the sphere of civil aviation. At least the two sides were now closer in principle if not so much so in practice. However, even here there was some convergence. By the end of 1985 the drive for deregulation in the USA was losing some of its impetus, though it was to revive again at the end of the decade. A Congressional report in 1983 indicated that some foreign airlines had gained more from US deregulation than US airlines. In the light of this, the USA became more cautious and pragmatic.[3] Thus, when the capacity provisions contained in annex 2 of the Bermuda 2 Agreement began to reach their expiry date in 1986, the US and British negotiators found it easier to reach a compromise than they had in 1977 when the issue of capacity control had been such a contentious issue.

The British negotiators in the Annex 2 Talks were led by Handley Stevens, Under Secretary at the DOT, and he was advised by R.C. Beetham, Head of the FO Maritime and Aviation Department. At the outset, the British were still worried about the possibility of British airlines being subject to US antitrust laws and they tried to persuade the Americans to change this and conduct negotiations in a broader context than capacity matters.[4] The Laker affair was over by now, but BA privatisation had still not been consumated.

The talks were not without difficulty. The Americans refused to undertake the job of trying to change the scope of the antitrust laws and some of them still harboured suspicion of the British. There were prickly personalities on either side, for instance in March 1986 British Aviation Minister, Michael Spicer, speaking before representatives of the American Chamber of Commerce, berated the USA for maintaining its cabotage and criticised other aspects of its aviation policy which he considered protectionist and discriminatory towards foreign airlines. Spicer was not held in high regard, but, fortunately for the sake of the Annex 2 Talks, British officials generally enjoyed good relations with their American counterparts.[5] There was particularly good rapport between the US delegation leader Jeffrey Shane and Beetham and by September 1986 a new capacity annex had been hammered out.

Summing up three years later, a senior FO official said: 'we both felt we'd got a satisfactory deal and indeed it has worked very well, no problems with it on either side [the Americans] certainly talked about our aviation relationship following that in a much happier way than previously.'[6] The British achieved their main goals, namely a degree of liberalisation, but with a safety net that would help to protect the rather ailing performance of B.Cal. on its route to the American south west. All scheduled airlines were granted a daily frequency as of right. Thereafter, capacity was controlled by mutual agreement with a top limit set in a proportional way between British and US airlines. On the same route one airline could not exceed more than 150 per cent of the other's subsonic capacity. If there were disagreement, then an airline could unilaterally increase its capacity by thirty and twenty flights respectively in the summer and winter season. The safety net for B.Cal. was soon redundant as BA took it over in 1988, but the rest of the agreement seemed to be a success.[7]

The appearance of the Annex 2 Agreement was, however, misleading. While it was true that up until the 1990s there were no serious problems with capacity on the north Atlantic, that was largely to do with the fact that the two US carriers operating into HR were not strong competitors and they did not use all the capacity available to them. This was because neither airline developed a domestic US hub and spoke system. Instead they remained wedded to an out of date operating system that relied on the traditional gateways and passengers finding their way there by means other than TWA or Pan Am. This was a very agreeable scenario for BA, because, as far as it was concerned, this put its main American competitors in the same relationship to the US domestic market as BA's, namely, no feeder lines to transatlantic gateway flights. However, the new US international carriers, AA, UA and Delta operated differently. They had prospered through developing domestic hub and spoke systems and increasing the volume of passengers they carried. As noted in an earlier chapter, more pasengers and more flights meant economies of scale in the new dispensation and that eventually pushed the traditional domestic US carriers into the international arena. But, that move out would not have been possible if the US government had not developed a policy in the 1970s of opening new international gateways. Initially this was not consciously done to help the new would-be foreign operators and their economies of scale. If anything, it was done in response to domestic political pressures for local international gateways and the strategy of trading access to the US market for liberal fare and capacity clauses in ASAs. With regard to Britain, that policy had only had a limited amount of succes, but nevertheless, opening US gateways away from the traditional ones, such as New York, Boston and Los Angeles, created the potential for AA, UA and Delta to operate from their hubs into the United Kingdom. In terms of the government's overall policy of opening new gateways, it allowed the US mega carriers to send their spokes fanning out into the international marketplace from hubs throughtout the USA. The position of these hubs was dictated by the ability to assemble large numbers of passengers from the US domestic market rather than historical importance or geographical propinquity to foreign destinations. Thus once airlines like UA and AA arrived on the scene, with corporate strategies that sought global economies of scale and a relentless pursuit of ever greater volumes of traffic, pressure was bound to arise on the capacity restrictions of Bermuda 2, even in the revised form of the 1986 agreement. It then became less convincing for the British to say that there had been no problems over capacity since 1986 as if annex 2 were not restrictive. As one American official put it in 1991: 'if annex 2 is not restrictive, why does Britain insist on having it?'[8]. But, in 1986 these problems still lay some distance in the future.

The problem, most characteristic of new developments in the airline industry, that arose between Britain and the USA in the 1980s was to do with CRSs. As deregulation created more routes, more fares and more complicated journeys, by feeding passengers into and out of hubs, computer information became vital both to the smooth operation of the system and to marketing. The cost of these vast computer systems was astronomical and added yet another dimension to the cost of running modern airlines. But, once in operation, the systems have enormous benefits for their airlines and have been extremely profitable. A US General Accounting Office (GAO) report in 1986 estimated that Sabre and Apollo, the CRS systems of AA and UA respectively, would each generate over half a billion dollars ($500m) profit from incremental revenues in the twelve years from 1978-90.[9]

While CRSs are an indispensable feature of the new more competitive airline industry, they have also had some anti-competitive effects. First of all, their costs are so high that small airlines find their development prohibitive. They thus have three choices: do without and be put at a competitive disadvantage with regard to the large airlines; make alliances with, or, pay fees to airlines that have a CRS, such an arrangement exists between Air UK and KLM; or enter a collaborative enterprise to develop a CRS. The classic examples of the latter are Amadeus with founder shareholders Air France, Iberia, Lufthansa and SAS;

and Galileo with founders BA, Covia, KLM, and Swissair. Clearly these co-operative ventures and alliances can pose competition problems between those who are dependent and those who supply CRS services and for those which collaborate in developing a shared CRS.[10]

Problems with CRSs first arose within the US domestic market with allegations of discriminatory screen displays at travel agents using the systems and excessive profits being made by the two largest CRSs, Apollo and Sabre: the latter by 1990 carried over 10 million individual airfares and was hugely successful. In November 1984, the CAB, in one of its last actions before its demise the following month, responded to the situation by issuing rules of conduct for CRS users. In January 1985 the DOT inherited from the CAB responsibility to oversee these regulations and generally ensure that the deregulated market did not lead to 'anticompetitive behaviour, unreasonable industry concentration or excessive market domination.'[11] However, problems persisted, as a report from the US GAO showed in 1986. The report was drawn up in response to requests from Senator Nancy Kassebaum, Chairman of the Subcommittee on Aviation of the Committee on Commerce, Science and Transportation, and Representative Norman Mineta, Ranking Minority Member of the Subcommittee on Aviation of the Committee on Public Works and Transportation. Its objective was to investigate the profitability and competitiveness of the CRS market and it recommended further studies by the DOT and action 'to enforce compliance with or to strengthen the CRS rules'.[12] The situation was clearly unsatisfactory, but attention on CRSs soon swithched from the domestic to the foreign field of operations.

The system that came into question was Sabre, which the British Government and BA felt was being used in a way that discriminated against BA. Towards the end of 1987 the Americans claimed that their DOT regulations had rendered Sabre and other US CRSs neutral, but the British remained unconvinced. While Sabre displays were in accordance with the CAB rules promulgated in 1984, BA still felt that they discriminated against its operations.[13] At the time AA used a display system that 'integrated both one-stop direct and connect flight schedules based on elapsed time' and gave emphasis to closeness to the specified departure time.[14] With its internal network and computerised connect flight schedule, this system favoured AA. BA decided to retaliate through the use of its own system Travicom-BABS."

Travicom was a means by which British travel agents could be patched into CRSs, including BABS, which BA had developed as a temporary stop-gap before the more advanced Galileo System came on line. However, BA refused to allow BA tickets to be issued by any other system in Britain, which encouraged travel agents to use BABS at the expense of both American CRSs and US airlines. By 1988 a serious dispute had arisen from this between AA and BA. The former under the aggressive leadership of Robert Crandall, brought legal action against BA under the fair trading clause of the Bermuda 2 Agreement, and also asked the US DOT to retaliate against BA for its discriminatory use of Travicom-BABS.[15]

The situation began to look ugly. As a Foreign Office official put it, 'I think the problem [was] one of our feeling that the way the American system operated favoured American airlines in the USA over ours and it got exacerbated because British Airways retaliated.'[16] The matter was taken up in Parliament by the Transport Committee and, just as had happened in the USA when difficulties arose with CRSs, it was decided that some regulatory code of practice should be adopted. In fact such matters had been under consideration at a European level in ECAC for some time. On 14 October 1988 proposals for a code of conduct drawn up by ECAC were brought before the EC Council and it was these proposals that constituted the accommodation arrived at between BA and AA.[17]

Before the Transport Committee Report was published on 28 July 1988, BA and AA agreed to an out of court settlement of their differences. As the AA Vice President for International Affairs later explained:

> To reach an agreement with BA we agreed and obtained US government approval to implement what amounts to the EC display [adopted from ECAC], not only in the EC, but we operate an alternative display in the US and more than half of all Sabre subscribers prefer it.[18]

The UK Transport Committee in its report explained the agreement as follows:

> BA has allowed Sabre to issue tickets although, outside the UK, this agreement will be subject to either a period of notice or to a moratorium and notice depending upon the region involved. The agreement opens up the UK market to Sabre and is in line with the ECAC code ..., American Airlines has agreed to abide by the ECAC code for screen displays, despite the USA not being a signatory to ECAC.
> Sabre has also agreed to improve the display of direct flights and interline connecting flights in the USA and the rest of the world. This will be of benefit to BA .... The issue of access to information is also resolved.

Within Europe Sabre will be subject to any future European Commission (Transport) regulations.[19]

" Problems with CRSs still arise from time to time. In 1991 yet another investigation into their operation was on-going in the USA and in 1992/93 serious abuses of computer data about Virgin Atlantic's operations was alleged to have been perpetrated by BA.[20] Access to information about markets and sales became ever more important as the airline industry moved towards globalisation. And of equal importance as the type of information CRSs could yield was expanded access to markets within which to operate. As the 1980s progressed the vast US domestic market thus became of great interest to foreign operators.

The importance of economies of scale persuaded BA that it must expand the boundaries of its playing field. In one sense it had done this over the years by becoming the world's largest international operator and by becoming a major gateway to Europe for US passengers. But this was no longer adequate for BA's ambitions and, in any case, its role of being the main foreign gateway airline to Europe for US passengers was somewhat under threat because direct flights to continental destinations, particularly France and West Germany, were expanding more quickly than to the UK. BA felt that it had to do three things in order to be a successful mega carrier, operating in all types of markets: develop a world-wide network of hubs and alliances; gain more access to Europe through liberalisation and the creation of a single European airline market; and thirdly, it had to get better access to the US domestic passenger market. By 1988 some progress was apparent with regard to Europe and in the following year BA managed to combine the other two strategies in one move."

In 1987 BA formed a limited alliance with UA. So far as Britain and BA were concerned the alliance was far from ideal, but at the time it seemed the only answer to the problem of greater access to the US market. US law prohibited BA from buying control of a US airline or from operating in US cabotage. Nevertheless, in 1988-89 BA developed ambitious plans for gaining a 15 per cent minority stake in UA and a merging of the two airlines' operations which would have created a hugely important airline alliance. It came close to success, but in the end was foiled by the bankers. There still remained, however, the successful code-sharing agreement which allowed UA to dovetail its domestic flights with BA's transatlantic flights bringing passengers to BA's gateways and taking inward coming passengers onwards to their final destinations in the USA.[21]

For the time being BA had to be satisfied with that. But, it was not only BA that wanted more access to markets, the US carriers did as well, including new routes to regional airports in the UK. It was in the context of talks about the latter problem that the next stage in the Anglo-American civil aviation saga unravelled. And it was one that exposed that both sides, while professing a desire for international liberalisation, also had areas of the market that they wished to protect. In addition, it became clear that now, more than ever, both the EC and the global implications of what the USA and the UK did had to be taken into account. Their policy decisions were affected by wider considerations than those in their bilateral relationship and whatever they agreed would also have impact that went wider than the routes between their two countries.

At the end of 1989 the Americans raised the possibility of broad liberalisation talks with the British. The idea was bruited in a situation where there were ongoing difficulties with the Bermuda 2 Agreement and a jostling for positions that would give more scope for the airlines of either side. Both countries professed commitment to liberalisation, but little progress was made between them, at least until 1994. Many of the reasons why there has been little progress can be well illustrated through a study of the HR Succession Rights Affair, but as useful as the HR affair is, it needs to be seen in the context of what has gone before and thus before entering the diplomatic details some summary of how things have broadly developed might help in the analysis of the important factors that arose out of the HR negotiations.

In particular, there are two overriding considerations that need to be fully appreciated. Firstly, the USA sees the EC and particularly Britain as protectionist in civil aviation. Of the Bermuda 2 Agreement, Jeffrey Shane of the US Department of Transport commented in the spring of 1991 that the only liberal aspect of the Bermuda 2 Agreement was the number of gateways available in the USA.[22] At about the same time a State Department official explained that the USA wants open skies between itself and other countries with no frequency, capacity, gateway, pickup or fare controls.[23] The two areas where the USA is not prepared to reform the marketplace are: cabotage - the exclusion of foreign airlines from US domestic routes; and the prohibition of foreign control over US airlines. The significance of these two reserved areas is enormous for other countries as they are barred from what amounts to 40 per cent of the world's airline market. It also makes it difficult for them to exploit the US market because of the advantages that American airlines have with their domestic feed systems.

The second factor is the possibilities that could be opened by the creation of a single European airline market. Britain is at a natural disadvantage in its relations with the USA because of its small domestic base. It cannot sustain more than one large international carrier and has no significant cabotage to trade in a liberalisation deal. While Britain has adopted a more competitive philosophy in recent years, it has had to contend with the dynamics released by US deregulation and the benefits that US airlines enjoy with their domestic hub and spoke systems and their enormous home passenger market. In this context Britain, and BA in particular, see liberalisation in terms, not just of open skies globalism, but in terms of removing artificial constraints on the operations of the market such as cabotage and controls over foreign owner-ship. Globalism should not stop at state boundaries. Not only would such reforms make a more level playing field, but, most crucially, it would enlarge the playing field for airlines such as BA, which is vitally important in the era of hub and spoke, and economies of scale. It is for these reasons that Britain and BA have pushed for liberalisation and the creation of a single European aviation market. Once that is in place, Britain and its partners would be in a position to negotiate on an EC basis with the USA, offering reciprocal entry into cabotage and an exchange of rights concerning ownership.

It would seem then that both Britain and the USA seek the same thing in principle, liberalisation, but differences in their market positions give them different priorities. Thus in December 1989, towards the end of talks about US access to Manchester Airport, Charles Angevine, head of the US delegation, proposed that Britain and the USA should consider an open skies agreement. The response he got was that this was fine, but the British would also like to discuss the removal of artificial distortions to the market such as cabotage and restrictions on inward investment. At this the US balked, claiming that such proposals would involve changes of US law which would be lengthy, and, given the climate in Congress, would probably fail. So far as the British were concerned, at that point, the Americans lost the moral high ground from which they like to negotiate. Nevertheless, the idea of liberalisation talks was accepted. Then, into all this, intruded HR succession rights.[24]

The problem of succession rights was first raised by the US Secretary of Transport Samuel Skinner with his opposite number Cecil Parkinson in Wash-ington in January 1990. Manoeuvring for the meeting had originated with British officials in the hope that a Parkinson/Skinner *tete a tete* would help resolve long-standing problems involving US desires for access to British regional airports. The situation was politically difficult for the British be-cause Manchester Airport Authority colluded with AA and US officials in the hope of getting US airlines into Manchester, while the British Government thought that the USA was not prepared to pay an adequate price. For a while, partly to defuse the situation, the British allowed AA into Manchester on the basis of a gentleman's agreement that that right would be paid for later. In the end, the payment was the right of Virgin to operate into Boston along with BA, but the exchange of notes authorising that was still seven months away in January 1990.[25]

In his talks with Parkinson, Skinner enquired about the possibility of transferring the London routes of TWA and Pan Am to other US airlines. Both TWA and Pan Am were in serious financial difficulty, especially the latter, and sales of valuable routes were of vital importance to their survival, but the matter of corporate successorship introduced into the Bermuda 2 Agreement in 1980 had to be clarified. Parkinson's reaction, according to American sources, was accommodating, so much so that: 'His officials ... got very nervous.' According to Angevine, Parkinson said that 'if there is a way it can be done, consistent with the idea of legal succession, then there would be entry for the successors without any payment.' Perhaps it was this kind of talk, along with Parkinson's charming manner, that led the Americans into false expectations.[26]

Once the British had drawn up their views of corporate succession, it became clear that the prospective buyers, AA and UA, could not accept what it would involve: namely, adopting both the names of Pan Am and TWA and enormous under funded pension liabilities. Furthermore, as Parkinson explained, in a letter to Skinner in July, there was also the problem of the TDRs. However, the Americans formed the impression that they would be changed. Thus, Skinner decided, as a contribution to what he understood to be foreward momentum, that he would implement the Manchester deal which by now had been agreed. He was exasperated when he later discovered that the TDRs matter had been referred to the British CAA and that a year or more was envisaged before it would complete its investigation. Meanwhile, Iraqui forces under the direction of Saddam Hussein invaded Kuwait on 2 August and the airline industry took a nose dive. The position of both Pan Am and TWA became critical and urgency for action on the HR succession matter increased. In October UA and AA made offers respectively for Pan Am's and TWA's routes to London.[27]

The attitude of the British Government was that they could hardly be held responsible for the misfortunes of US airlines, nor be expected to take action which would help BA's competitors without a *quid pro quo*. In working out the payment for rights of succession, eight main actors played parts. On the British side these were the DOT; the FO; BA; and the CAA. On the US side the departments of State and Transport; UA; and AA. In addition both President Bush and Prime Minister Major had some involvement.

Of all the actors BA's part was probably the most difficult. At the outset the British Government decided that cabotage and inward investment were not achievable in the likely timescale of the talks because they would require changes in US law. Instead of pursuing what could at best only yield promissory notes, the British sought secure bankable concessions. After apparently going along with this and co-operating closely with the government officials in charge of the negotiations, BA, towards the end of the talks and later, began to question the tactics that had been used and the results that had been achieved. BA argued that only inward investment rights and access to US cabotage could compensate them adquately for head to head competition at HR with AA and UA, and, as it transpired, Virgin Atlantic. If one BA official had had his way, he would have sought cabotage and inward investment until the end and then only let them go for major concessions instead of excluding them from the start. However, what he failed to explain, given that something was achieved on all aspects of BA's wish list bar one item, was what else could BA have desired?[28]

The FO and the DOT were close together in their approach to the negotiations, with the former marginally more accommodating. Basically they entered the talks with a willingness to find a solution to the problem at a price. Given that cabotage and inward investment were ruled out from the start (contrary to the impression given by most newspaper and periodical articles that appeared concurrently with the negotiations), the DOT and FO were under pressure to gain substantial concessions elsewhere. The purpose of those concessions was twofold: firstly, to gain advantages for British airlines; secondly, to manoeuvre Britain into a stronger position for forthcoming liberalisation talks by forcing the USA to make concessions which might otherwise be offered later as a sop to the British for not acting in the more important areas such as cabotage and inward investment.

The role of the CAA was rather marginal, but nevertheless important. For a long time it had been a liberalising force in British aviation and when it made its report in early 1991 it recommended the abolition of TDRs one, two and three, which would open up HR to all-comers (except US airlines, because of the succession clause), providing that they could get landing and take-off slots. That decision removed one obstacle to the entry of AA and UA into HR, but it did not overcome the problem of the corporate successor clause.

The State Department and the US DOT, like their British counterparts, had virtually no differences about the talks, though the latter tended to be more understanding of the British position. Judgement about such matters is difficult, perhaps the difference lay in that Angevine was more ready to show anger to the British than his Transportation colleagues. Things might have been similar on the British side except, unlike the USA, Transport take the lead with the FO in support (on the US side the situation is reversed), and David Moss, who led the British team, was completely unflappable.[29]

The US side understood that some payment was in order. Prior to the talks Shane said to Russell Sunderland of the British DOT:

> I think I understand that replacing Pan Am and TWA would represent to BA a different competitive picture and ... we are prepared to acknowledge that in negotiations. We won't sit here banging the table and insist that we simply have the right to replace those carriers. We'll pay for it. He [Sunderland] said that will make it a much easier proposition, so let's get going.[30]

However, the Americans thought that they could quantify the difference in revenue between AA and UA flying into HR and flying into Gatwick, for which they already held rights. The British, in contrast, wanted to introduce a qualitative element, namely, the superior competitiveness of AA and UA compared with Pan Am and TWA and that led them to make demands that shocked the Americans even with cabotage and inward investment off the table.[31]

UA and AA felt very hostile indeed to the British. UA in particular thought that payment was being asked for something the Americans should have as of right. According to Cyril Murphy of UA, the British argument was not tenable. If the interpretation of the corporate successor clause that was used by the British in the talks were accepted then, it would mean that, if BA went bankrupt the British would have no right to replace it with another carrier. Britain's main airport would be without a carrier operating to the USA. Murphy incredulously asked: Would the British really have accepted such a situation if BA had gone bust in the 1980s? His point was that the corporate successor clause was never intended to be used to do what the British did with it in 1991. It was intended to keep the Air Floridas of the world out of HR not AA or UA, neither of which is an Air Florida. For UA it was always HR or nothing. AA was more prepared to make do with Stansted and Gatwick, at least for a while, though if UA got into HR then it had to get in as well.[32]

These then were the positions of the main actors as the negotiations began.

The Americans were soon disabused of any hope that there was going to be significant give and take. Angevine presented a case for more US access to Stansted, but was forced to withdraw that. The British insisted that the only issue was the price the US was to pay for succession rights. Even on this the Americans believe that the British position hardened as the talks progressed.[33]

Whether or not British attitudes did harden is difficult to judge. The British DOT and the FO, after excluding cabotage and inward investment, asked BA and Virgin for a list of demands that might be made of the Americans. The American account of this wish list was that at the start it was a bit like a menu from which the British were likely to choose something from here and something from there. Later it changed to: We must have something from every item on the menu. In support of this interpretation is the fact that the negotiations were under the political auspices of Malcolm Rifkind on the British side. Mrs Thatcher fell from office on 22 November and Parkinson resigned a week later, just as the first round of talks began in Washington. Parkinson was seen by the Americans (and by some British officials) as being less cautious and more accommodating than his successor. Rifkind would have found it difficult to influence the initial talks much, but his tougher approach could account, so the American interpretation goes, for the more demanding approach to the wish list that developed later.

The British deny that their position hardened in the course of the talks as the US position deteriorated and Pan Am sank into what turned out to be fatal difficulties. Their account of events is that when the US balked at giving items on the wish list in their entirety, then the British responded by saying that in that case we must have something from each item. It was not a strategic change to damage the US position as some Americans seemed to think it was. It was a tactical change in order to try to get the same amount of benefit that would have been yielded if the USA had conceded some of the items in their entirety.[34]

The British asked for: a right for a second British carrier to operate from HR; unrestricted code sharing rights; more fifth freedoms; new options for double designation; capacity capping on AA and UA; and some seventh freedoms, which were actually offshore fifths as flights have to originate in Britain before going to a European country to pick up passengers for a direct flight to the USA. A true seventh would originate from the European country. Also, at a late stage in the talks, the possibility of British airlines participating in US airline frequent flyer programmes was raised.[35] In rounds of talks conducted successively in November and December 1990 and at both the beginning and end of January 1991 Angevine and Moss struggled to make progress. The situation was causing political concern to the extent that it was on the agenda for the Bush-Major meeting in December. The matter was discussed twice by the two leaders and subsequently as Wisgerhof of the State Department put it: 'I don't think we missed a single opportunity between January and March to take up the issue with appropriate British authorities, at all levels.'[36] The squabble was very inopportune as Britain was standing shoulder to shoulder with the USA in the Gulf Crisis and feelings in general about Anglo-American relations were good and there were political pressures for the aviation difficulties to be sorted out.

Progress was made and on 22 January the CAA announced its recommendation that the TDRs restricting access to HR should be abolished, which gave a significant boost to US hopes for a satisfactory outcome to the negotiations. By late January the US had conceded code sharing, a right for Virgin to operate from HR, and several fifth freedoms. However, other demands remained contentious, in particular the issues of capacity capping, seventh freedoms and the frequent flyer demand, which was not placed on the menu by the British until the talks had been under way for some time. It was at this point that impasse was reached. The Americans hoped that there would be some give on the British side, but it was not forthcoming and so on 30 January the Americans abruptly left the table at the DOT in Marsham Street and flew back to Washington.[37]

There followed a four week hiatus in which the protagonists could ponder upon events. While they did so Pan Am's position continued to get worse and Skinner took the unusual step of rejecting BA proposals for fare cuts. Normally the USA took a more positive line on such things, but this was a time for getting messages across to the British that the USA intended to play things hard.[38]

In fact, underlying all the difficulties of the HR talks was a realisation on both sides that in bilateral arrangements such as these there has to be give and take. Neither side can be the outright winner. Also both sides wanted an agreement. The British did not want to have Pan Am's life blood on its hands and in any case if things became too drawn out and Pan Am did fold up then Britain would lose much of its leverage. One of the compelling priorities on the US side was to get a deal done that would give Pan Am a chance to survive.[39]

Angevine believes that it was the possibility of US denunciation of Bermuda 2 that led the British to concede some ground when the talks were finally resumed in March. However, both sides also insist that matters never deteriorated to the extent that termination of air services was seriously considered as it was in the Bermuda 2 negotiations.[40]

The British did compromise in the end. Rifkind had accepted the CAA recommendation to allow free access to HR, but of course that applied to all-comers except the USA because of the succession clause. Under these conditions it would be politically unrealistic to expect the USA not to take retaliatory action as it would be the only country prevented from having strong carriers at HR. First of all, the British agreed to leave the frequent flyer issue for later. Providing that one sees this as a late addition, then, contrary to some US opinion, the UK did not get something from every item on the menu. On capacity capping they agreed that it should only be temporary. UA and AA were restricted for three years to the capacity allowed to TWA and Pan Am. The UK was allowed 'sevenths' from eight European countries, unrestricted code sharing rights, and the right to engage in joint ventures with European carriers in services to the USA.[41]

Apart from the British DOT and FO, and Virgin Atlantic, all the other major parties to the HR talks were unhappy with the outcome. The US DOT and the State Department felt dissatisfied and angry that they had had to pay such a high price for succession rights whilst leaving the highly regulatory Bermuda 2 in place. The European Commission was disturbed by Britain gaining new potential operating rights to the USA from Europe, without similar rights being extended to the other Members: this did not fit at all well with the aim of harmonising the way individual Members related to non-members in their ASAs. AA, UA and Delta were dismayed at the price the British had extracted and were particularly concerned that the capacity controls would prejudice their ability to compete effectively. Finally, BA felt that it had not been adequately compensated for now having to compete directly at HR with AA, UA and Virgin. Furthermore, its code sharing arrangements with UA - made in December 1987 in an attempt to develop a US feeder system for its gateways - was undermined because UA now competed directly with BA at HR. However, BA still had an important card to play: money.

BA was the only major world airline to make substantial profits in the deepening recession. US airlines in contrast were sinking into debt and were desperate for injections of cash to offset this: Delta, AA and UA together amassed losses of $1.4 billion in 1992. After numerous approaches from US airlines, BA finally agreed to a deal with US Air. In return for an investment of $750 million, BA would get a 25 per cent voting share, a US feeder system, and veto rights over company policy. As we shall see, Delta, AA, and UA were outraged.[42]

While BA was trying to redress its competitive disadvantage vis-a-vis US airlines, British and American officials took up liberalisation talks once again.

The British DOT and FO believed that incremental liberalisation was possible even without bringing the EC into the picture. BA thought otherwise. It wanted a single European airline market to play from before making any further concessions to the USA. Achievement of a single airline market would be difficult because of state owned and subsidised airlines and EC policy on community routes that are not profitable. But this was BA's preferred route and it was reluctant for further concessions to be made in the bilateral in the meantime.[43]

Although liberalisation talks were resumed, the legacy of the succession deal was to prove a major obstacle to progress. It was bad enough for US airlines to have to tolerate the capacity restrictions imposed by the HR deal and the continuation of the *status quo* regarding Bermuda 2, but once it looked as if BA were to get effective access to a domestic feeder system in the USA then matters became intolerable. Even so, at first, US Transport Secretary Andrew Card seemed to accept BA's move passively, but the outrage of UA, AA and Delta changed that.

It soon became clear that in return for approval of the US Air-BA deal the British would be expected to give concessions in the liberalisation talks. But, in late October there was stalemate and further discussion was postponed until after the presidential election. Neither side seemed to be getting very far. BA's deal looked ever more precarious and US hopes for liberalisation with Britain were fading fast. And the USA was not having much success with its open skies policy elsewhere either, except with Holland. With Germany severe problems arose, which were temporarily dealt with by a capacity freeze, but a new arrangement had to be worked out in 1993. France was so unhappy with its bilateral with the USA that it denounced it, and Japan threatened to do likewise. Within months France was to raise the prospect of renewed protectionism on a Community-wide basis. Almost everywhere the recession was encouraging protectionism and increases rather than decreases in regulation.

With opportunities closing down, or at least threatening to, there was less chance of an accommodation with BA's plans to penetrate the US domestic market via US Air. In November, Bill Clinton defeated Bush in the presidential election and there were growing fears that the USA was in danger of going protectionist, or, at least, that it would assert its economic interests more forcefully. In the aftermath of airline reports to Card in November about the BA-US Air deal prospects for its approval by the US DOT became dismal. In November the USA did give the go-ahead for a deal between KLM and NWA which looked similar to that between BA and US Air, but

215

it was in the context of an open skies agreement with Holland, whereas the much resented Bermuda 2 governed things with Britain. In late December, in order to pre-empt a formal disapproval of its arrangement with US Air, BA voluntarily pulled out.

In January 1993 BA came forward with a less ambitious plan for co-operation with US Air involving an initial $300 million investment, a 19.9 per cent stake in the company (possibly rising to over 40 per cent with more investment), three seats on the board of directors, and a code sharing arrangement that would give BA domestic US feed. The most significant change from the original deal was that this one did not include veto rights over company policy for BA. However, once again US airlines objected. They presented arguments to Transport Secretary, Federico Pena, that the code sharing provisions in the HR Agreement did not apply in all circumstances. They claimed that they should not apply with regard to US Air because BA would have a substantial investment in the company. They also raised the matter of anti-competitive practices arising from a long running dispute between BA and Virgin Atlantic that came to a head in the early months of 1993. They argued that this too was a factor that should prohibit the application of the 1991 agreement on code sharing.[44] In fact, the US DOT did give approval for the US Air-BA alliance, but there was a sting in the tail. The operation of the deal would be reviewed in twelve months time and that was interpreted to mean that the British Goverment would have to be more forthcoming in the liberalisation talks or else the review would result in damage to the BA-US Air deal.

While Britain, the USA and the EC proclaimed their commitment to liberalisation, though the latter with an increasing number of dissenting voices, the problem of actually achieving their objective remained elusive. This was partly because of differing views on liberalisation, partly because of special interests or advantages each wanted to protect, partly because of problems posed by CRSs which are difficult to deal with on a bilateral basis, and partly because of the adverse impact on the airlines of the recession. The HR negotiations threw many of these problems into stark relief. In particular, they exposed how the advocacy of liberalisation is restricted to areas which coincide with a state's interests. They also showed the importance of considering the airline market in global terms and that bilateral dealings were becoming more inadequate as a means of developing the international system. The calls for acces to the US domestic market and for the dilution of regulations over national ownership of airlines and the problems arising out of a need for harmonising EC ASAs all placed the inter-related shibboleths of nationalism and bilateralism, as manifested in the airline industry, under question. For how long could a bilateral system cope with the emergence of regional groupings such as the EC and the dynamics of an airline market that was moving to a globalisation of its operations?

Notes and References

1. Reportedly said by Cecil Parkinson.

2. Gialloreto (1988).

3. Jonsson (1987), pp. 144-5; Sampson (1984), p. 146.

4. Interview with senior FO official.

5. *Flight*, 29 March 1986, p. 4; Interview with senior FO official.

6. Ibid.

7. Ibid.; *Flight*, 20 Sept. 1986, p. 2.

8. Interview with Brendan Hanniffy, US Civil Aviation Attache, US Embassy London, conducted by the author, 13 Sept. 1991.

9. US General Accounting Office, *Airline Competition: GAO Report to Congress, May 1986* (GAO, Washington, 1986).

10. House of Commons Transport Committee, *Airline Competition: Computer Reservation Systems, 2 vols.* (HMSO, London, 1988).

11. GAO, *Competition*, p. 2.

12. Ibid., 14-15.

13. *Flight*, 23 Jan. 1988, p. 4; Interview with senior FO official.

14. Interview with Arnold Grossman, Vice President of AA for International Affairs, 12 April 1991, conducted by the author.

15. House of Commons Transport Committee, *CRSs*; Interview with senior FO official.

16. Ibid.

17. Proposal for a Council Regulation on a code of conduct for computerised reservation systems, COM(88)447, 14 Oct. 1988.

18. Grossman Interview.

19. House of Commons Transport Committee, *CRSs*, xxi.

20. *Sunday Times*, 30 Aug. 1992, 'Bizarre case of British Airways and the

217

rubbish bin snooper'.

21. Ibid., 10 Sept. 1989, 'BA tries to stall United's rivalry'; *Sunday Observer*, 28 Oct. 1990, 'Turbulence hits UAL deal'.

22. Shane Interview.

23. Wisgerhof Interview.

24. Official British Sources, interviews conducted by the author August/ September 1991; Angevine Interview; for another account of the HR Succession Rights Affair see John Newhouse, 'A Reporter at Large (Airline Gateway Rights)' in *The New Yorker*, 5 Aug. 1991; short articles also appeared in *Flight*; *Aviation Week and Space Technology*; *Business Travel News*; and in US and UK serious press.

25. Shane Interview; Angevine Interview; Official British Sources.

26. Angevine Interview; Shane Interview.

27. Ibid.

28. Ebdon Interview; Official British Sources.

29. Ibid.

30. Shane Interview.

31. Angevine Interview.

32. Ibid.; Murphy Interview.

33. Angevine Interview.

34. Ibid.; Official British Sources.

35. Ibid.

36. Interview with Paul Gretch, Director of International Aviation, US DOT, conducted by the author, 4 April 1991; Wisgerhof Interview.

37. Shane Interview; Official British Sources; *The Sunday Observer*, 10 Feb. 1991; Newhouse, *Reporter at Large*.

38. Official British Sources.

39. Ibid.; Angevine Interview; Shane Interview.

40. Official British sources; Angevine Interview.

41. Memorandum of Conversation 7-11 March 1991 and amendments to

US-UK Air Services Agreement, text courtesy of UK DOT.

42. *Flight*, 3 Feb. 1993, p. 8.

43. British Official Sources; King Interview and his Royal Aeronautical Society Speech, 16 May 1991, text courtesy of BA.

44. *Flight*, 10 Feb. 1993, p. 5.

Chapter 10
Competition in Crisis?

The Commission believes the United States should lead the way in vigorously pursuing this new multi-national approach to governing international aviation.
(Report to President and Congress August 1993)

1993 was a testing time for the fortunes of the airline industry, and that, generally, had adverse implications for the regulatory reform movement. Hardly any major airline made a profit in 1992 and the recovery rate in 1993 was slow and patchy. Most airlines continued to make enormous losses. Some governments sought readjustments to bilaterals to help their ailing airlines and gain a more favourable framework for their operations. Everywhere pressures mounted for protection and reregulation. Airlines were threatened by rising costs of operation from ATC authorities and airports and there was a danger of higher fuel taxes being imposed for both environmental and revenue raising reasons. The great aircraft leasing companies, that supplied many airlines and had created a degree of flexibility in the industry, began to falter. Airline debts continued to rise and there appeared to be no solution on the horizon to the problem of finding funds to replace old aircraft with ones straight from the production line, nevermind about meeting the costs of the futuristic planes that were on the drawing board for supersonic and extra large capacity aircraft. The existing commercial framework for international civil aviation, based on national policies and bilateralism, found it increasingly difficult to cope with the emergence of regional groupings such as the EC and the Andean Pact. The system's inadequacy was also exposed by problems arising from international difficulties of ATC and CRSs, from transnational airline

221

alliances and, generally, from the coming into existence of a global airline market. Governments and airlines had to take hard looks at their plans and it was soon clear that the airline industry stood at a possible departure point from how things had gone on in the past. In both the USA and in the EC, committees of investigation were set up to look at the future of the airline industry.

However, despite all the untoward developments in 1993, the year began promisingly in Europe with the acceptance of the third package of liberalisation. The proposals were made public in July 1991 and were intended to complete the single airline market, but the Commission observed that: 'a completely unregulated market may lead to abuse, and indeed to anticompetitive behaviour and certain regulation is therefore necessary to guard against such practices and to protect consumers.'[1] European faith in deregulation did not extend as far as the US model and some doubted whether the Commission had managed to weight the value of liberalisation heavily enough against arguments for the continuation of controls. Some controls could be genuinely beneficial for competition, but states with vested interests in maintaining a restricted and protected market sometimes cloaked their arguments in the garments of moderate liberalisation when their real intent was far more regulatory. Drawing the line between constructive and over-restrictive regulation involved some nice arguments. Given the reservations that were held by a number of Member States, the proposals were about as far-ranging as one could have expected. They covered route and airline licensing, ownership regulations and the fare regime. Karel van Miert, the Commissioner for Transport, thought that there would be problems over the proposed replacement of national with European cabotage and over fare liberalisation, but the real 'hot potato' were airline licensing provisions that would create a uniform regime to allow easy entry for new airlines which would erode the dominance of national flag carriers.[2]

For some, the proposals did not go far enough, or else failed to address obstacles to competition and efficient operations such as airport gateway slot allocations and congested and inadequately controlled airspace. The British and Dutch governments took the lead in wanting a more adventurous policy and the European Regional Airline Association was also less than sanguine about the proposals. The sceptics felt that too many possibilities remained for protectionist interference and also that the benefits of the proposals would be offset by other measures pending within the Community to impose vat on fares, to introduce a carbon tax, and to withdraw duty free shopping from the airlines. In addition to these fears, there were problems, brought about by the

222

economic recession of the 1990s, which were exacerbated by the Gulf War. The British, in particular, felt that the Commission was still far too willing to allow government financial assistance and bailouts for the airlines and did not know when to call a stop. Between 1990 and 1993, BA estimated that Sabena, Air France and Iberia, between them, received aid of about $3 billion. As 1993 drew to a close, it looked as if that was far from the end of the matter of financial packages for the airlines.[3]

Momentum for reform was slowed down by France, Belgium, Greece and others. There was a year of debate and argument on the third liberalisation package before a compromise finally emerged. Full European cabotage was delayed for four years. Regulations for public service routes and measures to deal with the problem of scarce slots at major airports were left for later decision. Unrestricted fifth freedom rights were created, but consecutive cabotage (e.g. the Frankfurt-Berlin leg of a London-Frankfurt-Berlin flight by a British carrier) was restricted to 50 per cent of the international leg of the route. More worryingly, there were other grounds for restricting foreign carrier access to domestic routes, namely: congestion; environmental concerns; and adequacy of alternative forms of high speed transport, such as fast rail links. Pricing was to be a single disapproval (one state could veto a fare) regime to avoid predatory or excessively high fares. Cases could be appealed to the Commission, but this was a retreat from the previous regime of double disapproval (both states had to disapprove of a fare before it was rejected). The most radical move was to introduce a common licensing policy, which facilitated the entry of new airlines, which were now defined in terms of Community rather than national rules of ownership. BA's response to all this was fairly representative of those who wanted liberalisation: 'the agreement leaves member states with too many powers to intervene, in too many ways.'[4]

Nevertheless, the third package did much to develop the EC airline market. It was a significant step forward and other moves were soon to follow on airport slots, on ATC and on the need for external competence for the Commission to negotiate on behalf of the EC.

As liberalisation has progressed in Europe, independent carriers, which have often been a catalyst for introducing competitive fares and higher standards of service, have increasingly complained about the obstacle to entry onto new routes posed by the scarcity of prime time, take-off and landing slots at major airports. Such constrictions on entry into the market must necessarily limit the effects of liberalisation. The Commission, realising this, brought forward proposals for a gradual redistribution of slots: it already had in place rules governing the distribution of new or abandoned slots. The reaction from the

Member States was hostile and in May 1991 van Miert confessed: 'It doesn't look as though we'll get an early decision. Some governments don't like it, and most airlines don't want it.'[5] In fact, there were many vested interests against the proposals. For example, while BA favoured EC liberalisation and the creation of a single European airline market, it saw slot redistribution as a form of reregulation rather than deregulation. Put more directly, it stood to lose valuable slots to competitors such as Virgin Atlantic and BM.

Despite widespread opposition, the Commission continued to press for action and in January 1993 the Council adopted a set of rules. States were to be responsible for placing a congested airport in the hands of a co-ordinator to allocate new or unused slots. Any slot not utilised over 80 per cent of the time could be confiscated and put in a pool, 50 per cent of which would be allocated to new entrants. These were hardly radical measures. Slots remained largely 'grandfathered': they stayed with those airlines that had had them for a long time. The possibilities of redistribution by market forces; by lottery; and by confiscation and redistribution through a regulatory authority were all laid aside.[6]

ATC appears to be largely technical, but a lack of national political will to deal with what is an international problem, and the question of which countries' companies get the lucrative high-tech contracts at stake in improving the system have lain at the heart of the matter. As with CRSs, ECAC has taken a leading role in stimulating a new approach to improve things. In 1990, the Transport Ministers of the members of ECAC asked Eurocontrol, which is based in Brussels and has the same membership as ECAC, to devise a plan to improve Europe's ATC system. The result was a programme named EATCHIP - the European Air Traffic Control Harmonisation and Integration Programme. In 1993 it had a budget of £300 million and some progress began to be made, but the scale of the problem is enormous: 'Europe contains 45 ATCCs and sub-centres, with Eastern Europe adding another 14. There are 31 different systems, using computers from 18 manufacturers, employing 22 different program languages.'[7] If nothing else, the problem with ATC systems highlights the need for a more international approach to deal with a problem of the airline industry for which a purely national approach has proven inadequate. In 1994 there were renewed calls for vigorous action in ATC reform in Europe and criticism of the lack of progress by Eurocontrol.

Perhaps the most important development in recent years, after the liberalisation programme, has been the growing competence of the Commission to negotiate on behalf of the Community in ASAs. Its authority is derived from article 113 and the articles in the transport chapter of the Treaty of Rome. Its most notable achievement so far has been to negotiate an airline association agreement with Norway and Sweden. However, the Commission feels that it is necessary to exercise more active authority than this. It wants the Member States to adopt, a model ASA in order to establish uniformity and, eventually, progress beyond bilateralism. It also wants to bring more negotiations under its own wing. The US granting of 'Sevenths' to Britain in 1991 and the Dutch-US open skies agreement of 1992 caused much unease in the Transport Commission. The Dutch-US protocol prompted van Miert to make a number of statements about the desirability of DG7 negotiating on behalf of Members to prevent discriminatory rights being gained by individual states at the cost of fellow Members, and of Community interests as a whole. *Flight* reported that: 'The EC Transport Directorate is adamant that open-skies negotiations should be carried out at EC level and not by individual states.'[8] But, so far, little progress has been made except to refer the matter to the Court of Justice for clarification after opposition from Members placed the Commission's policy in jeopardy. There are two major reasons for the lack of success. The first is reluctance by Member States to relinquish control over an aspect of their foreign affairs. Political inhibitions may have been overcome to bring about change within the domestic affairs of the EC, but there has generally been less success in doing that in the foreign field. Secondly, the Commission lacks the trained manpower to realise its ambitions. In early 1991 the Commission approved a reorganisation that would give DG7's aviation division the status of a full Directorate. However, as no extra money was provided for this and as there were only five full time members of the aviation division, the changes were more 'cosmetic than realistic'.[9]

Within the borders of the EC, significant progress has been made towards the creation of a single and more liberal airline market. One needs, however, to be clear exactly what the progress has been towards: US-type deregulation has never been on the official agenda. The aim has been to produce a flexible, safe and efficient market that responds to the main demands of the consumer, which can meet certain Community needs and which avoids abuses of the free market, such as predatory pricing and exploitation by dominant players. The Americans have similar goals, but have chosen to pursue them by a less interventionist regulatory system than the one being developed in Europe.

The EC, by increasingly bringing its competition rules to bear, has eroded the rigid structure in the European airline market that had developed since 1946. In May 1991 Malcolm Rifkind, UK Secretary of State for Transport, went so far as to say that 'bilateral barriers to aviation competition have largely gone [within the EC]'.[10] In theory he was right. The Commission, working in

225

conjunction with the Court of Justice and Member States such as Britain and Holland, has gradually broken down the political obstacles to reform. Having states which have been willing to lead the way in liberalising air services has been very important for the Commission. It has had willing players to demonstrate the benefits of a freer market. And so, capacity, frequency, fare and route restrictions and the division of whole markets by pooling arrangements have all been reformed. The most restrictive controls have been abandoned altogether, and the others can only be justified under specified circumstances and normally for only limited periods. These achievements amount to significant progress in allowing market, rather than political forces, to determine the character of the EC airline market.

As national political considerations were replaced by broader Community ones and freer competition developed, the specific characteristics of the European airline system also began to change. The most spectacular development has been the proliferation of new regional routes. In addition, there has been more fare competition, especially where a third airline has joined the traditional flag carriers on a route, and there have been cross-border alliances and the setting up of new or the purchase of old airlines in one state by airlines from another. Air France has a major stake in Sabena and alliances with Continental, Aero Mexico and Air Canada, and BA has bought both a French and a German regional airline (TAT and Delta Air respectively), has substantial stakes in Qantas and US Air and is developing an operation in Moscow. These are all part of the globalisation process and the strategy of developing worldwide hub and spoke operations and feeder services for long-haul routes.

Notwithstanding the importance of changes that have been wrought within the EC, problems remain and the potential for dangerous developments is still threatening. In particular, national factors can lead to the manipulation of protective reservations contained in EC regulations for the benefit of state carriers. The incidence of government-backed aid packages after the Gulf War was not encouraging in this respect. The continuation of national cabotage until 1997 provides further scope for protection, as do provisions about community routes, the environment and the adequacy of alternative types of high speed transport. There is also the matter of how effectively EC rules are implemented. BA's experience when negotiating both for an interest in Interflug and to transform its Internal German Services into Deutsche BA were not auspicious. In the former BA was told by German authorities that it would be wasting its time, in the latter, it came up against opposition from trade unions. But, the really galling thing was that the trade union official that BA had to deal with was also on the Lufthansa Board. In the end, BA abandoned the talks and bought Delta in order to try to realise its German ambitions, but, given the EC's establishment rules, this is not really what BA might have expected.[11]

Meeting the challenge from the airlines outside the EC is another thing that the Commission has still not met effectively.

The business of negotiating ASAs continues to be an area fraught with difficulties and one in which politics persists as a recalcitrant. In particular, reconciling the differences between the philosophy prevalent in the USA with that in Europe and designing an arrangement that equitably takes into account the different geographical positions and market structures in the EC and the USA is a mammoth task and one which the EC Commission is presently ill-equipped to address. The consequent danger is that EC interests will be undermined as individual Members try to safeguard their positions through bilaterals with the USA, which run contrary to to the emerging common airline policy. That, in turn, could have a damaging knock-on effect on what has already been achieved in the EC. All this raises questions, not just about airline policy within and between Member States, nor simply questions about relations between the EC and individual countries such as the USA: it raises questions about the adequacy of the present international airline system. In an important speech in April 1991, Frederik Sorensen observed: 'basic changes will be required in the traditional system of bilateral agreements because ... aviation is becoming more and more a global activity.'[12] It was with many of these ideas and worries in mind that the Commission established what became known as the Comite de Sages in June 1993 to look at the economic problems confronting the airlines of the Member States.

The committee was composed of ten members and was chaired by Herman de Croo, a former Belgian transport minister. EC officialdom claimed that the committee would not propose protectionism or reregulation. It was to look at structural problems afflicting European airlines and to consider to what extent the existing airline policy of the EC needed supplementing. It would also take up the issue of international agreements. Head of DG7's aviation division, Sorensen, thought that bilateral agreements were no longer acceptable. DG7 wanted to realise its ambition of negotiating ASAs on behalf of the whole EC.[13]

The submissions to and the hearings before the Comite de Sages fell into two main categories: infrastructure; and the character of commercial operations. The former had a large degree of unanimity and when the committee made its recommendations in early 1994 there was general agreement that the industry needed more infrastructure investment, an accelerated programme of ATC reform and some relief from ever rising user charges. On the way the airlines operate, matters were more fraught. By September, when the commit-tee received presentations from the airlines, there was a growing groundswell of opinion in favour of state aid and reregulation.

This groundswell arose for two interconnected reasons: competition, espe-cially from the USA; and the continuing failure of a number of European airlines to make profits. Germany and France resented US airline competition and objected to the capacity that they mounted into and out of Europe and within Europe because of fifth freedom rights. France felt so strongly about these matters that it denounced its bilateral with the USA in 1992 and Ger-many insisted on a capacity freeze. But, the main overall problem was a lack of profit making among European airlines and the problem with the USA was just a symptom of that.

Sabena and Air France made first half losses in 1993 of $42 million and $680 million respectively. Sabena had received a major revival package only eighteen months previously with Commission approval, but also with stric-tures that this would be the last time. Now Sabena was looking at the prospects of bankruptcy again and at the end of September the Belgian President of the EC, under pressure from Sabena, called an emergency meeting of transport ministers for the 27th to consider measures to help the airlines. Sabena was backed by Air France in its desire for new protection, and Aer Lingus, Iberia, Tap Air of Portugal and Olympic shared their concerns and were all in pretty dismal financial positions. Already on the 16 September, at the last session of the Comite de Sages, Bernard Attali of Air France had made the protectionist picture clear.[14]

The protectionist lobby led by Air France and Sabena made a three pronged case before the committee. Firstly, they called for a freezing of capacity and fares until 1996. Alitalia also proposed capacity co-ordination. Effectively this would mean the suspension of competition for two years, an entrench-ment of airlines in the *status quo* and the end of any hopes for further expansion in Europe of successful airlines like KLM, BA and the British independents BM, Air UK and Virgin. Secondly, there were calls for an EC fund to help with restructuring. In particular, the money would help airlines retire old or environmentally substandard aircraft which would also help reduce over-ca-pacity. Clearly such a fund would be a form of subsidy and would constitute a reversal of the EC's declared policy. Thirdly, there was an attack on Britain by the more strongly protectionist states alleging that it acted hypocritically in calling for liberalisation in Europe while at the same time retaining the most restrictive of bilaterals with the USA.[15] Colin Marshall and Sir Michael Bishop, in rare agreement, both attacked the idea of further EC subsidies for the airlines. Marshall said: 'As long as the European Commission continues to approve aid, there will be no sensible preparation to get Europe's airlines ready for world competition.'[16]

The recommendations of the Comite de Sages on the commercial were more controversial than on the infrastructure side. It still recognised the need for a 'last chance' financial aid package for some airlines, which did not please those that have to swim or sink according to market performance like SAS and BA. But, the Comite also noted that 'Capital injections and state aids have severely contributed to over-capacity and uneconomic pricing.'[17] De Croo said: 'The main lesson I have drawn from the exercise is that old habits die hard. Mentality changes are lagging behind technological, economic and regulatory changes.'[18] The spirit of the report was to try to maintain the momentum towards more liberalisation, but the future of that was doubtful. The French Government became obstructive of further developments and Air France was in deep financial trouble. In March 1994 a rescue package was produced involving government funding of $3.42 billion over three years in return for some rationalisation of the work force (i.e. job losses).[19] In such circumstances the French Government was unlikely to support any proposals for legislation to carry liberalisation further in the EC airline market because that would expose Air France to further competition with which it was patently unable to cope. And so the future of the EC airline policy hangs in the balance. After 1993 beginning auspiciously for further liberalisation, the forces of protection and reregulation mustered strongly and looked set to retake the initiative. States were still not willing to disengage political considerations from their airlines. Government owned still equated with government subsidised, as the British have rather self-righteously been so quick and ready to point out ever since they privatised BA. And as much as DG7 and DG4 might object to the protectionist and anti-competitive policies now being bruited by the airlines and some of their governments, if the Member States decide reregulation is what they want, it is going to be very difficult to resist that change of policy. The Comite de Sages may have been sage and skilful in its report, but the future of the EC airline market lies in the hands of the Member States, and those still supportive of liberalisation are in a minority and will have to be courageous and politically adept if EC airline liberalisation is not to lose its way.

In Britain, in 1992, John MacGregor took over at Transport from Rifkind: policy remained committed to liberalisation. Even the Americans began to hope that progress could be made with changing Bermuda 2, especially in 1993 after David Moss, who they regarded as an obstacle to further liberalisation, moved sideways in the Transport Department to a railway job.[20] The Americans also now, rather ironically, had more leverage on the British. After the striking of the BA/US Air deal, the USA made it quite clear that further development of the alliance would only be permitted if the British were more forthcoming in talks for an open skies regime between Britain and the USA. BA agreed in principle that such an arrangement was desirable, but their requirements and timescale differed somewhat from the Americans'. Talks took place during 1993 and were set to climax in October of that year. The British were willing to grant US airlines more access to regional British airports and to London, except to HR, but the talking continued inconclusively into 1994. How things would turn out still remained to be seen, but negotiations were extremely fraught at the time of writing in May/June 1994.

In the USA, the main development in 1993 was the appointment and report of 'The National Commission to Ensure a Strong Competitive Airline Industry: a Report to the President and Congress'. The Commission was set up on 7 April 1993 with Gerald Baliles, a former governor of Virginia, as its chairman. It was composed of fifteen voting and eleven nonvoting members. They included Herb Kelleher, chief executive of the most successful US airline in recent years, Southwest Airlines; Gina Thomas an executive of Federal Express; Randy Babbit of the Airline Pilots' Association; and representatives of the unions, the aerospace industry and the airports.[21]

Like the de Croo Committee that was appointed in Europe some three months later, the idea behind the Baliles Commission was prompted by crisis in the airline industry. Deregulation had had mixed blessings within the USA and had caused aggressive responses from foreign countries to increased US competition abroad. In addition to the denunciation of the French bilateral, there were continuing difficulties with Germany and threats of concerted action from the Orient Airlines Association, which claimed that bilaterals negotiated with its members in the 1950s and 1960s were too favourable to US interests. The bilaterals needed to be renegotiated on a fairer basis. And finally, there were also problems with capacity and fifth freedom rights with Japan and Australia. On the domestic front, all the big airlines were in financial difficulties and were deeply worried about their futures and the growing wave of, what they saw as, foreign protectionism that would restrict their market opportunities.

The Commission explained its view of the impact that deregulation had had on the airlines at the outset of its report.

The airline industry was found to be: 'more competitive than before deregulation in 1978 in that there is more head-to-head, city-pair competition:

and, [it] charges travellers and shippers less in real dollars than it did in 1978.'[22] On the negative side it had lost 'huge amounts of money in the past three years, and it has never made a sustained, substantial return on investment.' Furthermore, the industry has: 'Become uncertain about its freedom to compete in international markets because of foreign government restrictions and concerned about the erosion of its full participation in the fastest growing sector of the civil aviation market-place'[23] However, despite these concerns, since deregulation the more competitive oriented US airline industry had had considerable success on international routes. The US flag percentage of the international passenger market had risen from about 48 per cent in 1980 to approximately 54 per cent in 1992.[24] The evidence both within the domestic and the international context did not therefore point towards reregulation as a solution to the problems of the industry, but some new policy departures were called for.

Some of the Commission's recommendations were similar to ones later considered by the Comite de Sages in Brussels. ATC was to be improved with the technical help of satellites and the financial help of better and more consistent long-term funding to be organised by a revamped Federal Aviation Administration. Airlines should be exempted from proposed new taxes on fuel, and other charges should be kept under control. An investment fund should be set up to help the airlines modify equipment to meet environmental standards. Overseeing much of this should be a White House Committee. Finally, in the domestic sphere, there were recommendations that tighter controls over Chapter 11 bankruptcy protection should be introduced and also that the investment levels that foreign companies could make in US airlines should be raised, but this last proposal was linked with conditions that have a bearing on the foreign aspect of US aviation policy.

In the foreign field the Commission proposed that the negotiating status of ASAs should be raised with the appointment of a special ambassador to be placed in charge of American negotiating teams. More liberal bilaterals should be pursued and the granting of the right to foreign airlines to invest at the new higher level in US airlines should only be allowed if its government had negotiated a liberal bilateral with the USA.

> The Federal Aviation Act be amended to allow the U.S. to negotiate bilateral agreements that permit foreign investors to hold up to 49 percent voting equality in U.S. airlines, providing those bilateral agreements are liberal and contain equivalent opportunities for U.S. airlines; the foreign investor is not government owned; there are

reciprocal investment rights for U.S. airlines, and the investment will advance the national interest and the development of a liberal global regime for air services.[25]

This carrot and stick approach was evident throughout much of the section on international policy. The Commission emphasised the importance of the USA continuing to enjoy the rights granted to it by existing bilaterals and that it would retaliate through all means available, including renunciation, if they were restricted. At the same time, the Commission noted the inadequacy of the existing bilateral system and made a most radical proposal.

> We recommend: U.S. negotiating efforts focus on creating a multi-national operating environment for airlines free of discrimination and restrictions. ....
> We recommend: Liberal, multi-national agreements be negotiated that encompass provisions for passenger and cargo services; charters; cross-border investment and ownership; comparable traffic rights; fifth/sixth freedom traffic rights; fair market access and doing business opportunities; system capacity; government and customs and immigration facilities.[26]

It is however, one thing to come forward with an idea, it is quite another matter to put it into practice. Interestingly, a think tank, Global Aviation Associates Limited, which has a highly distinguished membership, came forward with similar ideas in 1991. They fully recognised the problem of creating a multilateral system and after much consideration of strategic options, they ruled out both action through the ICAO and the GATT as likely to be ineffective in the near future, and ruled in collective action by nation states.

> In the short term, ...the Think Tank believes that the most promising prospect for meaningful liberalisation is by agreement amongst those countries with a common recognition of the importance of liberal market access and a common commitment to achieving this objective.[27]

The most likely candidates to start the multilateralist ball rolling, according to the Think Tank, were the USA, Canada and the EC. However, in the intervening three years little progress has been made in bilateral talks between the USA and Canada and the EC is now teetering on the slope of reregulation and protectionism. Where the international system will go from here, despite the

US Commission's call for liberal multilateralism, is difficult to assess, especially as there has been little action to follow up the Commission's report.

Since the early 1970s the international airline industry has changed greatly because of deregulation or liberalisation, technological and infrastructure developments, and the emergence of regional actors, such as the EC. Three major problems now confront the airlines and the system in which they operate. The first is the poor economic condition of the industry and the revival of protectionism that it has helped to spawn. Secondly, developments over the last few years, such as CRSs, the need for greater access to markets for global hub and spoke operations, the emergence of an EC airline policy, and the technical and political problems of ATC, have highlighted the need for a more international structure. Multilateralism is not just a whim of those who desire a liberal market. There are dynamics within the inexorable globalisation process that also require that it be adopted in at least some form that is more adventurous than the current manifestations of it in IATA and the ICAO. And thirdly, there is the problem of defining liberalisation in a way that is acceptable to those of liberal inclination and yet does not damage, too badly, the self-interest of any particular state. This is the most intractable of the three, because it is the most political.

There are many possible scenarios for the future. Much will depend on how the USA and the EC respond to their respective airline inquiries and their recommendations. There is also likely to be an ever greater input into the determinants of international civil aviation policy from Japan and other Asian countries with vigorous economies and growing airlines. But, perhaps, the most important determinant will be the airline passenger market itself. If it moves out of its present depressed state, in response to a general improvement in the world economy, then that might create more room to manoeuvre for beleaguered airlines and give them the basis from which to act more adventurously in crafting a new international system.

From the present situation four scenarios, at least, are all possible. Firstly, there could be a move back to regulation and protection and highly politicised bilateral bargaining, reminiscent of the 1920s and 1930s, with no model to emulate and no clear direction to go except for a merry-go-round of bargaining for temporary advantages. Secondly, regional groupings may proliferate and strengthen, with liberal arrangements within and protectionist agreements with non-members. Thirdly, there could be a disintegration of regional groupings and a breakthrough with strong leadership from one, or a group of states, to a multilateral system enacted at an international conference. And fourthly, a variant on the second scenario, with liberal arrangements within and liberal agreements with non-members gradually developing into a liberal multilateral world order.

Whatever might happen, this present study has amply demonstrated that intense political arguments and complex diplomatic discussions will inevitably be involved and that things cannot be determined solely on the basis of economic analyses or abstract models of transportation systems. The fortunes of the international civil aviation system will continue to attract interest and attention from those sorts of inquiry, but any realistic appraisal or policy must take the political dimension into account as well. So often, policy is not determined by the 'objective' economics of the situation, but by political perceptions, accurate or otherwise, about the economics involved and by a multitude of other non-economic considerations. For the foreseeable future, the international airline industry is unlikely to become just a matter of commerce and business, whether it goes down the route of liberalisation or regulation and protection. It will remain highly political and involve complicated diplomatic negotiations for some time to come, whether they are conducted by national or regional representatives. It will thus also, no doubt, be the subject of this type of study again in the future.

Notes and References

1. 'Completion of the Civil Aviation Policy in the European Communities Towards Single Market Conditions', proposals for Council regulations COM(91)275, 18 Sept. 1991.

2. *Flight*, 24 July 1991, p. 8.

3. Ibid., 1 July 1992, p. 6 and 15 July 1992, p. 23, and 15 Sept. 1993, p. 5; *The Independent* 5 and 6 Aug. 1992, 'EC Airlines Still Clinging to State Subsidies'. Leon Brittan, alone of 16 Commissioners opposed £675m. cash injection for Iberia. *Financial Times*, 2 Sept. 1992, 'Softly, softly on EC fares'.

4. *Flight*, 1 July 1992, p. 6, 15 July 1992, p. 23; *Financial Times*, 2 Sept. 1992.

5. Ibid., 22 May 1991; King Interview; Bishop Interview; *Flight*, 11 Dec. 1991, p. 10, and 27 Jan. 1993, p. 14.

6. Ibid., 25 Jan. 1993, editorial and p. 8.

7. Ibid., 10 Feb. 1993, 'Controlling the World', p. 29.

8. Ibid., 16 Sept. 1992, p. 34; COM(90)17, 23 Feb. 1990; The opening of negotiations between the European Economic Community and EFTA countries on scheduled passenger services, COM(90)18, 14 Feb. 1990.

9. *Flight*, 24 April 1991, p. 13.

10. Malcolm Rifkind, Secretary of State for Transport, 'Speech to the Aviation Club, 21 May 1991: Aviation: A Framework for the Nineties', text courtesy of UK Department of Transport.

11. King Interview; Interview with Commission Official; *Flight*, 25 March 1992, p. 4.

12. Frederik Sorensen, presentation, 'European Airline Traffic After 1993', 8 April 1991, text courtesy of Sorensen.

13. *Flight*, 16 June 1993, p. 6.

14. Ibid., 21 July 1993, p. 6, and 22 Sept. 1993, pp. 5 and 20; *Daily Telegraph*, 25 Sept. 1993, 'Sabena Leads Move Against Open Skies'.

15. *Flight*, 29 Sept. 1993, p. 24.

16. Ibid., 15 Sept. 1993, p. 5 and 22 Sept. 1993, p. 5. In Germany, Lufthansa was making progress towards privatisation and after somewhat surprising progress in the talks for a new bilateral with the USA, which by October 1993 looked as if they would yield an open skies agreement, Lufthansa also looked set to deepen its co-operative alliance with UA.

17. *Flight*, 23 Feb. 1994, p. 25.

18. Ibid.

19. Ibid., 16 March 1994, p. 5.

20. Ibid., 12 May 1993, p. 8.

21. *Change, Challenge and Competition: the National Commission to Ensure a Strong Competitive Airline Industry: A Report to the President and Congress*, Washington, August 1993.

22. Ibid., p. 1.

23. Ibid.

24. Ibid., p. 21.

25. Ibid., pp. 22-23.

26. Ibid., p. 22.

27. Global Aviation Associates Ltd., *Free Trade in the Air: Report of the Think Tank on Multilateral Aviation Liberalization* (Jan. 1991), pp. 17-18.

Sources

British Command Papers

Cmd. 6747, 1946, 'US, UK Civil Air Services Agreement, Bermuda'.

Cmd. 4018, 1969, 'Report of the Committee of Inquiry into Civil Air Transport [Edwards Report]'.

Cmd. 4213, 1969, 'Civil Air Policy'.

Cmd. 4899, 1972, Civil Aviation Policy Guidance'.

Cmd. 6400, 1976, 'Future Civil Aviation Policy'.

Cmd. 7016, 1977, 'Agreement Concerning Air Services [Bermuda 2]'.

Cmd. 9366, 1984, 'Airline Competition Policy'.

Published Sources

Memoranda of Conversations 7-11 March 1991, correspondence and agreed amendments to US-UK Air Services Agreement (Bermuda 2), documentation courtesy of UK DOT.

House of Commons Transport Committee, 'Airline Competition: Computer Reservation Systems, 2 vols.' (HMSO, London, 1988).

House of Commons Debates, Hansard.

BA Reports and Accounts: 1979/80; 1980/81; 1989/90; 1990/91.

European Community, Official Publications and Documentation.

'Air Services Agreement Between the Government of the United States of

237

America and the Government of the United kingdom and Northern Ireland including Amendments thru 1980' (US DOT, Washington, 1981)

'US International Aviation Policy at the Crossroads: A Study of Alternative Policies and Their Consequences 2 vols.' (Harbridge House, Boston, 1975)

✓'Airline Competition: GAO Report to Congress, May 1986' (General Accounting Office, Washington, 1984)

'Change Challenge and Competition: the National Commission to Ensure a Strong Competitive Airline Industry: Report to President and Congress' (Washington, 1993)

'Public Papers of the President of the United States: Jimmy Carter Jan.-June 1978' (US Government Printing Office, Washington, 1979)

Congressional Digest

Congressional Quarterly

Documentary Sources

National Archives of the USA, Alexandria, Virginia, the Nixon Project.

White House Central Files [WHCF]

White House Special Files, WHCF [WHSF, WHCF]

Transitional Task Force Reports

Papers of Paul McCracken, Chairman Council of Economic Advisers [CEA]

Papers of Hendrix Houthakker, member CEA

Papers of Egil Krogh, Deputy Council and later Deputy Assistant to the President for Domestic Affairs

Gerald Ford Library

WHCF

Papers of William Seidman, Assistant for Economic Affairs

CEA/Greenspan Files [Alan Greenspan was Chairman of the CEA]

Papers of Philip W. Buchen, Presidential Counsel

Papers of J.M. Cannon, Assistant to the President for Domestic Affairs

Jimmy Carter Library

WHCF

Staff Offices, Domestic Policy Staff, Papers of Stu Eizenstat

Staff Offices Counsel, Papers of Robert Jerome Lipshutz

Interviews conducted by the author

Paul Wisgerhof, Director Office of Aviation Negotiations, US Department of State, (4 April 1991).

Jeffrey Shane, US Assistant Secretary of Transport for Policy and International Affairs, (5 April 1991).

Lord King, Chairman of BA, (17 May 1991).

Michael Colvin, MP, Chairman of the Conservative Backbench Aviation Committee, (7 Dec. 1989).

Charles Angevine, US Deputy Assistant Secretary of State for Transportation Affairs, (29 July 1991).

Frederik Sorensen, Head of Aviation Division, European Commission, DG7, (21 May 1991).

EC Commission Official, (22 May 1991).

Robert Ebdon, Head of Government Affairs BA, (5 Aug. 1991).

Cyril Murphy, Vice President for International Affairs, UA, (1 July 1991).

Raymond Colegate, former head of UK CAA economic and licensing branch, (25 March 1991).

Alan Boyd, sometime Chairman CAB, Secretary of Transport and Special Ambassador in charge of US delegation to negotiate Bermuda 2, (9 April 1991).

Rt. Hon. Edmund Dell, Secretary of State for Trade 1976-78, (8 Dec. 1989).

Rt. Hon. (now Lord) Callaghan, Prime Minister 1976-79, (26 Feb. 1987).

Sir Michael Bishop, Chairman BM, (15 March 1991).

Andrew Gray, Managing Director of Air UK, (26 March 1991).

Senior FO official, (8 Dec. 1989).

Brendan Hanniffy, US Civil Aviation Attache, US Embassy London, (13 Sept. 1991).

Arnold Grossman, Vice President of AA for International Affairs, (12 April 1991).

Paul Gretch, US DOT Director of International Aviation, (4 April 1991).

Various interviews with British officials cited simply as 'official British source'.

Weekly Publications, Ephemera and Miscellaneous

National Journal

Journal of Commerce

The Economist

The New Yorker

Aviation Week and Space Technology

Business Travel News

Flight International

Washington Flyer Magazine

Wall Street Journal

Daily Telegraph

Sunday Times

The Times

New York Times

The Independent

Sunday Observer

Financial Times

Remarks by Lord King, Royal Society 125th Anniversary Banquet, 16 May 1991: text courtesy of BA.

Frederik Sorensen, presentation, 'European Airline Traffic after 1993', Brussels, 8 April 1991: text courtesy of Mr. Sorensen.

Malcolm Rifkind, UK Secretary of Transport, 'Secretary of State's Speech to Aviation Club: Aviation a Framework for the Nineties', 21 May 1991: text courtesy of UK DOT.

Speeches by Robert Crandall, Chairman of AA at Allied Pilots Association Banquet, San Diego, California, 24 March 1991 and at Fuqua School of Business, Duke University, North Carolina, 28 March 1991: texts courtesy of AA.

Correspondence between the author and Patrick Shovelton, 18 Jan. 1993.

Correspondence between the author and Edmund Dell, 2 November 1993.

Global Aviation Associates Ltd., 'Free Trade in the Air: Report of the Think Tank on Multilateral Aviation Liberalization (Jan. 1991).

Bibliography

Adams, W., and Brock, J.W. (1991), *Antitrust Economics on Trial: A Dialogue on the New Laissez-Faire*, Princeton UP, Princeton.

Ashworth, M., and Forsyth, P. (1985), *Civil Aviation and the Privatisation of British Airways*, Institute for Fiscal Studies, London.

Atwood, James, R. (1980), 'International Aviation: How Much Competition and How?', *Stanford Law Review*, vol. 32, May, pp. 1061-74.

Baldwin, R. (1985), *Regulating the Airlines: Administrative Justice and Agency Discretion*, Clarendon, Oxford.

Callaghan, James, (1987), *Time and Chance*, Collins, London.

Campbell-Smith, D. (1986), *Struggle for Take-Off: the British Airways Story*, Hodder and Stoughton, London.

Carter, Jimmy, (1982), *Keeping Faith: Memoirs of a President*, Bantam, New York.

Chuang, R.Y. (1972), *The International Air Transport Association: A Case Study of a Quasi-Governmental Organization*, A.W. Sijthoff, Leiden.

Corbett, D. (1965), *Politics and Airlines*, Allen and Unwin, London.

Cramer, C. (1973), *American Enterprise: the Rise of US Commerce*, Paul Elek, London.

Daley, R. (1980), *An American Saga: Juan Trippe and His Pan American Empire*, Random House, New York.

Davies, R.E.G. (1982), *Airlines of the United States since 1914*, Putnam, London.

Dell, E. (1985), 'Interdependence and the Judges: Civil Aviation and Antitrust', *International Affairs*, vol. 61, no. 3, pp. 355-73.

Dell, E. (1991), *A Hard Pounding*, Clarendon, Oxford.

Dempsey, P.S. (1987), *Law and Foreign Policy in International Aviation*, Transnational Publishers, New York.

Dobson, Alan P. (1988), *The Politics of the Anglo-American Economic Special Relationship*, Wheatsheaf, Brighton and St. Martins New York.

Dobson, Alan P. (1991 A), *Peaceful Air Warfare: the United States, Britain, and the Politics of International Aviation*, Clarendon, Oxford.

Dobson, Alan P. (1991 B), 'The Special Relationship and European Integration', *Diplomacy and Statecraft*, vol. 2, no. 1, pp. 79-102.

Dobson, Alan P. (1993), 'Aspects of Anglo-American Aviation Diplomacy 1976-93', *Diplomacy and Statecraft*, vol. 4, no. 2, pp. 235-55.

Dobson, Alan P. (1994), 'Regulation or Competition? Negotiating the Anglo-American Air Services Agreement of 1977', *Journal of Transport History*, vol. 15.

Doganis, R. (1985), *Flying off Course: the Economics of International Airlines*, Allen and Unwin, London.

Dierikx, M. (1992), 'Shaping World Aviation: Anglo-American Civil Aviation Relations 1944-46', *Journal of Air Law and Commerce*, vol. 57, no. 4, pp. 795-840.

Drake, William J., and Nicolaidis, Kalypso, (1992), 'Ideas, Interests and Institutionalization: "Trade in Services" and the Uruguay Round', *International Organization*, vol. 46, no. 1, pp. 37-100.

Ellison, A.P., and Stafford, E.M. (1974), *The Dynamics of the Civil Aviation Industry*, Saxon House, Farnborough.

Erdmenger, Jurgen, (1983), *The European Transport Policy*, Gower, Aldershot.

Ford, G.R. (1979), *A Time to Heal: the Autobiography of Gerald Ford*, W.H. Allen, London.

Friedman, Milton and Rose, (1981), *Free to Choose*, Avon, New York.

Gardner, R.N. (1980), *Sterling Dollar Diplomacy in Current Perspective*, Columbia UP, New York.

Gialloreto, L. (1988), *Strategic Airline Management: the Global War Begins*, Pitman, London.

Gidwitz, B. (1980), *The Politics of International Air Transport*, Heath, Boston.

Gunston, Bill, (1988), *Diamond Flight: the Story of British Midland*, Henry Melland, London.

Haanappel, P.P.C. (1984), *Pricing and Capacity Determination in International Air Transport: a Legal Analysis*, Kluwer, Deventer.

Hargrove, Erwin, C. (1988), *Jimmy Carter as President: Leadership and the Politics of the Public Good*, Louisiana State UP, Baton Rouge.

Hayek, Frederich Von, (1944), *The Road to Serfdom*, Routledge Kegan and Paul, London.

Hayek, Frederich Von, (1960), *Constitution of Liberty*, Routledge Kegan and Paul, London.

Ikenberry, John, G. (1992), 'A World Economy Restored: Expert Consensus and the Anglo-American Post-war Settlement', *International Organization*, vol. 46, no. 1, pp. 289-321.

Jonsson, C. (1978), 'Sphere of Flying', *International Organization*, vol. 35, no. 2, (1981), pp. 273-303 .

Jonsson, C. (1987), *International Aviation and the Politics of Regime Change*, Francis Pinter, London.

Keegan, William, (1984), *Mrs. Thatcher's Economic Experiment*, Penguin, Middlesex.

Kent, R.J. (1980), *Safe, Separated, Soaring: A History of Civil Aviation 1961-72*, US DOT, Washington.

Krieger, Joel, (1986), *Reagan, Thatcher and the Politics of Decline*, Polity Press, Cambridge.

Lowenfeld, Andreas, F. (1975), 'A New Take-off for International Air Transport', *Foreign Affairs*, vol. 54, no. 1, pp. 36-50.

Lyth, Peter, J. (1990), 'The 1946 Decision to Create a Separate British European Airline and its Effects on Civil Aircraft Production', *Journal of Transport History*, vol. 11, no. 2, pp. 1-18.

Lyth, Peter, J. (1993), 'The History of Commercial Air Transport: A Progress Report, 1953-93', *Journal of Transport History*, vol. 14, no. 2, pp. 166-180.

Mackenzie, D. (1991), 'The Bermuda Conference and Anglo-American Aviation Relations at the End of the Second World War', *Journal of Transport History*, vol 12, no. 1, pp. 61-74.

245

Majone, G. (ed.), (1990), *Deregulation or Re-regulation? Regulatory Reform in Europe and the United States*, Pinter, London, St. Martins New York.

McGowan, F., and Trengove, C. (1986), *European Aviation: A Common Market?*, Institute for Fiscal Studies, London.

Newhouse, J. (1983), *The Sporty Game*, Alfred Knopf, New York.

Nicholl, W., and Salmon, T.C. (1990), *Understanding the European Communities*, Philip Allen, London.

Nixon, R.M. (1978), *The Memoirs of Richard Nixon*, Book Club Associates, London.

Noll, Roger G., and Owen, Bruce M., (eds), (1983), *The Political Economy of Deregulation: Interest Groups in the Regulatory Process*, American Institute for Public Policy Research, Washington.

Penrose, Harald, (1980), *Wings Across the World: An Illustrated History of British Airways*, Cassell, London.

Preston, E. (1987), *Troubled Passage: The Federal Aviation Administration During the Nixon and Ford Term 1973-77*, US DOT, Washington.

Pryke, R. (1987), *Competition Among International Airlines*, Gower, Aldershot.

Rand, Ayn, (1967), *Capitalism the Unknown Ideal*, New American Library, New York.

Reichley, A.J. (1981), *Conservatives in an Age of Change*, Brookings Institute, Washington.

Richardson, E. (1976), *The Creative Balance: Government, Politics, and the Individual in America's Third Century*, Hamish Hamilton, London.

Sampson, A. (1984), *Empires of the Sky: the Politics, Contests and Cartels of World Airlines*, Hodder and Stoughton, London.

Shaw, S. (1985), *Airlines and Management*, Pitman, London.

Shoenebaum, E.W. (1979), *Political Profiles of the Nixon/Ford Years*, Facts on File Inc., New York.

Sochor, E. (1991), *The Politics of International Aviation*, Macmillan, London.

Solberg, C. (1979), *Conquest of the Skies: A History of Commercial Aviation*, Little Brown, Boston.

Spero, J.E. (1990), *The Politics of International Economic Relations*, Unwin

Hyman, London and St. Martin's, New York.

Stockman, D. (1987), *The Triumph of Politics*, Avon, New York.

Swann, D. (1983), *Competition and Industrial Policy in the European Community*, Methuen, London.

Swann, D. (1988), *The Retreat of the State: Deregulation and Privatisation in the UK and the US*, Harvester/Wheatsheaf, Hemel Hempstead.

Swann, D. (1992 A), *The Economics of the Common Market*, Penguin, London.

Swann, D. (1992 B), *The Single Market and Beyond: a Study of the Wider Implications of the Single European Act*, Routledge, Andover.

Taneja, N.K. (1988), *US International Aviation Policy*, Heath, Lexington.

Wassenbergh, H.A. (1970), *Aspects of Air Law and Civil Air Policy in the Seventies*, Nijhoff, The Hague.

Wassenbergh, H.A. (1976), *Public International Air Transport in a New Era*, Kluwer, Deventer.

Wassenbergh, H.A. and Fenema, H.P. van (1981), *International Air Transport: a Legal Analysis*, Kluwer, Deventer.

White, T.A. (1965), *The Making of the President 1964*, Jonathan Cape, London.

Index

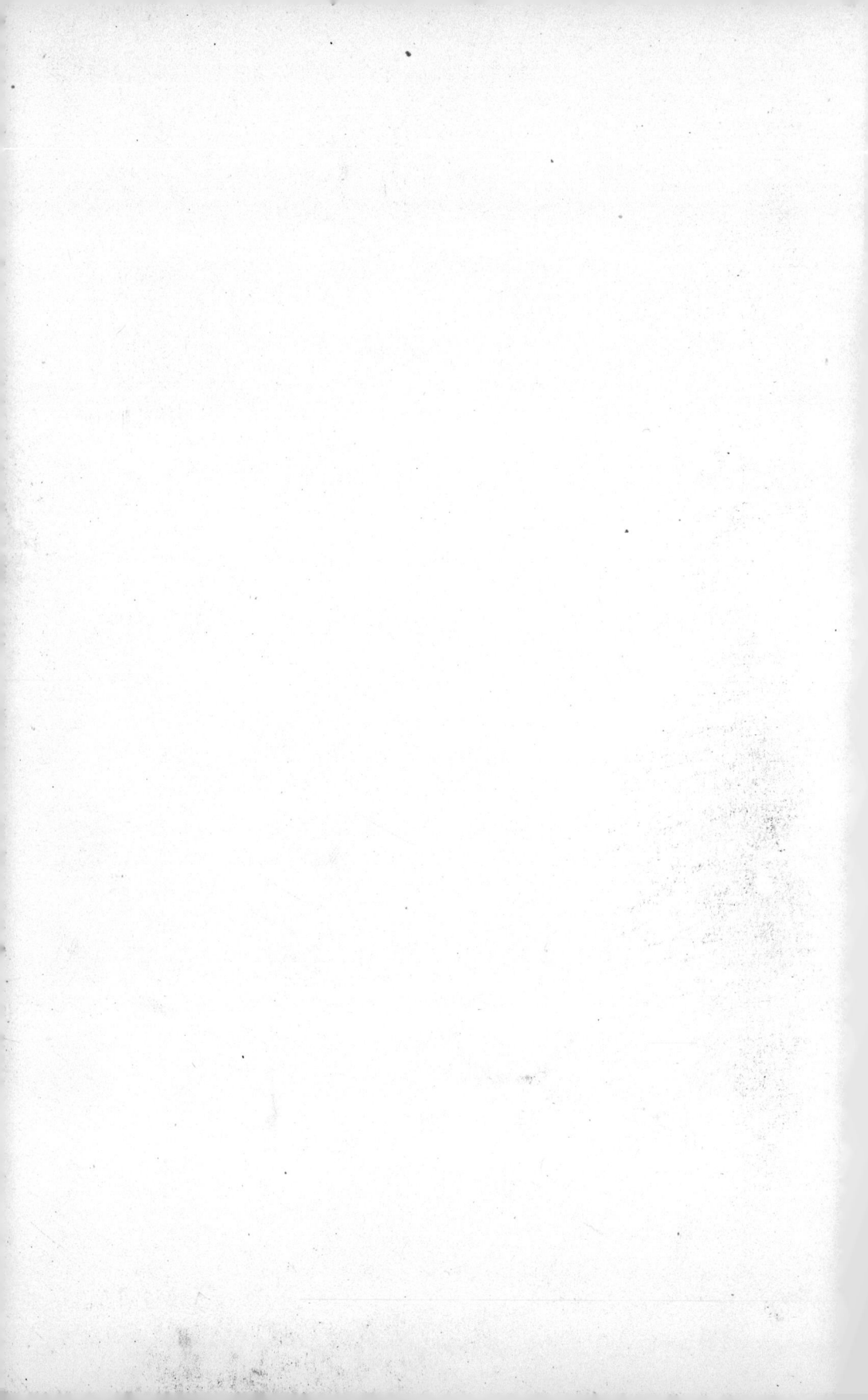